PENGUIN BOOKS

NASTY, BRUTISH, AND SHORT

Scott Hershovitz is director of the Law and Ethics Program and professor of law and philosophy at the University of Michigan. He holds a BA in philosophy and politics from the University of Georgia, a JD from Yale Law School, and a D.Phil. from the University of Oxford, where he was a Rhodes Scholar. Professor Hershovitz served as a law clerk for Justice Ruth Bader Ginsburg of the U.S. Supreme Court. He is married to Julie Kaplan, a social worker, whom he met at summer camp. They live in Ann Arbor with their two children, Rex and Hank.

NASTY, BRUTISH, and SHORT

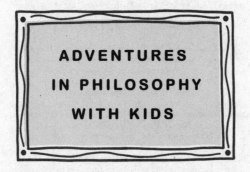

ADVENTURES
IN PHILOSOPHY
WITH KIDS

SCOTT HERSHOVITZ

PENGUIN BOOKS

PENGUIN BOOKS
An imprint of Penguin Random House LLC
penguinrandomhouse.com

First published in the United States of America by Penguin Press,
an imprint of Penguin Random House LLC, 2022
Published in Penguin Books 2023

Passages adapted from "Taylor Swift, Philosopher of Forgiveness"
(*The New York Times*, September 7, 2019) reprinted by
permission of *The New York Times*.

"The Death of Big Bob" (Letter to the Editor, *The Globe and
Mail*, March 4, 2008) by Derek Wilson reprinted
by permission of the author.

ISBN 9781984881830 (PAPERBACK)

THE LIBRARY OF CONGRESS HAS CATALOGED THE HARDCOVER EDITION AS FOLLOWS:
Names: Hershovitz, Scott, author.
Title: Nasty, brutish, and short : adventures in philosophy
with my kids / Scott Hershovitz.
Description: New York : Penguin Press, 2022. |
Includes bibliographical references and index.
Identifiers: LCCN 2021035834 (print) | LCCN 2021035835 (ebook) |
ISBN 9781984881816 (hardcover) | ISBN 9781984881823 (ebook)
Subjects: LCSH: Philosophy—Study and teaching. | Children and philosophy.
Classification: LCC B52 .H47 2022 (print) |
LCC B52 (ebook) | DDC 107—dc23
LC record available at https://lccn.loc.gov/2021035834
LC ebook record available at https://lccn.loc.gov/2021035835

Printed in the United States of America
1 3 5 7 9 10 8 6 4 2

DESIGNED BY MEIGHAN CAVANAUGH

To Julie, Rex, and Hank

CONTENTS

———

PART III

MAKING SENSE
OF THE WORLD

NASTY, BRUTISH, and SHORT

THE ART
OF THINKING

I nee a philosopher." Hank was standing in the bathroom, half-naked.

"What?" Julie asked.

"I nee a philosopher."

"Did you rinse?"

"I nee a philosopher," Hank said, getting more agitated.

"You need to rinse. Go back to the sink."

"I nee a philosopher!" Hank demanded.

"Scott!" Julie shouted. "Hank needs a philosopher."

I am a philosopher. And no one has ever needed me. I rushed to the bathroom. "Hank, Hank! I'm a philosopher. What do you need?"

He looked puzzled. "You are *not* a philosopher," he said sharply.

"Hank, I *am* a philosopher. That's my job. What's bothering you?"

He opened his mouth but didn't say anything.

"Hank, what's bothering you?"

"DER'S FOMETHING FUCK IN MY FEETH."

A flosser. Hank needed a flosser—one of those forked pieces of plastic with dental floss strung across it. In retrospect, that makes sense. A flosser is something you could need, especially if you are two and your purpose in life is to pack landfills with cheap pieces of plastic that provided a temporary diversion. A philosopher is not something that people need. People like to point that out to philosophers.

⁘

"WHAT DO PHILOSOPHERS DO, EXACTLY?"

"Um, uh . . . we think, mostly."

"What do you think about?"

"Anything, really. Justice, fairness, equality, religion, law, language . . ."

"I think about those things. Am I a philosopher?"

"You might be. Do you think about them carefully?"

I cannot count the number of times that I've had that conversation. But that's because I've never had it. It's just how I imagine things would go if I were to tell a stranger that I'm a philosopher. I almost always say that I am a lawyer. Unless I am talking to a lawyer; then I say that I'm a law professor, so that I can pull rank. If I am talking to another law professor, though, then I'm definitely a philosopher. But if I am talking to a philosopher, I'm back to being a lawyer. It's an elaborate shell game, carefully constructed to give me an edge in any conversation.

But I am a philosopher. And I still find that improbable. I didn't set out to be one. As a first-semester freshman at the University of Georgia, I wanted to take Intro Psychology. But the class was full, and Intro Philosophy fulfilled a requirement. If a spot had come open in that psychology class, then I might be a psychologist and this book might be full of practical parenting advice. There is a bit of parenting advice in this book, but most of it is not so practical. Indeed, my main advice is just this: talk to your kids (or somebody else's). They're funny as hell—and good philosophers too.

I missed the first day of that philosophy class, because my people—Jews, not philosophers—celebrate the New Year at a more or less random time each fall. But I went to the second class, and by the second hour I was hooked. The professor, Clark Wolf, asked each of us what mattered, and as he went around the room, he scratched our answers on the board alongside our names and the names of famous philosophers who had said something similar.

> Happiness: Robyn, Lila, Aristotle
>
> Pleasure: Anne, Aristippus, Epicurus
>
> Doing the Right Thing: Scott, Neeraj, Kant
>
> Nothing: Vijay, Adrian, Nietzsche

Seeing my name on the board made me think that my thoughts about what mattered might matter—that I could be a part of a conversation that included people like Aristotle, Kant, and Nietzsche.

It was a crazy thing to think, and my parents were not happy to find me thinking it. I remember sitting across from my father in a rotisserie chicken restaurant, reporting that I planned to major in philosophy. "What's philosophy?" he asked. That is a good question. He didn't know the answer because when he registered for classes, there was a spot left in psychology, and that became his major. But I realized that I had a problem: I didn't know the answer either, and I had been in a philosophy class for several weeks. What *is* philosophy, I wondered, and why do I want to study it?

I decided to show my dad rather than tell him. "We think we're sitting at a table, eating rotisserie chicken and having a conversation about how college is going," I started. "But what if we aren't? What if someone stole our brains, put them in a vat, hooked them up to electrodes, and stimulated them so as to make us think that we're eating chicken and talking about college?"

"Can they do that?" he asked.

"I don't think so, but that's not the question. The question is how do we know that they didn't? How do we know that we aren't brains in vats, hallucinating a chicken dinner?"

"That's what you want to study?" The look on his face was something other than encouraging.

"Yeah, I mean, don't you see the worry? Everything we think we know could be wrong."

He did not see the worry. And this was before *The Matrix* came out, so I couldn't appeal to the authority of Keanu Reeves to establish the urgency of the issue. After a few more minutes of muttering about brains and vats, I added, "The department has lots of logic classes too."

"Well," he said, "I hope you take those."

• ————— •

I SAID THAT IT'S improbable that I'm a philosopher. But that's not right. What's improbable is that I'm *still* a philosopher—that my dad didn't put a stop to it, at that dinner or long before. Because I was a philosopher almost from the time that I could talk, and I am not alone in that. Every kid—every single one—is a philosopher. They stop when they grow up. Indeed, it may be that part of what it is to grow up is to stop doing philosophy and to start doing something more practical. If that's true, then I'm not fully grown up, which will come as a surprise to exactly no one who knows me.

It's not for lack of trying on my parents' part. I remember the first time I pondered a philosophical puzzle. I was five, and it hit me during circle time at the JCC kindergarten. I thought about it all day, and at pickup time I rushed to tell my mother, who taught a preschool class down the hall.

"Mommy," I said, "I don't know what red looks like to you."

"Yes, you do. It looks red," she said.

"Right . . . well, no," I stammered. "I know what red looks like to me, but I don't know what it looks like to you."

She looked confused, and to be fair, I may not have been clear. I was five. But I struggled mightily to get her to see what I was saying.

"Red looks like that," she said, pointing to something red.

"I know that's red," I said.

"So what's the trouble?"

"I don't know what red looks like to you."

"It looks like *that*," she said, increasingly exasperated.

"Right," I said, "but I don't know what that looks like to you. I know what it looks like to me."

"It looks the same, sweetheart."

"You don't know that," I insisted.

"Yes, I do," she said, pointing again. "That's red, right?"

She didn't get it, but I was not deterred. "We call the same things red," I attempted to explain, "because you pointed to red things and told me they were red. But what if I see red the way you see blue?"

"You don't. That's red, not blue, right?"

"I know we both call that red," I said, "but red could look to you the way blue looks to me."

I don't know how long we went round on that, but my mother never did see the point I was making. (Mom, if you're reading this, I'm happy to try again.) And I distinctly remember her concluding the conversation: "Stop worrying about this. It doesn't matter. You see just fine."

That was the first time someone told me to stop doing philosophy. It was not the last.

PHILOSOPHERS CALL THE PUZZLE I pressed on my mother the *shifted color spectrum*. The idea is typically credited to John Locke, the seventeenth-century English philosopher whose ideas influenced the

Framers of the United States Constitution. But I'd bet that thousands of kindergarten-aged kids got there first. (Indeed, Daniel Dennett, a prominent philosopher of mind, reports that many of his students recall pondering the puzzle when they were little.) Their parents probably didn't understand what they were saying, or see the significance in it. But the puzzle *is* significant; indeed, it's a window into some of the deepest mysteries about the world and our place within it.

Here's how Locke explained the puzzle (it's easier to follow if you read it out loud in an English accent):

> Neither would it carry any Imputation of Falshood . . . if . . . the same Object should produce in several Men's Minds different Ideas at the same time; v.g. if the Idea, that a Violet produced in one Man's Mind by his Eyes, were the same that a Marigold produces in another Man's, and vice versâ.

I know what you're thinking: at five, I had a better grasp of the English language than Locke. At the least, I didn't capitalize letters like a crazy person. But don't worry: I won't make you slog through lots of passages from long-dead philosophers. The point of this book is that anyone can do philosophy and every kid does. If a kindergartner can do philosophy without reading Locke, we can too.

But we did read Locke, so let's see if we can make sense of it. What was he on about? There are lots of mysteries lurking in that short passage: about the nature of colors, about the nature of consciousness, and about the difficulty—or perhaps impossibility—of capturing some of our experiences in words. We'll think about some of those mysteries later on. But the last one points toward an even bigger worry: that other people's minds are, in a fundamental sense, closed to us.

Other people might see the world differently than we do, and not just in the metaphorical sense that they might have different opinions about controversial topics. They might actually *see* the world differently. If I could pop into your head—see through your eyes, with your brain—I might discover that everything is, from my perspective, topsy-turvy. Stop signs might look blue; the sky might look red. Or perhaps the differences would be more subtle—off by a shade, or a bit more vibrant. But since I can't pop in, I can't know what the world looks like to you. I can't even know what it looks like to the people I know best: my wife and kids.

And that is a lonely thought. If Locke is right, then we are, in an important sense, trapped in our own heads, cut off from other people's experiences. We can guess what they're like. But we can't know.

I don't think it's an accident that this thought occurs to many kindergarten-aged kids. Kids that age are working hard to understand other people—to learn to read their minds. You won't make it very far in the world if you can't figure out what other people think. We have to be able to anticipate other people's actions, and their reactions to our actions. To do that, kids are constantly generating and testing theories about the beliefs, intentions, and motivations of those around them. They wouldn't put it that way, of course. It's not something they do reflectively. But neither was dropping their sippy cup from their high chair, even though that too was an experiment—in physics and psychology. (It fell every time, and someone always picked it up.)

I don't know why I was thinking about colors that day in kindergarten. But what I discovered—simply by thinking it through—was a limit on my capacity to read other people's minds. I could learn a lot about my mother's beliefs, motivations, and intentions just by watching the way she behaved. But no matter what I did, I couldn't learn whether red looked to her the way it looked to me.

We'll return to this problem. As I said, it's a window into some of the deepest mysteries about the world. Kids peer through that window all the time. Most adults have forgotten that it's even there.

PEOPLE ARE SKEPTICAL when I say that kids peer through that window. Sure, *you* came up with the shifted color spectrum, they say. But *you* turned out to be a philosopher. That's not a normal thing for a kid to do. I might have believed them if I didn't have kids myself. I've got two boys: Hank, whom you've already met, and Rex, who's a few years older. By the time Rex was three, he was saying things that implicated philosophical issues, even if he didn't yet see them himself.

As the kids got older, philosophy was right on the surface of what they said. One day, Julie asked Hank (then eight) what he wanted for lunch, and she gave him two options: a quesadilla or a hamburger left over from the night before. Hank was tortured by the choice—you'd think we'd asked him which parent to save from certain death.* It took him a while to decide.

"I'll have the burger," he said, decades later.

"It's already on the table," Julie replied. Hank *always* chooses a burger if one's available.

Hank was *not* happy with this development. He started to cry.

"What's wrong, Hank?" I asked. "That was what you wanted."

"Mommy didn't let me decide," he said.

"Sure she did. You said you wanted a burger and you have a burger."

"No," Hank said. "She predicted me."

"Yeah, but she got it right."

"*It's still insulting,*" Hank insisted. And his burger got cold while he wailed.

The following week, my philosophy of law class talked about *prepunishment*—the idea that we might punish someone before they commit a crime if we know, beyond a reasonable doubt, that they'll do

---

*Actually, he could answer that instantly—and it wouldn't go well for me.

it. Some people doubt that it's possible to predict well enough to know. I don't, actually. But there's another objection that's a lot like Hank's.

It's disrespectful, some say, to treat a person as if he's already made a decision when he hasn't—even if you know what he'll decide when he does. It's his decision that ought to make the difference, and he's free to go in a different direction until he's decided, even if you know he won't. (Or is he? Does the fact that you can predict what he'll do imply that he doesn't have free will?) I told my class about Hank, and we talked about whether he was right to feel disrespected. Many thought that he was.

I do that a lot when I teach. I share a story about my kids that illustrates the issues we're talking about. Then we debate whether the kids are right in what they say. I do that when I talk with my colleagues too, since the kids give me such great examples. By now, Rex and Hank are famous among philosophers of law.

For years, people would tell me that my kids weren't normal—that they were doing philosophy *because* they have a philosopher for a dad. I didn't think so. Often their ideas came out of nowhere; they didn't track any conversations we'd had. One night at dinner, four-year-old Rex wondered whether he'd been dreaming his entire life. Philosophers have asked that question for ages. But none of them had ever put it to Rex—or even discussed it around him. (We'll take up the question in chapter 8, when we inquire into the nature of knowledge.) If there was a difference between my kids and others, I thought, it was down to the fact that I noticed when they were doing philosophy—and encouraged it.

My view was confirmed when I discovered the work of Gareth Matthews, a philosopher who dedicated most of his career to kids. He passed away in 2011, when Rex was just one. I never met him, but I wish I'd gotten the chance, because Matthews knew more about kids' philosophical abilities than anyone else.

Matthews's interest started the way mine did. His kid said something philosophical. Their cat, Fluffy, had fleas, and Sarah (age four) asked how she got them.

Fleas must have jumped from another cat onto Fluffy, Matthews told her.

"How did *that* cat get fleas?" Sarah asked.

They must have come from a different cat, Matthews said.

"But Daddy," Sarah insisted, "it can't go on and on like that forever; the only thing that goes on and on like that forever is numbers!"

At the time, Matthews was teaching a class that covered the Cosmological Argument, which aims to show that God exists. There are many versions of the argument, some quite complicated. But the basic idea is simple: Every event has a cause. But that can't continue back forever. So there must be a First Cause, which was itself uncaused. Some say that's God—most famously, Thomas Aquinas.

The argument has problems. Why does the chain of causes have to come to an end? Perhaps the universe is eternal—endless in both directions. And even if there was a First Cause, why think it was God? But it doesn't matter whether the argument works. (We'll ask whether God exists in chapter 12.) The point is simply to see that Sarah reproduced its logic. "Here I am teaching my university students the argument for a First Cause," Matthews wrote, "and my four-year-old daughter comes up, on her own, with an argument for the First Flea!"

That caught Matthews off guard, since he knew a little developmental psychology. According to Jean Piaget, the Swiss psychologist famous for his theory of cognitive development, Sarah should have been in the *pre-operational stage*, so called because kids in it can't yet use logic.* But Sarah's logic was exquisite—far more compelling than the Cosmological Argument. Whatever you make of an infinite regress of causes, it's hard to imagine an infinite regress of cats.

Okay, I can hear you say: Matthews is yet another philosopher with a

---

*Matthews documents several instances in which Piaget simply fails to understand what kids are saying—and so misses the subtlety of their thought. Often the problem is that Piaget isn't as creative as the kids.

philosophical kid. That doesn't tell us much about kids in general. But Matthews didn't stop with his kids. He talked to people who weren't philosophers—and heard many similar stories about their kids. Then he started to visit schools to talk to more kids himself. He'd read stories that raised philosophical questions to the kids—then he'd listen to the debate that ensued.

My favorite of Matthews's stories came from the mother of a little boy named Ian. While Ian and his mother were at home, another family came to visit, and the family's three kids monopolized the television, keeping Ian from seeing his favorite show. After they left, he asked his mother, "Why is it better for three people to be selfish than for one?"

I love that question. It's so simple—and subversive. Many economists think that public policy ought to maximize the satisfaction of people's preferences. Some philosophers think so too. But Ian invites us to ask: Should we care about preferences if they're simply selfish? There's a challenge to democracy lurking here too. Suppose Ian's mother put the question what to watch to a vote? Is counting selfish kids a good way to settle the question?

I don't think so. Had Ian been my child, I would have explained that we let guests choose what to watch because they're guests—not because there are more of them. It's a way of showing hospitality, so we'd do just the same even if the numbers were switched.

What about democracy? We'll think about it later on, since Rex thinks our family ought to be one. For now, I'll just say: Democracy shouldn't be a way of summing people's selfish preferences. Voters ought to be public-spirited. They should seek to promote the common good—and important values, like justice and fairness—not their own individual interests. Don't get me wrong. I believe in democracy, even when it doesn't live up to that ideal. But I stand with Ian in thinking that more people acting selfishly is just more selfishness—and not a good way to make decisions.

Ian's mother was confused by his question. She had no idea how to answer. And I suspect most adults would find themselves just as flummoxed. Little kids often question things grown-ups take for granted. Indeed, that's one of the reasons they make good philosophers. "The adult must cultivate the naiveté that is required for doing philosophy," Matthews said, but "to the child such naiveté is entirely natural."

At least, it is for the littlest kids. Matthews found that "spontaneous excursions into philosophy" were common between the ages of three and seven. By eight or nine, kids seem to slow down, publicly if not privately. It's hard to say why. It may be that their interests shift, or that they feel pressure from peers or parents to stop asking childish questions. Still, Matthews found it easy to prompt philosophical conversations among kids that age and older—and he was struck by the clever ways in which they reasoned. Indeed, Matthews claimed that, in some ways, kids are better philosophers than adults.

<hr>

I SUSPECT THAT SOUNDS ODD. The very idea of child development seems to presuppose that kids' minds mature—get more sophisticated as they grow older. In Matthews's view, just the opposite is true, at least in relation to some skills.* Kids do philosophy with "a freshness and inventiveness that is hard for even the most imaginative adult to match." The freshness stems from the fact that kids find the world a puzzling place. Several years back, a psychologist named Michelle Chouinard listened to recordings of young children spending time with their parents. In just over two hundred hours, she heard nearly twenty-five thousand questions. That works out to more than two a minute. About a quarter of those questions sought explanations; the kids wanted to know *how* or *why*.

Kids also like to puzzle things out. In another study, researchers found that kids who don't get answers to *how* or *why* questions cook up their

---

*As we'll learn in chapter 10, many developmental psychologists now agree with Matthews. Kids' minds are different—not better or worse.

own explanations. And even when they do get answers, they often aren't satisfied. They follow up with another *why* or challenge the explanation offered.

But we haven't yet hit the most important reason kids make good philosophers: they aren't worried about seeming silly. They haven't learned that serious people don't spend time on some questions. As Matthews explains:

> The philosopher asks, "What is time, anyway?" when other adults assume, no doubt unthinkingly, that they are well beyond the point of needing to ask this question. They may want to know whether they have enough time to do the week's shopping, or to pick up a newspaper. They may want to know what time it is, but it doesn't occur to them to ask, "What is time?" St. Augustine put the point well: "What, then, is time? Provided that no one asks me, I know. But if I want to explain it to a questioner, I am baffled."

I've spent years attempting to answer a question that sounds equally silly: What is law? I'm a law professor, so you'd think I'd know. (I teach at the University of Michigan, where I hold appointments in the law school and philosophy department.) But if we're honest, most lawyers are like Augustine: we know what law is, right up until you ask, then we're baffled.

Most of my colleagues happily ignore their ignorance. They have important business to get on with. And I think they think I'm silly for getting stuck on the question. But I think we should all be silly like that sometimes. We should take a step back from our practical concerns and think like little kids. It's a way of recapturing some of the wonder they have at the world—and a way of reminding ourselves how little we understand of it.

ON THE FIRST DAY of second grade, Rex was asked to write down what he wanted to be when he grew up. The teacher sent home a list of the kids' career ambitions, but she didn't say which kid was aiming at which career. Still, it wasn't hard to pick Rex's entry from the list. There were a few future firemen, several doctors, some teachers, a surprising number of engineers. But there was only one "math philosopher."

At dinner that night, I asked Rex the question I still couldn't answer: "Ms. Kind says that you want to be a philosopher of math. What is philosophy?"

Rex pondered for a half second. Then he said, "Philosophy is the art of thinking."

I called my dad. "Remember when we had dinner at that rotisserie chicken place, when I first came home from college? I told you I wanted to study philosophy, and you asked what it was. Well, now I know!"

He didn't remember, and he didn't much care. But Rex was right. Philosophy is the art of thinking. A philosophical puzzle is one that requires us to think about ourselves and the world in an effort to understand both better.

Grown-ups and kids do philosophy in different styles. Adults are more disciplined thinkers. Kids are more creative. Adults know a lot about the world. But kids can help them see how little they actually know. Kids are curious and courageous, where adults tend to be cautious and closed down.

David Hills (who teaches at Stanford) describes philosophy as "the ungainly attempt to tackle questions that come naturally to children, using methods that come naturally to lawyers." That's an apt description of professional philosophy. But it presupposes a division of labor we don't need. Grown-ups and kids can do philosophy together.

Indeed, they should. Conversations between kids and adults can be collaborative, since each brings something different to the table. And they can be fun too. Philosophy is partly play—with ideas. For sure, we should think like little kids. But we should also think *with* them.

• ────── •

THIS BOOK IS INSPIRED BY KIDS, but it's not for them. In fact, kids are my Trojan horse. I'm not after young minds. I'm after yours.

Kids will do philosophy with or without you. I'm hoping to get you to try it again. And I'm hoping to give you the confidence to talk to kids about it, by helping you to see the philosophical issues latent in every-day life—and teaching you a bit about them.

I'm going to tell you stories, mostly about Rex and Hank. In some of the stories, Rex and Hank do philosophy. They notice a puzzle and try to puzzle it out. In others, they say or do something that presents a philosophical puzzle, but it's not one they notice themselves. Still other stories are just about our hapless parenting; philosophy provides some perspective on what went wrong.

Sometimes we'll think with the boys. Sometimes we'll think about them. And sometimes we'll go off on our own and do some grown-up thinking about the questions they raise. But the boys will never be too far away, since they have a lot to say.

Together Rex and Hank will take us on a tour through contemporary philosophy. But like many of the best tours, this one's a bit quirky. Some of the questions we'll encounter are universal. They'd pop up in parent-ing any kid. In that category, we could put questions about authority, pun-ishment, and God. Others reflect interests Rex and Hank happen to have, like the size of the universe. Different kids get interested in different things.

When parents hear about this project, they often share questions their kids ask. Some are *amazing*. Every night at bedtime, for weeks on end, one little girl would ask her mother: *Why do the days keep coming?* Her mom explained the rotation of the earth, but it was clear the mechanics weren't what interested her. I might have told the girl about *continuous creation*—the idea (common to some Christian thinkers) that God creates the world at every moment, not just at the start. I don't know whether that would have satisfied her, though. It's possible that the girl's question came from someplace dark—from angst about the world and what it was throwing at her.

My boys aren't dark—at least not yet. But they're constantly curious, so we're going to cover a lot of ground. This book comes in three parts. The first is called Making Sense of Morality. In it, we'll ask what rights are—and what it takes to override them. We'll ask how we ought to respond to wrongdoing. In particular, we'll wonder whether revenge is ever warranted. And we'll ponder punishment too—what it is and why we do it. Then we'll think about authority. We'll ask whether *because I said so* could really be a reason for a kid to follow orders. Finally, we'll think about the words we're not supposed to say—the bad bits of language. (I should warn you: I swear a bit, maybe more. Don't judge me too harshly. I defend myself in chapter 5.)

In the second part, Making Sense of Ourselves, we'll turn to questions about identity. We'll ask what sex, gender, and race are. But we won't be leaving morality behind. When we think about sex and gender, we'll ask what role they should play in sports. And when we consider race, we'll ask whether it's a ground of responsibility—and whether reparations are owed for slavery and segregation.

The third part is called Making Sense of the World. It starts with questions about knowledge. With Rex, we'll wonder whether we might be dreaming our entire lives. And we'll consider skepticism—the worry that we can't know anything about anything at all. After that, we'll take up questions about truth—and we'll think about the tooth fairy too. Then we'll train our minds on our minds, as we wonder what consciousness is. We'll also ponder the infinite. And at the end of our journey, we'll ask whether God exists.

We're going to move fast, at least for philosophers. You could spend a lifetime studying any of the topics we'll take up. The best we can do is hit the highlights. But if all goes well, by the end of the book, you'll be well equipped to think through the puzzles we'll see—with a kid or on your own. That's one of the things I love about philosophy: you can do it anytime, anywhere, in conversation with others or all by yourself. You just have to think things through.

To that end, I want you to read this book a bit differently than you would many others. Most nonfiction writers want you to believe the things they say in their books. They're hoping that you'll accept their authority and adopt their way of thinking about the world.

That's not my aim at all. Sure, I'd like to persuade you to see things my way. But the truth is: I'm happy for you to think differently—as long as you've thought it through. In fact, I suggest that you approach the arguments I offer skeptically. Don't assume that I'm right. In fact, assume that I've gone wrong somewhere, and see if you can spot the spot.

But do me a favor. Don't just disagree. If you think I'm wrong, work out the reasons why. And once you've done that, think through what I might say in response. And how you'd reply, and what I'd retort. And so on, until you feel like you aren't learning anything anymore. But don't give up too quick; the further you go, the more you understand.

That's how philosophers work (at least the grown-up ones). I tell my students: when you have an objection to another philosopher's work, you should assume that she already thought of it—and that she thought it so misguided it wasn't even worth mentioning. Then you should try to work out why. If you give it a good try and you can't figure out where you've gone wrong, it's time to tell other people about it. The goal is to get in the habit of treating your own ideas as critically as you treat other people's.

That advice shows up in the way I talk to the boys. In our house, you're not "entitled to your opinion," as Americans like to say. You have to defend it. I ask the boys lots of questions. Then I question their answers, so they have to think critically about their own ideas. That annoys them sometimes, but I see it as an important part of parenting.

We're all accustomed to supporting kids' interests—and helping them discover new ones. We expose them to art, literature, and music. We encourage them to try sports. We cook with them. We dance with them. We teach them about science and take them to nature. But there's one task lots of parents neglect, because they don't see it as a separate task: supporting their kids as thinkers.

Over the course of this book, you'll learn lots of ways to do that. The simplest is to ask questions—and question answers. But you don't have to play teacher. Indeed, it's better if you don't.

Jana Mohr Lone directs the Center for Philosophy for Children at the University of Washington. Like Matthews, she visits schools to talk philosophy with kids. But she doesn't teach them philosophy. Instead, she does philosophy with them. The difference is subtle but important. Kids can already do philosophy—in some ways, better than you. So treat them like collaborators. Take their ideas seriously. Try to solve problems with them, not for them. When you're talking philosophy, that shouldn't be so hard, since chances are, you don't know the answers yet either.

That leads me to my last ask: set your grown-up sensibilities aside. Most adults are like my dad. They have little patience for the sorts of puzzles that philosophers ponder. They're the opposite of practical. Worrying that the world is not what it seems will not get the laundry done. But I hope the boys and I can flip that script, at least for a little while. Why do the laundry when the world may not be what it seems?

- ⁓ -

LATELY REX AND HANK have been wondering why this book is called *Nasty, Brutish, and Short.* You might have heard the phrase before. It comes from Thomas Hobbes, who lived at roughly the same time as

Locke. Hobbes was curious what life would be like without any government at all—a condition philosophers call the *state of nature*. He thought it would be awful. Indeed, he thought it would involve a "war of every man against every man." In the state of nature, Hobbes said, life would be "solitary, poor, nasty, brutish, and short."

I don't know about the state of nature. But a "war of every man against every man" is an apt description of what a house with little kids is like.

We are lucky. Our lives aren't solitary or poor. But our kids are nasty, brutish, and short.

They are also cute and kind. And actually, we are lucky on that front too. Rex and Hank are uncommonly cute and kind. But all kids are, at times, nasty and brutish. That's why we're going to think about revenge and ask whether punishment can be used to build better creatures.

The kids are willing to accept the characterization, at least in part.

"Are you nasty and brutish?" I asked Hank.

"I can be nasty," he said, "but I'm not British."

Rex lobbied for another title. He wanted to name the book *Not Nasty or Brutish, Just Short*. Having lost that battle, he's begging to blog under that title. So watch out. He might be coming to an Internet near you.

For now, though, he's the star of this show, alongside his little brother, Hank. They are two of the finest philosophers I know. They're among the funniest. And the most fun too.

PART I

MAKING SENSE OF MORALITY

1

RIGHTS

I love drawing a bath. Not for me, of course. I'm a straight man socialized in the last century, so I don't take baths. Or express the full range of human emotions. But my children take baths, and someone has to draw them. Most nights, I make sure that someone is me.

Why? Because the bath is *up*stairs. And *down*stairs is a fucking madhouse. As kids get tired, their kinetic energy increases and their self-control self-destructs. The noise rivals a rock concert. Someone is screaming because it's time to practice piano, or because there's no time to practice piano. Or because we didn't have dessert, or because we did have dessert but he got it on his shirt. Or simply because there must be screaming. Screaming is the cosmological constant.

So I escape. "I'll start Hank's bath," I say, bounding up the stairs, on the way to the best part of my day. I close the door, start the water, and tinker with the temperature. Not too hot, not too cold. Back and forth, as if I might get it right. But make no mistake: The water will be too hot.

Or too cold. Or both, because kids reject the law of noncontradiction. I will fail. But I am at peace. Because the bath muffles the screams. There, alone on the tile floor, I sit with my thoughts (and by *thoughts*, I mean *phone*), soaking up the solitude.

My wife has figured me out, so sometimes she strikes first. "I'll start Hank's bath," she says, crushing my soul. But she's a straight woman socialized in the last century, so she wastes the opportunity. She turns on the bath, but instead of fiddling with her phone while the water fills, she does something sensible, like laundry. Or something inexplicable, like return to the room the children are in to . . . parent?! I know that I should feel bad about this. And I do. But not for the reason I should. Solitude is the greatest luxury we can afford. Someone should soak it up. Better Julie than me. But if not her, definitely me.

So there I am, sitting on the bathroom floor, dimly aware that the downstairs crazy is crazier than normal. Hank (age five) is full-on wailing, so it must be something serious (and by *serious*, I mean *trivial*). When I cannot let the water rise any longer, I shut it off and shatter my serenity.

"Hank, the bath is ready," I shout down the stairs.

No response.

"HANK, THE BATH IS READY!" I scream over his screams.

"HANK, THE BATH IS READY!" Rex relays, with great satisfaction.

"HANK, THE BATH IS READY!" Julie says, with great irritation.

And then the sobs are ascending upon me. Slowly. One. Step. At. A. Time. Until Hank arrives, out of breath and out of his mind.

I try to calm him down. "Hank," I say softly, "what's wrong?" No response. "Hank," I whisper, even more softly, "what's bothering you?" He still can't collect himself. I start taking off his clothes as he tries to catch his breath. Finally he's in the bath, and I try again. "Hank, what's bothering you?"

"I don't . . . I don't have. . . ."

"What don't you have, Hank?"

"I DON'T HAVE ANY RIGHTS!" Hank wails, bursting back into tears.

"Hank," I say softly, still hoping to soothe him but also now curious: "What are rights?"

"I don't know," he whimpers, "but I don't have any."

———————

THIS TIME, Hank did need a philosopher. And lucky for him, he had one.

"Hank, you do have rights."

That got his attention. The tears slowed a tiny bit.

"Hank, you do have rights. Lots of them."

"I do?" Hank asked, starting to catch his breath.

"Yeah, you do. Would you like to learn about them?"

He nodded.

"Well, let's talk about Tigey," I said. Tigey is the Hobbes to Hank's Calvin—the white tiger that has been his constant companion since birth. "Can people take Tigey away from you?"

"No," he said.

"Can people play with Tigey without asking first?"

"No," Hank said, "Tigey's mine." The tears were almost gone.

"That's right," I said. "Tigey's yours. And that means you have a right to him. No one can take Tigey or play with him unless you say it's okay."

"But someone *could* take Tigey," Hank objected, teetering back to the edge of tears.

"That's right," I said. "Someone *could* take Tigey. But would that be okay? Or would it be wrong?"

"It would be wrong," he said.

"That's right. That's what it means to have a right. If it would be wrong for someone to take Tigey, then you have a right that they not take him."

Hank's face brightened. "I have a right to all my aminals!" he said, swapping the *n* and *m* to make my favorite of his mispronunciations.

"That's right! You do! That's what it means for them to be yours."

"I have a right to all my toys!" Hank said.

"Yes—you do!"

And then his cute face collapsed. Sobbing again, soaking wet.

"Hank, why are you sad?"

"I don't have a right to Rex."

That was the source of the downstairs crazy. Hank wanted to play with Rex. Rex wanted to read. And Hank did not, in fact, have a right to Rex.

I explained: "No, you don't have a right to Rex. He gets to decide whether he wants to play or not. We don't have a right to other people unless they make a promise."

That's a bit too simple. Sometimes we have claims on others even when they haven't promised us anything. But I decided to save a more detailed conversation until the student was less distraught. Instead, we talked about what Hank could do on his own when Rex wanted to read.

· ⌒⌒⌒ ·

WHILE TEETERING AT THE EDGE of tears, Hank made a sharp observation about rights. I started by asking whether someone could take Tigey without his permission. He said no. But a split second later, he thought better of it. Someone could take Tigey without his permission. In fact, Hank had done just that to Rex. Rex's Tigey is named Giraffey. (Before you criticize my boys' naming conventions, you should know that I was even less creative; my companions were Monkey and Giraffe.) When Hank first learned to crawl, he'd zoom into Rex's room at every opportunity, put Giraffey under his chin, and scoot out as quickly as he could. Rex had a right to Giraffey, every bit as much as Hank has a right to Tigey. But Hank could and did take Giraffey.

What does that tell us about rights? Well, Hank's right to Tigey protects his possession of him. But the protection the right provides is not physical. There's no force field around Tigey that prevents others from taking him. Rather, the protection a right provides is, in philosopher-speak, *normative*. That is, it is generated by the norms, or standards, that govern good behavior. Someone who is aiming to act well would not take Tigey without Hank's permission (at least not without a really good reason—more on that in a moment). But not everyone aims to act well. The protection that a right provides depends on the willingness of others to recognize and respect it.

◆ ———— ◆

BEFORE WE MOVE ON, a brief note about language and the people who are pedantic about it. I asked Hank whether someone could take Tigey without his permission, and he said no. Then he thought better of it and said yes. He was right the first time. And the second.

Wait, what? How could that be? Words like *can* and *could* are super flexible. Here's a quick story to show you what I mean.

When I was a student at Oxford, a friend took me to his college bar. He asked for two pints.

"Sorry, mate, can't do it. We're closed," said the guy tending bar.

My friend looked at his watch. It was 11:01; the bar closed at 11:00. "Aww, come on, just two pints."

"Sorry, can't. Rules."

"Well, you *coooould*," my friend said.

Now pause the story. Was my friend pointing out that the guy tending bar was confused about the meaning of the word *could*? No. There's a sense in which he couldn't sell us the drinks. And a sense in which he could. And my friend's long, drawn-out *could* was an attempt to shift his attention to the second sense. The bartender was telling us that it wasn't *permissible* for him to sell us two pints; my friend was pointing out that it was *possible*. No one else was around, so he wouldn't get caught.* The gambit worked: the guy gave us two pints, even though he couldn't (permissibly), because he could (without consequence).

Hank made the same sort of shift in the middle of our conversation. He understood that I was asking whether someone could (permissibly) take Tigey, and he answered (correctly) no. But then he worried that someone could (possibly) take Tigey, and he teetered back toward tears.

Why spend time picking this apart? Well, that's what philosophers do; we pay careful attention to the way that words work. But also, there's almost surely someone in your life who thinks this the height of wit:

"Can I have a cup of tea?" you ask politely.

"I don't know—can you?"

That person thinks you should have said, "May I have a cup of tea?" And he is an asshole. Cut him out of your life. And when you do, tell him that he can, may, and should take English lessons from a toddler, since he doesn't speak the language as well as one.

·———~———·

But back to rights. What are they, exactly? It's hard to say. Hank and I talked about that one day. He was eight, and he'd spent the afternoon cleaning his room. He called me in to see his progress.

"Wow, this looks good," I said.

"Thanks! I put almost everything away."

"Where'd you put your rights?" I asked.

"What do you mean?"

"Your rights—like your right to Tigey. Where's that?"

"I didn't put that away," Hank said. "It's inside me."

"Really? Where? In your belly?"

---

*It was possible in another sense too. The bartender had beer, glasses, and functioning hands, so he was capable of pouring two pints. As this suggests, the meaning of the word *possible* also shifts with context.

"No," Hank said. "It's not in a particular spot. It's just inside me."

"Why don't you take it out? So it doesn't weigh you down."

"It's not the kind of thing you can take out," Hank said. "You can't even hold it."

"Could you burp it out?" I asked.

"No," Hank said. "Rights are *not* burpable."

And then he ran away. So we never sorted out what rights are, beyond their inburpability.

But I can finish the task. Hank had it half-right. Rights aren't the sort of thing you can hold. But they're not inside you either. Rights are relationships.

Let me show you what I mean. Suppose that you have a right that I pay you $1,000. Your right is a claim to that money. That claim is good against me, and if I'm the only person who owes you the money, then only me. But sometimes you hold a right that's good against several people (perhaps Julie and I owe you the money). And sometimes you hold a right that's good against absolutely everyone. For instance, you have a right not to be punched in the face. If *anyone* proposes to punch you in the face, you can remind them of their obligation not to do it.

As that last sentence indicates, when you have a right, someone else has an obligation. That's why I said that rights are relationships. At least two people are party to every right: the right holder and the obligation bearer. Rights and responsibilities travel together. They are the same relationship described from different sides.

What's the nature of that relationship? Here we can get help from one of my all-time favorite philosophers, Judith Jarvis Thomson. Thomson was an expert in ethics. She had a knack for crafting thought experiments, the short stories philosophers use to test ideas. We'll see some of her stories in a bit. But Thomson was also famous for her theory of rights.

When you have a right, Thomson said, you stand in a complex relationship with the person who has the corresponding obligation. That relationship has many features. To name just a few: If I owe you $1,000 next Tuesday, I should warn you if I don't think I'll be able to pay. If the time comes and I don't pay, then I should apologize and seek to make it up to you somehow. But most important: all things equal, I ought to pay you $1,000 next Tuesday.

What do I mean when I say *all things equal*? That's a philosophers' phrase meant to capture the fact that sometimes stuff happens. I owe you $1,000 on Tuesday. But Tuesday is here and it turns out I need that money to pay my rent or my family will be put out on the street. Should I pay you? Maybe. You might suffer even worse if I don't. But if nothing so serious is at stake for you, then I ought to pay my rent, apologize for failing to pay you, and seek to make it up to you as soon as I can.

One of the most pressing questions in moral philosophy is: Just how much stuff has to happen to override a right? One answer is: not much. Maybe we should ignore people's rights whenever doing so would turn out better than respecting them. On this view, you ought to punch me in the face if the good from doing so would outweigh the bad.

That strikes some people as sensible. But notice: it renders rights irrelevant. Instead of worrying about who has what rights, we could just ask: Would the action you're pondering have good or bad consequences? If good, go ahead. If not, hold back. Rights don't make a difference to what you should do.

There's a name for this sort of view. It's called *consequentialism*, since it insists that the moral status of an act depends on its consequences. The most famous version of consequentialism is *utilitarianism*, which suggests that we should aim to maximize *welfare*, or *utility*, as it's sometimes called. What's that? There are many different ways to construe it. On one common view, it's the balance of pleasure over pain in the universe. If you want to know whether you should punch me in the face, a utilitarian (of a certain sort) would encourage you to ask whether the pleasure that people would experience as a result of the punch would outweigh the pain it would cause. Rights wouldn't enter the equation at all.

Ronald Dworkin did not like that way of thinking about morality. Indeed, he wrote a book called *Taking Rights Seriously*, in which he argued that we ought to, um, take rights seriously. (Dworkin was a philosopher of law—arguably the most influential of the last several decades. My work in philosophy is, in some ways, an extension of his.) Dworkin borrowed a concept from card games, like bridge, to explain the relevance of rights. In a moral debate, he said, rights *trump* concerns about welfare.

To see what Dworkin had in mind, consider this story, commonly called Transplant: You work at a hospital and times are tough. You've got five patients desperately in need of transplants. Each needs a different organ. And all five will die if they don't get the organ they need immediately. Just then, a man walks into the emergency room. He's got a broken arm. It's not life threatening. But it occurs to you: if you kill him, you can harvest his organs and save the other five. You ask if he minds, and he says he does, a lot.

Should you do it anyway? Arguably, overall welfare will increase if only one life is lost instead of five.* But so what? The man has a right to life. And his right trumps the well-being of the other patients.

◆⸻◆⸻◆

OR DOES IT? We've arrived at the doorstep of the most famous puzzle in contemporary philosophy. It's known as the Trolley Problem.

To see the problem, we need new stories—indeed, we need Thomson's stories. She called the first Bystander at the Switch. It goes like this:

---

*I say *arguably* because there could be secondary effects. If people start to worry that they will be killed in emergency rooms so that their organs can be harvested, they'll avoid them when they can. And that may lead to a decrease in overall welfare. Philosophers try to limit secondary effects like this by adding features to the case. In Transplant, for instance, we might suppose that the killing can be done in secret, so that no one will ever know. That helps highlight the relevant question: whether the killing is wrong, even if it enhances overall welfare.

A runaway trolley is racing down its track. It's headed toward five workers, who are making repairs further on. If the trolley keeps going, it will kill all of them. But good news: you're standing near a switch that can divert the trolley onto a different track! Alas, there's bad news too: there's a worker on that track—just one, but he'll surely die if you divert the trolley.

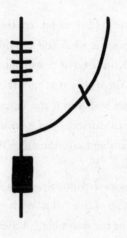

What would you do?

Most people say they would throw the switch, so that the trolley would kill just one person instead of five.

But wait! Didn't we just say that the guy in Transplant had a right to life, even though killing him would help save five others? Why doesn't the lonesome trolley worker have the same right?

⁓

I RECENTLY TAUGHT A CLASS on the Trolley Problem. It met at my house, so the boys could participate. They built Bystander at the Switch out of a toy train set. And as we discussed variations on the story, they'd adjust the model.

Their favorite version comes from another story Thomson told. This one's called Fat Man. (No, the name isn't great, but his corpulence is key to the case.) It runs like this. The trolley is out of control again, heading down the track toward five workers. But this time you're nowhere near the switch. You're standing on a bridge, watching the whole thing play out beneath you. Then you notice that, right next to you, a large man is leaning against the rail. If you give him a little push, he'll fall over and land on the track. His heft will stop the trolley, saving the workers. But the impact from the trolley will kill the fat man if the fall doesn't do it first.

What would you do? Push the man to his death and save the workers? Or let the trolley crush the five?

Most people say that they would *not* push the fat man. They'd let the five die.

But why? The moral calculus—let five people die or kill one instead—is the same across all the cases we've considered. In Bystander at the Switch, most think it's okay to kill. In Fat Man and Transplant, most don't.

Why? What's the difference? *That* is the Trolley Problem.

＊

THE TROLLEY PROBLEM REQUIRES us to rethink what we said about Transplant. We said that it was wrong to kill the patient, on account of his right to life. But the single worker on the track also has a right to life, and most people are comfortable killing him in Bystander at the Switch. Sometimes, it seems, the right to life gives way, when the lives of many others are at stake. So we need a new explanation of why, in Transplant and Fat Man, it's impermissible to kill.

What we're hoping to find is a right that's breached in Transplant and Fat Man but not in Bystander at the Switch.

Is there such a right? Maybe. For inspiration, some look to Immanuel Kant.

Kant lived in Germany in the eighteenth century. And he's on the short list for most influential philosopher ever, alongside people like Plato and Aristotle. Kant lived rather rigidly; it's said he was so consistent in his schedule that his neighbors would set their watches by his walks.

Kant insisted that we shouldn't treat people *merely as means* to achieve our ends. Instead, we should treat people *as people*. That requires that we recognize and respect their humanity—the stuff that separates them from ordinary objects (which *are* appropriately used as means to ends). What separates people from objects? Well, people have the capacity to set ends for themselves, to reason about what their ends should be, to work out how to pursue them, and so on. To treat people *as people*, we have to respect those capacities.

It's important to say: Kant thought it was okay to use people as means to ends sometimes. When a student asks me to write her a recommendation, she's using me as a means to her end. She hopes the letter I write will help her get a job. But she's not *just* using me, in the way she might use her computer to send the application in. In asking me to write for her, she engages me as a person. She lets me choose whether to adopt her end as mine. The computer gets no say in the matter. I do.

Can Kant help us solve the Trolley Problem? Some think so. The relevant right, they suggest, is the right to be treated as a person, not merely as a means to an end.

Let's consider our cases again. In Transplant, you'd clearly infringe that right if you killed the guy with the broken arm. You asked if he'd sacrifice himself for the others, and he said no. If you kill him anyway, you're treating him like a bag of body parts, not as a person, entitled to make his own decisions.

The same is true in Fat Man. If you push the man over the rail, you're treating him like an object, not like a person. All that mattered to you was that he had the heft to get the job done.

What about Bystander at the Switch? On first glance, it looks bad, because you're not getting permission from the single worker on the spur—there's no time for that. But: you're not using him as a means to an end, either. He's not part of your plan at all. If he wasn't there, you'd still divert the trolley. His death is just an unfortunate by-product of your plan to save the five by directing the trolley to a different track. If he somehow escaped, you'd be overjoyed.

That makes this case rather different from Fat Man and Transplant. In those cases, escape would frustrate your plans. So it seems like maybe, just maybe, we've found the solution to the Trolley Problem.

<hr />

OR MAYBE NOT. Thomson knew about Kant, of course. And she considered the solution we just worked up. But she rejected it.

Why? Well, Thomson had another story to tell.

This one's called Loop. And it's just like Bystander at the Switch, except this time there's a twist or, rather, a loop. The trolley is headed toward five workers. If you pull the switch, you direct it to a different stretch of track, where there's only one worker. But that different stretch of track loops back and connects to the first. If the single worker wasn't there, the trolley would go around the loop and hit the five from the

other side. As it happens, the single worker is hefty enough to stop the trolley. But he'll be killed by the collision.

Is it permissible to turn the trolley in Loop? Notice that, this time, you *are* treating that worker as a means to an end. If he wasn't there (say, if he somehow escaped), your plan to save the five would be frustrated. Once again, you need his heft to stop the trolley; otherwise the five workers will die. That makes Loop look a lot like Fat Man.

And yet, it struck Thomson that it *is* permissible to turn the trolley in Loop. She didn't see how adding a bit of extra track behind the worker could make a moral difference. In her view, Loop was just like Bystander at the Switch. The extra track was irrelevant. The trolley would never even touch it!

If Thomson's right, then the Kantian solution—which rests on the right to be treated as a person, not merely as a means to an end—does not solve the Trolley Problem.

. ⁓ .

SOME PHILOSOPHERS THINK THOMSON is right. Rex is one of them. We talked about Loop recently.

"Would you pull the switch?" I asked.

"Yeah, it's just like the first case," he said. He meant Bystander at the Switch. "The track is longer. But that doesn't change anything."

"Well, something's changed," I said. Then I explained that, with the loop in place, you're using the worker's body to stop the trolley. "That makes it like Fat Man."

"Well, it's sorta like Fat Man," Rex said. "But it's different."

"How?"

He hesitated. "You're using him, but you're not."

"What do you mean?"

"He's already on the track. In Fat Man, you have to put him there. You have to push him. I think that's different."

Rex is right. That's different. The question is: Does the difference matter? Some philosophers think it does. In Transplant and Fat Man, you'd make physical contact with the people you'd kill. At the least, that's icky.

But does it matter morally? To test the idea, let's try one more case. We'll call it Fat Man Trapped. It starts the way Fat Man does: runaway trolley, five workers, and a fat man on a bridge. But as luck would have it, he's standing on a trap door, right above the track. If you pull a lever, he'll fall onto the track below, stopping the trolley and saving the five. Also, he'll die. But you'll never lay a finger on him.

Does that redeem the story? I don't think so. It might feel less icky to pull a lever than push him over. But either way, you're dropping him to his death. The mechanism hardly seems to matter.

The literature on the Trolley Problem is vast.* It contains a dizzying array of cases. And they quickly become convoluted. They involve avalanches, bombs, second trolleys, and lazy Susans that turn tracks.

This corner of philosophy is sometimes called Trolleyology. The name is partly pejorative, a signal that something has gone off the rails. We started with serious moral questions—about the scope and limits of our rights—and somehow ended up in endless arguments about trolleys, set in stories that could not come to pass.

To outsiders, this looks like madness. Indeed, my favorite critique of Trolleyology was written by a train engineer named Derek Wilson. He sent this letter to the *Globe and Mail*:

> The ethical dilemmas involving a runaway trolley
> illustrate the uninformed situations that cause people's

---

*Perhaps the most surprising bit of it was Thomson's last word on the topic. Toward the end of her life, she changed her mind. Thomson decided that it wasn't permissible to divert the trolley in Bystander at the Switch after all. She came to think that case just like Transplant and Fat Man. If Thomson's right, that means that there's no Trolley Problem to solve, since the problem was all along aligning our judgments about those cases. Most people, however, continue to think it permissible to divert the trolley in Bystander at the Switch, leaving the Trolley Problem intact.

eyes to glaze over in philosophy class. Trolleys and
trains are unlikely to run away because they're
equipped with a "dead man's pedal" that applies the
brakes if the driver is incapacitated.

The potential rescuer would not have the choice of
"throwing the switch" because track switches are
locked to prevent vandalism. And the rescuer's
response would depend on the speed of the trolley.
If the speed were less than 15 kilometers an hour,
the rescuer could jump onto the trolley, sound the
bell and save all five lives. If the speed were less than
30 km/h, then the rescuer (with a switch lock key)
could throw the switch and kill only the one person
on the branch line.

If the trolley were moving faster than 30 km/h,
throwing the switch would cause it to derail, which
would injure or kill the passengers but save the
workers on the tracks. So the better choice is to allow
the occupied trolley to run through on the main track
and, regrettably, kill the five workers.

I love that letter, for two reasons. First, it's a reminder that the real
world is never so simple as a philosopher's hypothetical.

Sometimes it's simpler. That's the way Wilson sees it. If you know a
bit about trolleys, he thinks, you'll see that the Trolley Problem is easy
to solve.

At the same time, Wilson shows us that the real world is more complicated than the stories philosophers tell. Look how much we left out:
dead man's pedals, the speed of the trolley, and crucially, the fact that
the switch would likely be locked.

Actual trolley problems look nothing like the Trolley Problem! And
yet philosophers have good reason to tell too simple stories. We're trying
to isolate one problem, when the real world has a nasty habit of throwing
up several at the same time.

The second reason I love Wilson's letter is that, even as he criticizes philosophers, he's doing philosophy. His instincts are utilitarian—save as many people as possible—so he'd throw the switch and kill the one if the trolley was traveling less than 30 kilometers per hour. But if the trolley was going faster, he'd let it kill the five, so as to save the (presumably greater number of) people on the trolley from dying in a derailment.

Wilson thinks it's obvious that this is what we should do, so obvious that it doesn't require an argument. But it's far from obvious. If Wilson was in my class, I'd ask him what he thinks about Transplant. I'd want to know: If Wilson would kill one worker to save five (when the trolley is traveling between 15 and 30 kilometers per hour), would he also take a life in Transplant? If he said no, we'd be off to the races, working with just the sorts of stories that irk him.

———

WHAT IS THE ANSWER to the Trolley Problem? Hank asks all the time. He's used to hearing about legal cases, since I tell him about the ones I teach.

"Tell me another case, my daddy," he says when he's bored.

He knows that, after a bit of back-and-forth about how he thinks the case should have come out, I'll tell him what the court decided. So ever since I first taught him the Trolley Problem, he keeps asking: "What did the judge say?" And he will not accept my attempts to explain that the story is not real. He desperately wants to know the answer.

I do too. But in philosophy, there's no answer key. You've got to work things out yourself, as best you can. If you gave me an afternoon and a whiteboard, I'd try to convince you that Rex is wrong about Loop—and that Thomson is too. I'd argue that the extra bit of track does make a difference. I'd throw new cases on the board. And I'd defend a version of the Kantian idea—that we're not allowed to use one person to save five.

Once I wrapped that up, I'd spring my surprise. In a roundabout way, our collection of cases sheds light on the debate about abortion. If the state forces a woman to carry a pregnancy to term, it's using her body as a means to an end. That's not permissible, even when a life is at stake. (Or so I'd argue. As I said, it would take a while.)

In making my case, I'd close the loop on the Trolley Problem. Trolleys were introduced to philosophy by an English philosopher named Philippa Foot—in a paper about abortion. Thomson made trolleys famous by refining Foot's story and introducing others. But the point was never to sort out what Derek Wilson—or anyone else who works with trolleys—should do when they're out of control.

For philosophers, trolleys are tools for thinking about the structure of morality—for thinking about what rights we have, and when those rights yield to the needs of others. They're tools for thinking about serious issues, like abortion and . . . the laws of war.

Imagine, for a moment, that you're Harry Truman, trying to decide whether to drop an atomic bomb (called Fat Man) on the city of Nagasaki. The bomb will kill tens of thousands. But it will shorten the war, saving many more.*

When are you permitted to kill some people to save others? *That* is an important question. And the Trolley Problem helps us think about it. If it seems silly to outsiders, that's because the trolleys crossed into popular culture without the serious questions that called them forth.

Trolleys may not matter much. But rights do.

·—~—·

ESPECIALLY WHEN YOU LIVE with little kids. Hank did not know what rights were when he worried that he didn't have any. But he was already adept at asserting them. Every time he said "mine" as a way of warding

---

*Or so you believe. You might be wrong, and there's another moral question lurking there: How should you make decisions when you aren't certain about the outcomes?

off a kid who wanted to play with a toy, he was staking a claim to an object—and the right to exclude others from it, even if only for a bit.

When you first bring a baby home from the hospital, your main job is to keep the kid alive. It's custodial care: feed, burp, bathe, and change an endless series of diapers. Then wake up and do it all again, assuming you even slept. The task that comes after that—more than a year later—is integrating the kid into the community. To do that, you have to introduce the kid to the idea of rights and responsibilities—even if you aren't yet using those words. When Hank would kidnap Giraffey, we'd explain that he had to ask first, since Giraffey was Rex's. We also taught Hank what was his—and when Rex needed to ask his permission.

Those early property lessons were soon supplemented by lessons in promising, privacy, and personal space. Sometimes it felt like we were running a little law school for students who had no idea what their rights and responsibilities were. In contracts class, the boys learned to keep their promises. In torts, they learned to keep their hands to themselves—and knock on doors that are closed. In criminal law, they learned that there are consequences for bad behavior.

There's more to morality than rights and responsibilities. Indeed, one of the most important lessons a kid can learn is that you shouldn't always stand on your rights. You should share what's yours, at least some of the time, even though you have the right to exclude others from it. That's kind and caring, and when kids acquire those virtues, rights recede in importance. But the early years of parenting are mostly about morality, in one form or another. That's why we've started our journey with questions about rights—and are soon to turn to revenge, punishment, and authority, topics that are each, in their own way, connected to rights.

⁘

As the boys learned about rights, they became little lawyers—ready to assert their rights and (as we'll see in chapter 3) defend themselves from allegations that they'd breached the rights of others. Indeed, as soon as Hank knew what rights were, he saw them everywhere.

One night, we took the boys out for tacos. Hank (then six) noticed the Fanta in the soda cooler. And he asked, six or seventeen times, whether he could have one. We said no, and we sat down to eat. Hank was not happy, and he mounted a protest. Indeed, he declared that we were violating his rights.

"What right is that?" I asked.

"The right to decide what to drink."

"Is that a right that you have?"

"Yes!" he said emphatically.

"Why?" This is one of my favorite parenting tricks.

Kids wield *why* like a weapon. Often they ask out of genuine curiosity, so it's good to offer explanations when you can. But there's no such thing as a complete explanation. Every explanation leaves a lot left unsaid. That means kids can always ask why again. Over and over, ad nauseam.

At the start, they do it for fun; they want to see how many explanations you'll offer. But as they get older, they start to realize that a well-placed *why* can expose the shaky foundations of your authority. Or just drive you insane.

But grown-ups can turn the game around: ask *why* and make a kid make an argument.

So that's what I did with Hank. I asked: "Why do you have a right to decide what to drink?"

"I don't know," he said with a shrug. "I just do."

"No, that doesn't work," I said. "If you say you have a right, you better have a reason."

The gears in Hank's head started to turn, and sure enough he gave me a reason—two, in fact.

"If you get to decide what I drink," Hank said, "you might make me drink something that I don't like." Let's call this the *argument from self-*

knowledge. To that he added: "*You* get to decide what *you* drink, so *I* should be able to decide what *I* drink." Let's call that the *argument from equality.*

Are these arguments any good? No, not at all.

Start with the argument from self-knowledge. There's little risk that I'll demand Hank drink something he doesn't like. Most nights, Hank has just two options: milk or water. He likes milk just fine, and though he wouldn't say he likes water, he doesn't dislike it.

Moreover, the argument from self-knowledge assumes that it matters whether Hank has a drink he likes. And perhaps it does matter. But there's something else that matters more. Hank needs a healthy diet. That's why we offer him water and milk. Sugary drinks are a special treat. Left to his own devices, Hank would have diabetes within a week.

What about the argument from equality? Equality arguments are compelling when people are similarly situated. But Hank and I are not. I know a lot more than he does. For instance, I know about diabetes and how he might get it. I also have capacities for self-control that Hank hasn't yet acquired. But most important, I have responsibility for him that he doesn't have for me. Hank will inevitably grow up, but it's my job to make sure that he's a grown-up grown-up, not an overgrown child. To do that, I need to set limits, not least to the amount of Fanta Hank can consume.

These are all reasons to think that Hank does not, in fact, have a right to decide what to drink. Indeed, they are reasons to think that I have a right to decide what he may drink (or, rather, that Julie and I do jointly, as Hank's parents).

I explained some of that to Hank. And I reminded him that, when he's grown up, he'll get to make his own choices. But for now, he's stuck with us.

I cut the kid a deal, though. I wanted the war to end.

"If you stop arguing about it," I said, "then you can have a soda when our friends come over Saturday night."

"Do you promise?" Hank asked.

"Yes."

"Okay," he said.

Saturday arrived, and so did our friends. Hank set off to claim his soda as soon as they came in.

As he went, he announced: "I have a right to a root beer."

2

REVENGE

Hank had the day off, so I did too. And we were in the midst of one of his favorite activities. I was tossing him around the bed while he had a giggle fit.

Then, all of a sudden, Hank went quiet.

"What's up, Hank? Are you okay?"

"Yesterday," Hank started, "Caden called me a floofer doofer, and then Kelly came to talk to me."

There are lots of questions you could ask about that sentence. Some of them are easy to answer. Caden was a kid in the Sycamore Room at school, where Hank had recently taken up residence, just shy of his fourth birthday.* Kelly was the lead teacher. Since I knew all that, I went with: "What's a floofer doofer?"

"Daddy, it's bad."

"Are you sure? Maybe floofer doofers are cool. Should we Google it?"

---

*For the record, Caden's name isn't Caden. I've changed the names of kids that aren't mine to protect the innocent—and Caden.

"Daddy! Floofer doofers are *not cool*."

We argued about that for a while, because it's fun to say "floofer doofer" and even more fun to hear Hank say it. But of course, Hank was right. It's awful to be a floofer doofer, even though no one knows what the fuck a floofer doofer is. You might as well be a fuckface. (Fun fact: no one knows what a fuckface is either. Insults are weird that way.)

In any event, it was the second part of the story that Hank really wanted to talk about. The part where Kelly comes to talk to him.

"Did Kelly talk to Caden too?"

"No," Hank said, indignant. "She only talked to me."

"Why? Did you tell her what Caden called you?"

"Not until after."

"Not until after what?"

At that point, the witness went silent.

"Hank, did you do something to Caden?"

Silence.

"Hank, did you do something to Caden?"

"Kelly talked to me."

"About what, Hank?"

The witness would not crack. And I respect that. So I shifted tactics.

"Hank, did you think it was okay to do something mean to Caden because he said something mean to you?"

"*Yes*," Hank said, as if I were stupid. "*He called me a floofer doofer*."

~

AT THAT POINT, a good parent would have taught their kid the Motown classic "Two Wrongs Don't Make a Right,"* which sits just behind "The Golden Rule" on *Billboard*'s Pop Morality chart.

---

*Seriously. Berry Gordy Jr. and Smokey Robinson wrote a song called "Two Wrongs Don't Make a Right," which was recorded by Barrett Strong in 1961 and Mary Wells in 1963.

Alas, I am not a good parent. I am an *awesome* parent. So we spent the next twenty minutes rocking out to revenge songs, starting with James Brown's 1973 funk fantasia "The Payback." ("Revenge! I'm mad! Got to get back! Need some get back! Payback!")

Actually, I'm not that cool. At least, not in real time. So I didn't play James Brown *or* teach Hank that two wrongs don't make a right. And I regret the Brown bit, because it took me years to learn that kids think his lyrics are hilarious. Which they are. ("Uh! Ha! Good God! Darn good!") They also love his music. Which they should. (Just be careful which song you play, or you'll replicate the conversation Hank and I had about sex machines.)

But you know what I don't regret? Passing up the chance to teach Hank that two wrongs don't make a right. That's my least favorite piece of parental propaganda, because two wrongs *can* make a right. Or, rather, the second wrong can set things right. And we're lying to our kids—and maybe ourselves—when we say otherwise.

* * *

WHY ARE WE SO QUICK to reject revenge? Well, to start, it's risky. If you attempt to hurt someone, you might get hurt yourself. But worse than that, revenge can lead to reprisal, and then revenge, and then reprisal, and then revenge, and then reprisal. So you might find yourself in an endless cycle of violence.

But risk is not the only reason we reject revenge. The violence strikes many people as senseless. Take the Old Testament formula *an eye for an eye*, and let's amp up Caden's attack on Hank. Suppose that Caden put Hank's eye out. How, exactly, would Hank taking Caden's eye make anything any better? Hank wouldn't get his eye back. We'd just have an extra kid who had to learn to live with one eye.

So why do we seek revenge if it's so senseless?

One possibility is that we're just wired up to want it whenever someone wrongs us. Indeed, there's evidence that little kids in particular are prone to seek revenge. In one study, kids between four and eight were asked to play a computer game in which other participants (controlled by the researchers) would either steal their stickers or give them stickers as gifts. When the kids got the chance, they took revenge on the sticker stealers, stealing from them at much higher rates than they did from other participants. But they did not show the same reciprocity when it came to kindness. A kid who'd received a gift was no more likely to give one to the giver than to give one to anyone else. Getting even, it seems, comes more naturally than giving back.

And there's more evidence for the revenge-is-hardwired hypothesis. Scientists say that insults arouse an appetite for revenge, in a rather literal sense. They activate the same part of the brain—the left prefrontal cortex—that lights up when people seek to satisfy hunger and other cravings. So Homer was onto something when he suggested that revenge is sweet. And he might have undersold it. I saw a T-shirt once that said revenge is better than sex. And Joseph Stalin turned that up to eleven, insisting that revenge is life's greatest pleasure.*

I don't know about that. Sex can be pretty great. And Stalin was a sociopath. But revenge can sure satisfy, and the pleasure we take in it might well be a function of some circuitry buried deep in our brains. But even if we're disposed to seek revenge by an animal instinct, we can still ask what purpose it serves—and whether, on reflection, we should act on that impulse or restrain it. That is, we can ask whether revenge is really as senseless as it seems.

---

*Simon Sebag Montefiore relays the story: "At a boozy dinner, Kamenev asked everyone round the table to declare their greatest pleasure in life. . . . Stalin answered: 'My greatest pleasure is to choose one's victim, prepare one's plans minutely, slake an implacable vengeance, and then go to bed. There's nothing sweeter in the world.'"

WILLIAM IAN MILLER is my most entertaining colleague. He's one of the world's leading experts on revenge—and the cultures that practiced it. And he's every bit as fun as that sounds, for the stories he knows and the way he sees the world. Miller once told me that he took out too little life insurance *on purpose*. "I don't want my family to be destitute if I die," he explained, "but I want to make sure they'll miss me." He asked if I was well insured, and I said reasonably so. He told me to watch my back. (Rex was still a toddler when we had that chat.)

Miller doesn't have the least bit of patience for those who think revenge irrational. On its own, Caden's eye isn't helpful to Hank. But taking it surely is. If people expect Hank to strike back, they'll think twice about striking first. A reputation for revenge is an insurance policy; it protects you from injuries. And it's even better than ordinary insurance, since it prevents the injuries entirely, instead of paying cash to help you cope with them.

So revenge can be rational. But cold calculation can't account for the pleasure that people take in it. Or the fact that they're willing to pursue it past the point at which it's rational. The pleasure, it seems, is a form of schadenfreude—pleasure at the suffering of another, specifically the person who made you suffer.

But why take pleasure in that? A common answer is: he deserves it. Indeed, some think that there's a special form of justice—*retributive justice*—that demands that those who (wrongfully) cause others to suffer should suffer themselves. Unless and until that suffering is inflicted, some cosmic account is out of whack. The pleasure, on this picture, is pleasure at seeing justice done.

That sounds a bit impersonal, though. Those who seek revenge want to inflict the suffering themselves, not just see it done. It's not a cosmic account that's out of whack. It's an interpersonal one. *It's payback time,* we say. *He's got to pay for what he's done.* Those are accounting metaphors, and they're inconsistent, since they swap the roles of debtor and creditor. But that doesn't matter. The point is: the books aren't in balance, so it's time to *get even.*

SHOULD WE TAKE THAT sort of talk seriously? Over the course of human history, many people have, maybe even most. So I'm reluctant to say we shouldn't. And yet I've got serious reservations. I don't know where the cosmic account books are kept, or why we should care what's in them. If they belong to God, he'll surely balance the books. ("Vengeance is mine," saith the Lord.) And I think we need more than a metaphor to justify putting eyes out ourselves.

Some philosophers reject the idea of retributive justice. They think there's nothing more to it than misguided metaphors, and that we'd do well to leave it behind. I think we can redeem it. But we won't try until the next chapter, when we take up punishment. For now, I want to focus on a different sort of justice. In fact, let's put two on the table.

Long ago, Aristotle drew a distinction between *distributive justice* and *corrective justice.* When we worry about inequality, we're worrying about distributive justice. We've got a pie, and we're arguing over how to split it. If your slice is bigger than mine, I might complain that we didn't distribute it equitably. Now suppose that we each have our slices, however large. And you steal mine. I want it back. Aristotle says that *corrective justice* demands that you return it to me. It demands that you make good my loss.

Is revenge a way of doing corrective justice? It sort of seems like it. *An eye for an eye* isn't far off from *give me back my pie.* If Hank takes Caden's eye, he gets back what he lost—an eye. But he doesn't get *just* what he lost, and that matters. Caden's eye isn't much use to Hank, since he can't see with it.

Nevertheless, Miller says, an eye for an eye is a way of doing corrective justice, and a rather genius one at that. The key is to see that compensation doesn't always have to be paid in kind. Sometimes you return my pie. Sometimes you pay for it. So too, it turns out, with eyes.

The aim of an eye for an eye, Miller says, was not to see more eyes put out. Rather, the *law of the talion* (that's the fancy name for the rule exemplified by an eye for an eye) gives victims leverage over the people who wronged them. If Caden and Hank had lived in biblical times (and were all grown up), then as soon as Caden put Hank's eye out, the talion would make Hank the owner of one of Caden's eyes. He could take it if he wanted it. And he'd sure want Caden to think that he would. But chances are, Hank wouldn't actually take Caden's eye, because Caden would *buy it back* from him. The price that Caden paid to keep his eye would compensate Hank for losing his.

In other words, the prospect of losing his own eye pushes Caden to satisfy the demands of corrective justice by compensating Hank for his. The talion is, in a funny way, all about empathy. It's a way of forcing you to feel other people's pain. If you injure someone, you're subject to exactly the same injury that you inflicted. That gives you reason to imagine suffering an injury before you inflict it on someone else. The hope is that holds you back, so that no one gets injured at all. But if deterrence doesn't work, the talion gives you reason to compensate the injuries that you cause, since you're soon to suffer them yourself if you don't pay up.

"Hey, Rex, can I tell you a story about revenge?" I asked one day at lunch. Rex was ten.

"Will it be gross?" he asked.

"No," I assured him.

"Okay."

"Well, maybe a little," I admitted.

"Do you have to tell me?"

"Yeah, I really do."

"You're writing about revenge, aren't you?"

The kid is onto me. "Yeah, I am."

"Okay, fine."

The story I told Rex comes from an Icelandic saga—*The Saga of Gudmund the Worthy*.

"There's a guy named Skæring," I started, "and he's down at the port doing business with some Norwegian merchants. The deal goes bad, and they chop off his hand."

"Dad! That's gross. A lot gross."

"Yeah, okay. But that's the only part that's gross. I promise. Do you want to know what happens next?"

"Yeah," Rex said.

"Skæring goes to get help from a relative—a guy named Gudmund. Gudmund gathers up a group of men, and they ride to the port to confront the Norwegians. What do you think they do when they get there?"

"Kill them."

"Nope. When Gudmund gets there, he demands that the Norwegians compensate Skæring for his hand. Do you know what that means?"

"No."

"It means that he wants them to pay Skæring some money to make him feel better about losing his hand."

"Okay. Do they pay?"

"They say they'll pay whatever price Gudmund says is fair. But then Gudmund sets the price, and it's big. Like, really big."

"How big?"

"*Thirty hundreds.*"

"Is that a lot?"

"The saga says so. It says that's how much people would've expected to pay for killing someone like Skæring, not for chopping off his hand."

"Do they pay it?"

"Nope. They get mad at Gudmund. They think he's asking too much."

"What does Gudmund do?"

"Guess."

"He kills them," Rex said seriously.

"Nope."

"He chops off their hands!" Now he was getting a feel for the talion.

"No, but you're getting closer. Gudmund was pretty clever. What do you think he'd do before chopping anything off?"

"He'd tell them he was gonna do it if they didn't pay!"

"Exactly! Gudmund said that he'd pay Skæring the thirty hundreds himself. Then he'd pick a Norwegian guy and chop off his hand. He said the Norwegians could compensate that guy as cheaply as they liked."

"Did that work?" Rex asked.

"What do you think?"

"I bet they paid," he said.

"That's right—they paid the thirty hundreds."

"Gudmund was *smart*," Rex said.

GUDMUND *WAS* SMART. And so was the talion. The Norwegians paid up because Gudmund recast the significance of the payment. It was no longer the price to purchase Skæring's hand; it was the price to keep one of their own. And as Miller observes, most people "are willing to pay more to save their own hands than they would be willing to pay to take someone else's." Which makes sense. Hands are more helpful when attached to their original owners.

Gudmund was sharp in another way too. He didn't just get the Norwegians to pay. He humiliated them in the process, by suggesting that they were cheap. They attempted a grand gesture by allowing Gudmund to set the price for Skæring's hand. Then they balked at the price he set, allowing Gudmund to get in a grand gesture of his own by volunteering to compensate Skæring at the sky-high price himself. Finally, Gudmund cast the Norwegians as cowards, since their willingness to pay shifted as soon as their own hands were at risk.

In doing all that, Gudmund increased his honor. But what's that? And why did it matter? Honor defies simple definition. It was the abstract quality that set a person's place in the social hierarchy. And it was all important in societies like saga Iceland. As Miller explains:

> Honor was what provided the basis for your counting for something, for your being listened to, for having people have second thoughts before taking your land or raping you or your daughter. It even governed how you spoke, how loudly, how often, and to whom and when, and whether you were attended to when you did; it governed how you held your shoulders, how tall you stood—literally, not figuratively—and how long you could look at someone or even dare to look at him at all.

In short, honor was a measure of your value in the eyes of others. I'll say more about it later on. But before we leave Gudmund behind, let's compare the way he settled Skæring's claim with the way that courts would do it today.

——— ∾ ———

WE DON'T FOLLOW THE LAW of the talion anymore. But courts still try to do corrective justice. If you suffer an injury, you can sue the person who caused it. And if you show that the injury resulted from a wrong, the court will award compensation.

Officially, courts set compensation without any appeal to emotion, empathy or otherwise. Jurors are instructed to award fair and reasonable compensation for the injuries suffered by a successful plaintiff. In practice, however, plaintiffs' lawyers seek jurors' sympathy for their clients. They describe the plaintiff's injuries in dark detail, making them sound as pitiful as possible to drive up damage awards.

But sympathy turns out to be less powerful than empathy. I teach my students a case about Kay Kenton. She was in the lobby of a Hyatt Regency Hotel when two poorly designed skywalks, weighing more than fifteen tons, collapsed on the guests below. More than a hundred people were killed. Kenton survived. But she suffered devastating injuries: a broken neck; lost sensation throughout her body; impaired breathing, bladder, and bowel function; plus tremendous pain and psychological trauma, among many other problems.

The jury awarded Kenton $4 million. That sounds like a lot. At least, until you think about what it covers. Kenton's medical expenses were estimated to run more than a million dollars. At the time of the accident, she was in law school. The evidence suggested that she'd never work again, in any job, let alone as a lawyer. Her lost wages were estimated at roughly $2 million over the course of her career. Finally, the jury was invited to put a price on Kenton's pain and suffering; subtraction suggests that they pegged it at something like $1 million.

Spelled out that way, the award doesn't seem so generous (and it's even less generous than it seems, since her lawyer likely took a quarter of it, maybe more). Would you agree to suffer Kenton's injuries if someone agreed to cover your costs and kick in another million for your pain and suffering? I wouldn't. Not a chance.

And yet Hyatt had the audacity to ask the court to cut the award in half, arguing that it was excessive. The court shut that down. But ask: How much would Hyatt have been willing to pay to prevent someone in its C-suite from suffering Kenton's injuries? Suppose that we followed the law of the talion, so that Kenton had the right to drop a skywalk (or similarly heavy object) on Hyatt's CEO. How much would the company pay to prevent her from doing it?

If your guess is more than $4 million, I'm pretty sure you're right. I could see them paying $40 million. Or more. Maybe *much* more. That's the power of empathy. And the power of the talion lies in its ability to harness it.

I'm sure the jurors felt sorry for Kenton—sympathized with her situation. But I doubt they felt her pain. The Hyatt executives would have if they feared it for themselves.

—————~——

EMPATHY IS NOT THE only attraction of an eye for an eye. It sets a limit on revenge, since it also means *no more than* an eye for an eye.

Evolution seems to have endowed us with an appetite for revenge. But appetites can get out of hand. Just think how often you overeat. (Perhaps I'm projecting here. Rex says *I ate too much* is the motto of Hershovitz men.)

Some people want more than an eye for an eye. They overvalue themselves. Or undervalue others. Or simply go berserk at the slightest slight.

Revenge cultures had no tolerance for these types, since there was little possibility of peace in their presence. An eye for an eye helped rein them in by establishing what counted as reasonable compensation. And so did characters called *oddmen*, who would step in to settle disputes when people couldn't reach an agreement on their own. They were *odd* because they were third parties to disputes. As Miller puts it, "You needed odd to get even or you would forever be at odds."

Juries are descended from oddmen. They do the same job. They represent the community and decide what counts as reasonable compensation. But they set that compensation differently than oddmen did. Oddmen enforced an eye for an eye. They didn't sell body parts on the cheap, like juries tend to do.

I suspect that sounds a bit off. In popular imagination, American juries are out of control—they award too much compensation, not too little. But I don't see it that way. Courts routinely set damages well below what anyone would accept for suffering an injury if you asked them in advance.

Sometimes I ask my law students what they would want in return for agreeing to suffer Kenton's injuries. Most say there's no price at which they would do it. A few say that hundreds of millions of dollars might entice; they're willing to sacrifice themselves for their families. But I've never had a single student say she'd accept the injuries for the $4 million that Kenton actually received.

We like to think that we're more refined than those for whom revenge was a regular part of life. We imagine that life was "cheap, nasty, and brutish among such violent souls." But that's a mistake, Miller says. Indeed, life was expensive in communities committed to the talion. Take one and pay with your own. We are the people who put little value on life and limb.*

That said, there's no chance I'd want to live by the talion. Much of modern life is possible only because we let juries sell bodies on the cheap. As Miller points out, we wouldn't drive cars if "every road fatality gave the victim's kin a right to kill." And it's not just cars that we'd have to give up. It's all the machinery of modern life: planes, trains, trucks, power tools—more or less everything with a motor. All that is made possible by our willingness to abandon an eye for an eye and accept more meager compensation.

But the conveniences of modern life are far from the only reason to reject revenge culture. Earlier I suggested that Caden could buy his eye back from Hank. But he'd need money to make that work. If he didn't have it, he'd have to give up his eye. Or let Hank have something else he valued—likely Caden's labor, as a debt slave, until he'd worked off the cost of his eye. So an eye for an eye was not really a recipe for equality.

And slavery was not the only repugnant feature of societies that ad-

---

*At least in court, where the question is how to respond to wrongdoing. As Miller points out, we spend staggering sums on health care, especially at the end of life. But that, he adds, bespeaks "less of our virtue than of our vice, less of our commitment to human dignity than of our lack thereof. We are so afraid of death and pain that we will bankrupt our grandchildren's generation to add on more useless years at the butt-end of our days than we know what to do with." I think Miller's off the mark on the money bit; our grandkids won't be bankrupted by Medicare. But it's worth wondering what the juxtaposition he observes says about our values.

hered to an eye for an eye. The very idea of honor was another. Remember when I said that Gudmund set the price for Skæring's hand at roughly what people expected to pay for killing someone like Skæring? The value of people—and their parts—varied with their honor. Some people (women, servants, slaves) didn't count at all, or counted only because they belonged to someone who did. And everyone who did count was constantly competing to increase their honor—or keep it from being captured by someone else.

Which sounds exhausting. We should be grateful to live in a society where a person's worth is a function of something worthwhile, like the number of Likes on her latest Facebook post.

Oh, wait. I meant to say: We should be grateful to live in a society that values everyone equally.

Shit. That's still not right. I meant to say: We should be grateful to live in a society that *says* that it values everyone equally.

And I mean that. We don't live up to that ideal. But at least it *is* our ideal. That is, in itself, a moral achievement, since few societies have shared that ambition. Of course, it would be leagues better if we actually managed to build a society that valued everyone equally.

But the point for now is just this: we can reject revenge culture and still recognize that an eye for an eye was, in its time, a genius way of doing justice.

———

BUT LITTLE KIDS KNOW nothing of that genius, and still they seek revenge. Why? Hank wasn't so articulate about his reasons. When pressed to explain himself, he repeatedly referenced a fact already in evidence—that Caden had called him a floofer doofer—as if that were explanation enough.

It's not. But it's no mystery why Hank took revenge. He was standing up for himself. But what does that mean? And why did Hank need to do it?

For the reasons we saw earlier, it's in Hank's interest to make sure that other kids don't think he's an easy mark. That is, it's in his interest to develop a reputation for revenge. Hank couldn't articulate that, of course. But he might have sensed it. Indeed, if we're wired up to want revenge, that's likely the reason why.

But I think there's more to it than that—that Hank has something else at stake beyond his future safety. For help here, we can turn to the philosopher who shaped my thinking on these subjects. Pamela Hieronymi was a consultant for *The Good Place*; in fact, she had a cameo appearance in the last episode. Hieronymi is a sharp observer of our moral lives. She's interested in the way that we respond to wrongdoing. In particular, she's interested in the messages that wrongdoing sends and the reasons we have to respond to them.

Suppose that Caden pushes Hank. Hank might get hurt. He might not. But the push is bothersome either way, because it sends a message. It says that Hank is the kind of kid that Caden can push around.

Hank has reasons to resist that message. Indeed, Hieronymi says his *self-respect* is at stake. Hank won't want to see himself as the kind of kid that can be pushed around. And on top of that, his *social status* is at stake. Hank won't want others to see him as the kind of kid they can push around.

To defend his social status—and restore his self-respect—Hank has to respond to Caden. If he lets it go—and nobody else responds either—he runs the risk that people will conclude that Caden can push him around. Indeed, he may come to think so himself. All too often, people become accustomed to abuse and start to see it as something they must live with—or, worse yet, as something they deserve.

How should Hank respond? Hieronymi suggests that he ought to feel anger and resentment. Those aren't attractive emotions, and lots of people react reflexively against them. But Hieronymi subscribes to a long tradition in philosophy that sees resentment as a matter of self-respect.

Resentment is a protest against the message implicit in wrongdoing. If Hank resents Caden, he insists, if only to himself, that it's not okay for Caden to push him around.

But resentment is just a first step. The next step is to make the protest public. That's what you do when you stand up for yourself. And there are several ways Hank could do it. To start, he could simply tell Caden: *You can't push me around.* But simply saying it may not be enough. If Caden doesn't suffer a consequence for pushing Hank, he might continue to think that he can push Hank around, regardless of what Hank has to say about it. And other kids might get the same impression.

So Hank has reason to see to it that Caden suffers a consequence. How? He can push Caden back. That's a way of saying: *You can't push me around.* But more than that, it's a way of saying: *I am your equal. If you can push me, I can push you.*

Caden didn't push Hank. He called him a floofer doofer. But that just means his message was more explicit.

Caden named the low status Hank held in his eyes. Hank was a floofer doofer. Or at least a kid who could be called one. And he communicated that to Hank and every other kid in earshot of the insult.

I don't know what Hank did in response. It couldn't have been that bad, because we didn't get an incident report. If I had to guess, Hank returned the insult in kind, calling Caden a floofer doofer or something similarly ridiculous. But whatever Hank did, he was standing up for himself—saying to Caden and every other kid in earshot: *I'm not the kind of kid you can call a floofer doofer.*

<hr>

SUPPOSE YOU HAD FRONT-ROW SEATS to that fight. Would you pull Hank aside to tell him that two wrongs don't make a right? I wouldn't. In fact, I'd feel good about the guy—like he was gonna be okay in the world.

Way back at the start, I said that the second wrong could set things right, and I stand by that. The two wrongs don't have the same symbolic significance. In calling Hank a floofer doofer, Caden hoped to show that he was Hank's superior. In returning the insult, Hank hoped to show that he was Caden's equal.

Indeed, if I have any reservation about the slogan *the second wrong can set things right*, it's that the second wrong really isn't a wrong at all, so long as you don't take it too far. The moral quality of an act is partly a function of what it communicates. There's a world of difference between standing up for yourself and cutting others down, even if you say the same words.

***

"HAVE YOU EVER TAKEN REVENGE?" I asked the boys recently. (Hank has no recollection of L'Affaire du Floofer Doofer.)

"Yeah," Rex said. "When Hank hits my butt, I hit his butt back."

"Me too!" Hank said, super proud. "When Rex hits my butt, I hit his butt back."

"Is that okay?" I asked.

"Yeah, we're brothers—we can touch each other's butts," Hank said, missing the point.

"Have you ever taken revenge on someone at school?" I asked.

"No," Rex said. "Two wrongs don't make a right."

"Why do you say that?"

"If someone does something wrong, and then you do something wrong back, you're just as bad," Rex said.

"Are you sure about that?"

"Yeah."

"Well, what if the first person was just being mean, and the second person was standing up for himself?"

"Oh, I see," said Rex. "I guess it's not just as bad. It's just not good."

"Why's that?"

"Well, there's always something else you can do."

There's truth in that. You don't have to strike back to stand up for yourself. You can *use your words*, as we tell toddlers. And you can ask others to stand up for you too. Kelly, for instance, could have made clear that Caden can't call Hank a floofer doofer. And she might have done that had Hank appealed to her for help.

But I don't share Rex's optimism that there's always another way to respond. Hank could probably count on Kelly to correct Caden. But teachers don't always come to the rescue. And sometimes you look weak when you look to others for help. If you rely on Kelly for protection, what do you do when she's not there? I don't want my kid to hurt others. But I do want him to be capable of standing up for himself, at least when it comes to everyday insults and indignities.

I also want my kid to stand up for others. Resentment and revenge are ways for victims to resist the messages implicit in wrongdoing. But bystanders can play a role in rejecting those messages too. And when they do, they relieve victims of the work—and reassure them that not everyone sees them the way the wrongdoers do. One night when Hank was in kindergarten, he told us that he wasn't playing with some of his friends anymore, since they were treating another boy badly on the playground. He didn't want to be a part of it. And he wanted to know how he could make them stop. We were happy—that he was doing what he could to stand up for his friend and that he knew he needed to ask for help.

GROWN-UPS NEED HELP responding to wrongdoing too. They can't turn to parents and teachers like kids can. But they can turn to courts. Earlier I said that courts attempt to do corrective justice in response to wrongdoing. They don't succeed much, at least not in Aristotle's sense. Hyatt took a lot from Kenton—her ability to work, to live independently, to live pain-free, and much more. The money she was awarded might have helped her cope. But it didn't return what she lost. And revenge wouldn't have either. Injuring a Hyatt executive would not have erased her injuries.

There's another way to think about corrective justice, though. All too often, we can't repair injuries. But we can correct the messages that wrongdoing sends. When she went to court, Kenton called on her community to reject the message implicit in Hyatt's misconduct. At her request, the court made clear that Hyatt had a duty to watch out for her safety—and the safety of all its guests. And it made clear that Hyatt's failure to care for Kenton mattered—and that it would not be tolerated.

I think that's what lots of people are looking for when they go to court: vindication as much as compensation. They want the court to affirm that they were wronged—that they had a right not to be treated the way they were. And they want the court to make clear that their mistreatment matters.

When I pitch this point to my students, I tell them about Taylor Swift. In 2013, a radio host named David Mueller grabbed her butt as they posed for a picture. She complained about it, and he lost his job. He sued her for defamation, saying he'd never groped her. Swift counterclaimed for battery. She asked for a single dollar in damages, and she won.

What was the point? Swift didn't need another dollar. But money wasn't what her suit was about. Swift sued to make clear that her body was not public property, available to any man who wanted to touch it. In other words, she asked the court to reject the message Mueller's groping sent. The verdict told Mueller—and every man listening—that no one had a right to Swift's body but her. And because the court applied general principles of battery law, it sent a message about everybody's butt: hands off.

Litigation gets a bad rap. But courts give us a chance to call on our community to reject the messages that wrongdoing sends. *That* is corrective justice. And it's the best substitute for revenge.

· ⌒⌒⌒ ·

I'D BE REMISS if I didn't mention another piece of parental propaganda from *Billboard*'s Pop Morality chart: "Sticks and Stones May Break My Bones, but Words Will Never Hurt Me."

My mother was fond of that one. Whenever a kid said something mean to me, she'd trot that out—and try to persuade me that I should too. But even as a kid, I knew it wasn't true. Some words hurt. A lot more than broken bones.

I won't teach my kids "Sticks and Stones," because I want them to feel okay about the fact that words hurt. But I do think there's something to learn from it. At its best, "Sticks and Stones" is a subtle bluff. Words might hurt, but sometimes you're better off acting as if they don't.

A kid who calls you a floofer doofer is hoping to get a rise out of you. So it's best not to give it to him, even if you're bothered by what he said. And it's even better if you can communicate that there's nothing he can say that will insult you. That's a way of flipping his script. Ignoring him signals that he's so insignificant, you don't care what he says. It's hard to pull that off. But if you can make it work, it's the best way to make him stop.

I taught Hank that one night when we were talking about a kid who'd said something mean. I told him I could teach him one of the most powerful sentences he could possibly say.

"Are you ready for it?" I asked.

"Yeah."

"Are you sure? It's really powerful."

"I'm ready," he insisted.

"When someone says something mean to you, you can say, *I don't care what you think*."

"Daddy doesn't care what I think!" Hank shouted, hoping to attract his mother's attention.

"No, goofball. I care what you think. That's what you can say when someone's mean. Do you want to practice?"

"Yeah."

"You're so short, even ants look down on you."

He giggled. Then he said, "I don't care what you think."

"Are those your eyebrows, or did caterpillars park on your face?"

More giggles. "I don't care what you think."

"Did you brush your teeth? Your breath smells like your face farted."

Wild laughter. Then: "I don't care what you think."

We went a few more rounds, but I was running out of kid-friendly cut-downs. So we called it quits and said our good nights.

I wrapped up the way I always do: "Good night, Hank. I love you."

"I don't care what you think."

Floofer doofer.

3

PUNISHMENT

"AIEEEEEEEE!"

"Quiet down, Rex. It's time to eat."

"AIEEEEEEEEEEEEEEEEEEEE!"

Rex was barely two, and he was finding his voice. Or, rather, finding out just how loud his voice could be. And he would not stop.

Finally, Julie snapped. "You need a break," she said, removing Rex from his high chair and carrying him to the living room. This was his first time-out. But there was no chance that he'd sit on his own, so Julie sat down with Rex in her lap. "We are taking a break because you are being too loud," she said.

"Why we takin a break?" Rex asked.

"We are taking a break because you are being too loud," Julie said again.

"We takin a break!" Rex said, with way too much glee for a kid who was supposed to be suffering.

A time-out, my social worker spouse would tell you, should be about as long as a kid's age. So two minutes later, she was back at the table with Rex.

"I want mo takin a break," Rex said, as she strapped him into his chair.

"It's time to eat, Rex."

"I want mo takin a break!"

"No, Rex, it's time to eat."

"AIEEEEEEEEEEEEEEEEEEEEEEEEEEEEEE!"

⁘

THAT DIDN'T GO WELL, and it's not hard to figure out why. Punishment is supposed to be unpleasant. But Rex found his time-out fun; it was a break from his routine, and he certainly didn't mind sitting in his mother's lap. If we really wanted to punish Rex, we'd have to be harsher.

But wait a minute. Why would we treat a child harshly? Or, better: Why would we treat *anyone* harshly? Just what is the justification for punishment?

A standard answer is *retribution*. That's the idea we encountered in the last chapter—that some people deserve to suffer, on account of the wrongs they've committed. Why? It's hard to say, and some retributivists decline to say. It strikes them as obvious that the morally wicked should suffer for their sins. Others offer metaphors, like the ones we met in the last chapter. Wrongdoers incur a debt to society, they say. They have to pay for what they've done.

As I said last go-around, we need more than a metaphor to explain why we'd inflict suffering on anyone, even those who have acted wrongly. And we certainly need more than a strongly felt feeling that we should. We need to know what we'd accomplish—what good we'd do—if we are to justify the bad that clearly comes with punishment.

Later on, I'll attempt to redeem the idea of retribution by explaining why it might make sense to make some people suffer. But let's put that on pause for a moment, since we can be sure that retribution does *not* play a role in explaining why we would treat a two-year-old harshly. Perhaps we could wrap our heads around the idea that some adults deserve to suffer. But it's hard to imagine that a little kid could—especially not a kid as little as Rex.

So what were we up to with the time-out? Well, we desperately wanted Rex to stop screeching. And eat lunch. But mainly, we wanted him to stop screeching so that we could eat lunch. The immediate point of the time-out was just that: get him to shut up by showing him that it wasn't in his interest to scream.

The two-dollar word for what we were trying to do is *deterrence*. It's the same thought we had with revenge. People respond to incentives, kids included. Rex was having fun screeching at the top of his lungs. If we wanted him to stop, we'd have to make it *no fun*. Unfortunately for us, Rex found the time-out more fun than the fun he started with, so he doubled down and screeched again.

At two years old, distraction would have been a better strategy than deterrence. And if that didn't work, ignoring the screeching would probably have squelched it sooner than punishing it. At least, that's the lesson I've learned from the trainer we consulted about our puppy, Bailey. She's a mini goldendoodle, and she likes to screech too. And jump on people. And nip at their hands. The trainer taught us a game called Invisible Dog. It couldn't be easier. When Bailey jumps or nips, we ignore her completely—act like she's not even there. The game ends the second she pulls back. Then we praise her wildly and give her a treat. The aim is to teach her that good things happen when she doesn't jump or nip. In other words, we're parenting through positive incentives, not negative ones.

And it works. Like, shockingly well. Like, if I had it to do all over again, I'd put little Rex on a leash and take him to the trainer. She knows what she's doing, so much better than we did. And she's not alone. Animal trainers are terrific at extinguishing bad behaviors and encouraging good ones. And for the most part, they do it without punishment. Or at least they do if they know what they're doing.

So why do we punish people? Why don't we just train them, in the way that we train animals? That's a good question. In 2006, *The New York Times* ran an essay by Amy Sutherland. She was writing a book about a school for animal trainers. And as she'd watched them work, she had a flash of inspiration: she could train her husband.

His name also happens to be Scott. And, at least at the time, he had a shocking set of habits. He left his clothes on the floor. And he lost his keys a lot. And, worse yet, he lost his mind when he did. These are things that I have never, ever done. At least not in the last day or two. So it was not at all a problem for me when my wife read Sutherland's article.

Actually, it was a huge problem, and I knew it as soon as I saw it. I disappeared our copy of the paper. And I resolved never to speak of what I'd read. Alas, I could not disappear the internet, and inevitably Julie saw Sutherland's article herself. Here's what she found. The article was called "What Shamu Taught Me About a Happy Marriage." In it, Sutherland explains that, before she started her study, she would nag her husband about his faults. That didn't work. In fact, it made things worse. The animal trainers gave her a way forward.

"The central lesson I learned from exotic animal trainers," Sutherland reported, "is that I should reward behavior I like and ignore behavior I don't. After all, you don't get a sea lion to balance a ball on the end of its nose by nagging." At SeaWorld, a dolphin trainer taught Sutherland *least reinforcing syndrome*. If a dolphin does something wrong, the trainer ignores it completely. She doesn't even look at the dolphin, since behaviors that don't get a response tend to die away. Sutherland also learned about a technique called *approximations*—rewarding the least little step toward the behavior one wants to encourage. And after that, the next little step. And then the next. And on and on, until the sea lion balances the ball on its nose.

At home, Sutherland put her new skills into practice. She thanked her husband if he put his laundry in the hamper. And she ignored the clothes that didn't make it in. Sure enough, his piles of clothes started to shrink. Before too long, her sea lion was balancing the ball on his nose.

Soon I noticed Julie running the same experiment. Suddenly, her complaints about my clothes stopped. I'd pick some up, and she'd thank me, way too enthusiastically. The same scene played out in the kitchen, whenever I'd put my dirty dishes into the dishwasher instead of piling them by the sink. I started to run little tests, and sure enough, the least step in the right direction yielded positive reinforcement.

"Are you Shamu-ing me?" I asked.

"Oh, shit," she said. "You saw that?"

"Everyone saw that," I said. It was one of the most emailed articles ever.

"Well, it works," she said, with a smile that suddenly slipped from her face. She'd just realized that she might have a problem too. "Have you been Shamu-ing me?" she asked.

I had no comment. And I still don't.

We laughed about the fact that we'd both attempted to keep the article secret. Then we negotiated a ceasefire. We agreed not to Shamu each other. But the truth is, Julie still Shamus me. I ignore it completely. Which, when you think about it, is some serious Shamu jujitsu. If she ever stops, I'll give her a treat.

～

DOES THAT IMAGE BOTHER YOU? Me giving Julie a treat, in an effort to induce good behavior? It should. And so should the reverse. It's a messed-up way for spouses to relate to each other. Indeed, it's a messed-up way for *people* to relate to each other. And seeing why will help us get a grip on a different way of thinking about punishment.

Peter Strawson was the Waynflete Professor of Metaphysical Philosophy at Oxford. He wrote one of the most influential papers in twentieth-century philosophy. It's called "Freedom and Resentment." In it, Strawson describes two different ways of looking at people. We can see them as objects, subject to the laws of cause and effect—as things we might manipulate or control. To look at people that way is to see them in roughly the way you see the appliances in your house. You fiddle with the thermostat to get the temperature you want. You mess with the settings on the microwave so that it warms your food without burning it. You swap the filter in your furnace so that it runs more efficiently. In all this, you adjust inputs to affect outputs. And that's just what Sutherland was doing with her husband.

To see a person as an object, Strawson said, is to see them as something "to be managed or handled or cured or trained." Sutherland wasn't shy about seeing her husband that way. In explaining her experiment, she said she wanted to "nudge him a little closer to perfect" and "make him into a mate who might annoy me a little less." Notice the verbs: she wanted to *nudge* him in a new direction, to *make* him something better than he was. Her husband was, in every sense, the object of her project—a thing to manipulate with her newfound skills.

Strawson called the attitude Sutherland took toward her husband *objective* (since it involved seeing him as an object). He contrasted it with the attitudes we display in ordinary relationships, which he labeled *reactive*. These are attitudes like anger, resentment, and gratitude. When we're in a relationship with someone—as spouses, colleagues, friends, or even just as fellow human beings—we have expectations for how the other person ought to behave. Most fundamentally, we expect people to treat us with goodwill. When they go beyond, we are grateful. But when they fall short—when they treat us badly—we feel anger and resentment.

Strawson said that reactive attitudes are central to seeing each other *as people* rather than as objects. People are responsible for what they do, in a way that mere objects are not. I don't get angry when my thermostat breaks. Or if I do, I don't get angry *at* my thermostat. I might get angry at the people who made it, the person who installed it, or even at myself for failing to buy a better one. Anger makes sense only when directed at a person who is (or at least might be) responsible. That's because anger conveys a judgment—that the person should have done better.

I know what you're thinking: Sometimes you get angry at inanimate objects. So do I. I have cursed my computer for crashing on more than one occasion. But when we get angry at an object, we're anthropomorphizing it. We're treating it like a person, responsible for what it does, even though we know it's not.

Sutherland was running that gambit in reverse—treating a person like an object. And actually, that makes more sense, since people *are* objects, subject to manipulation and control. But we are not *just* objects. We are also responsible for what we do. Or at least we can be. And reactive attitudes, like anger, are one way in which we hold each other responsible.

——————

"WHAT IS PUNISHMENT?" I asked the boys one night at dinner.

"It's something bad," Hank said. Followed by: "Can we not talk about that while I'm eating?" Hank doesn't like to talk about anything unpleasant—or really anything at all—while he's eating.

But Rex picked up the baton. "It's something bad someone does to you," he said. "Or it's something they make you do that you don't want to do."

"So if I say you need to practice piano when you'd rather play outside, I'm punishing you?" I asked.

"No," Rex said.

"Why not?"

"Because I didn't do anything wrong."

"So punishment is a response to wrongdoing?"

"Yeah!" Rex said. "It's when someone does something bad to you *because* you did something bad."

"Can we NOT talk about that while I'm eating?"

HANK CUT OFF THE CONVERSATION prematurely. But Rex still put together a pretty good account of punishment. Indeed, before Joel Feinberg came along, it was common to define punishment in roughly the way Rex did: harsh treatment, inflicted by an authority, in response to wrongdoing. (Or, as Rex put it: something bad someone does to you because you did something bad.)

Feinberg taught philosophy at the University of Arizona. One of his students, Clark Wolf, was my very first philosophy professor. Another, Jules Coleman, was my mentor in law school. So Feinberg is more or less my grandfather, as far as philosophy goes. And he was a leading thinker about criminal law too—the author of magisterial books about its proper scope and aims.

Feinberg saw a problem with the standard account of punishment. And we can see it too, if we think about pass-interference penalties in football. The penalty for pass interference—a first down at the spot of the foul—is harsh. Sometimes the outcome of the game hangs in the balance. And the penalty is imposed by an authority (the referee) for a wrong (pass interference). So the penalty is punishment if Rex's definition is right. But something seems off. Pass interference is a penalty, for sure. But we don't *punish* players for it.

Here's another example. You forget to move your car in a snowstorm, and it's towed when the plows come through. Again, that's harsh treatment. You'll have to trek to the impound lot and pay to get the car back. But again, it seems like you've been penalized, not punished. Indeed, if the fine is limited to the cost of towing and storing your car, it's not even clear that you've suffered a penalty; you've just been asked to pay the costs of your mistake.

What Rex's definition misses, according to Feinberg, is the symbolic significance of punishment. Punishment expresses reactive attitudes, like resentment and indignation. When a state brands someone a criminal and puts him in prison, it condemns what he's done. "Not only does the criminal feel the naked hostility of his guards and the outside world," Feinberg explained, "that hostility is self-righteous," since it is seen as a proper response to his wrong.

If punishment is what Feinberg says it is—a way of expressing reactive attitudes—two things follow. First, Julie didn't really punish Rex when she gave him a time-out. She was just trying to stop him from screeching. She didn't mean to condemn what he did. From Feinberg's perspective, Julie penalized Rex (and not all that well either). So maybe we've had our sports metaphor wrong all along. We shouldn't give kids time-outs; we should put them in penalty boxes.

Second, and more serious: the fact that punishment expresses reactive attitudes constrains who we can properly punish. Reactive attitudes, we saw before, are ways of holding people responsible for what they do. So we should only punish people who *are* responsible for what they do. That's why the criminal law contains lots of doctrines that aim to determine whether a defendant is, indeed, responsible for what he's done. We don't (at least officially) punish people who are insane or otherwise incompetent.* We don't punish people who were coerced into committing a crime. We only punish people we think should have done better.

~

WHY ARE PEOPLE RESPONSIBLE for what they do? That's a hard question, and I cannot give a comprehensive answer here. But I can give a quick one. People are capable of recognizing and responding to reasons, in a way that mere objects—and even sophisticated animals—are not. Our trainer likes to say that Bailey will do what it takes to get what she wants. If nipping gets her the attention she's after, she'll keep at it. If it

---

*The parenthetical is there to mark the fact that our actual criminal practices don't succeed on this score. There are many people in prison who suffer serious mental illness, such that we ought to doubt their moral responsibility.

doesn't, she'll stop and try something else. To be sure, she can restrain her impulses, at least for a bit. She's learned to sit and wait for a treat. But she restrains her impulses only when she thinks it in her interest.

How are people different? Well, you meet some you suspect aren't. We all know people who have difficulty acting on anything other than their immediate desires. But people can act on reasons instead. What are reasons? That's another complicated question, to which I can only give too quick an answer. But roughly, reasons are *shoulds*, not *wants*. *That you're hungry* is a reason for me to feed you, even if I'd like to see you starve. *That you're in pain* is a reason for me to stop standing on your foot, even if I'd like to stay there. *That I promised* is a reason to do what I said, even if I'd like to do something else.*

Some deny that there's a difference here. David Hume, the leading philosopher of the Scottish Enlightenment, said that "reason is, and ought only to be the slave of the passions, and can never pretend to any other office than to serve and obey them." The idea is that we're all more like Bailey than we might seem. Sure, I can get off your foot, even if I'd like to stay there. But I'll do it, Hume thought, only in service of a different desire—like the desire not to be punched in the face. Reason, according to Hume, helps us figure out how to satisfy our desires. It doesn't compete with them.

Hume has his fans, but I'm not one of them. I think that reason and desire operate independently. Our desires don't always generate reasons. (That Hitler wanted to exterminate Jews was *not* a reason to do so.) And our reasons are not always—or even typically—grounded in desires. (I should pay my debts, even if I don't want to do it—and not just because I'll suffer if I don't.) Indeed, I'd go a step further and say that our hu-

---

*To say that these things are reasons is not to say that they are *conclusive* reasons. That Hank's hungry is a reason for me to feed him, but as Hank often discovers, competing reasons can win out. For instance, if dinner is close, we'll make Hank wait, since we think it worthwhile to eat together whenever we can.

manity lies partly in our capacity to distinguish what we ought to do from what we want to do.

You can't reason with Bailey. The only way to shape her behavior is to adjust her incentives. But we can reason with each other. And reactive attitudes are a way in which we do so. When you're angry with someone, you're telling them that they should have done better. They won't find that pleasant. But at least you're treating them as a person, responsible for what they do, and not like an object or an animal.

• ⁓ •

AND NOW WE CAN SEE what's so worrisome about Sutherland's experiment. When she set out to train her husband, she stopped seeing him as a person and started seeing him as an object that she was entitled to manipulate and control. (I hope you are hearing echoes here of the Kantian idea we encountered in chapter 1—that we should treat people *as people*, not as objects.) She stopped *reasoning* with him and started *shaping* him. Or at least she did to the extent she was trying to train him. I'm sure that, in other ways and at other times, Sutherland did see her husband as a person. And I don't want to be too hard on her. Later on, I'll suggest that we should sometimes take an objective attitude toward people, even the ones we love. But still, I want to insist: you should not Shamu your spouse.

• ⁓ •

WHAT ABOUT YOUR KIDS? Should you Shamu them? You bet. All day, every day. At least when they are little. Because little kids *are not people*. At least, not in the relevant sense. You cannot reason with a two-year-old about rights and wrongs. Sometimes you say words and they say words back. And it sure seems like you're reasoning with them. But I assure you, you're not. Because they can't yet comprehend the difference between what they want to do and what they ought to do.

I cannot tell you how many conversations I've had with little kids that went like this:

ME: Why did you [take that/hit him/pull down your pants in public]?

KID: Because I wanted to.

ME: Yeah, but why did you want to?

KID: I just did.

ME: Yeah, but *why*? What were you trying to accomplish?

KID: I just wanted to.

ME: How many times do I have to tell you? Desires are not reasons for action.

KID: Ok, Boomer. I've read Hume.

ME: What? I'm not even a Boomer. I'm Gen X.

KID: Reason is a slave to my passion, Xoomer.

I'm kidding. Sort of. But there's a serious point here: Little kids aren't responsible for what they do. They can't reliably distinguish right from wrong. And even when they can, they can't always regulate their behavior. They don't have the relevant capacities. And that's not their fault. It's who they are.

The upshot is that you can't get angry at a little kid. Of course, you get angry anyway. I got mad at Rex almost as soon as he came home from the hospital. He hardly slept at first. And Julie had a rough delivery, so I was handling everything aside from feeding for several nights. As I held him, crying, for hours on end, I cycled through many emotions, including anger *at* Rex. But it wouldn't last, because it wasn't his fault. It couldn't be. Rex wasn't the kind of creature one could be angry at, since he wasn't responsible for what he was doing.

You have to take an objective attitude toward little kids. And they are little, in the relevant sense, for longer than you might think—at least until four or five. But actually, it's somewhere around six or seven that they start to become real people. Before that, they're animals. Awfully cute animals. Who look like people. And sort of sound like people. But they're definitely not people. Little kids are things "to be managed or handled or cured or trained."

AND DO IT RIGHT, PLEASE. When Hank was a toddler, I would take him to preschool playtime at Gym America. He loved a runway that led to a foam pit. Hank would zoom down at full speed, come to a complete halt, and then carefully jump into the foam. (Hershovitz kids are cautious.) Hank wasn't the only one who loved that runway, so the start was chaos as kids struggled to sort themselves into some semblance of a line. But the rule was strict: you can't start down the runway until the kid before you has wiggled free from the foam.

Once, I was perched on the edge, helping kids climb out. Off to the side, there was a little boy (age three or four) who didn't want to bother with the line. He kept launching himself into the foam. There were several midair misses. But more than once, he landed on top of a kid climbing out. I looked to his mother for help. She shrugged and said, "That's just how he is. He's a wild one."

Well, yes. That is how he is. "And it's your job," I definitely didn't say, "to make him something else—something better."

With adults, we sometimes talk about *rehabilitation* as an aim of punishment. When it comes to kids, the *re* is out of place. That boy needed to be *habilitated*—made fit to live with the rest of us—for the very first time.

What should his mother have done? Well, to start, she should have stopped him in his tracks. *Incapacitation* is yet another purpose of punishment. An upside of putting an arsonist in prison is that he cannot burn anything down while he's there. If that little boy were mine, I'd grab him by the shirt and hold him back so that he couldn't hurt other kids. Then I'd get down on his level, look him in the eye, and . . . anthropomorphize him.

Seriously. I just told you that little kids aren't people. But you have to treat them as if they are. You have to give kids reasons, even if they'll struggle to act on them. You have to explain: "You may not jump in the pit *because you are going to hurt someone.*" And you need to display a reactive attitude. Anger isn't the right one, since the kid hasn't slighted you. Instead, you need to tell the kid that you're disappointed—that you are sad about what he's done. If, after all that, the kid continues to fling himself into the foam, it's time for the penalty box. Or maybe just a premature end to preschool playtime.

When it comes to punishment, a parent's primary job is to raise a child the rest of us can resent. I was annoyed by that boy, and concerned he might hurt another kid. But I wasn't angry at him. What he was doing wasn't his fault, as he wasn't yet the kind of creature that could be expected to recognize and act on reasons. His parents' job was to make him that kind of creature. To do that, they needed to introduce him to reasons and reactive attitudes.

⁘

HAVING SAID ALL THAT, I should sound a note of caution. Kids need to experience reactive attitudes. But it's easy to overdo it. If you're angry—actually angry—you're the one who needs a time-out.

Julie and I gave each other time-outs all the time. She'd hear me screaming, sense that I was actually angry, and summarily dismiss me: "I got it. You're on a break," she'd say. Then she'd calmly talk to the kid about whatever he'd done wrong. I did the same for her, but far less frequently than she had to do it for me. There are upsides to parenting with a social worker.

But even when you're in the right frame of mind, you have to be careful what you say. You don't want kids to feel shame—to think of themselves as bad. The standard advice is to talk to kids about their actions, not their character. But that's not quite right. When a kid does something good, you should praise their action as a reflection of their character. As in: "Wow, it was so nice that you shared that toy. You are a really kind person who wants to include everyone." When a kid does something bad, you should criticize their action as inconsistent with their character. As in: "Taking that toy was not nice. And that makes me sad, because you're a kind person who likes to share." The point is to help the child build a positive sense of self. You want them to see good behavior as built into who they are—and bad behavior as an aberration they can correct.

Some combination of Julie's social work experience and sheer luck helped us hit on these strategies when our kids were little. But it turns out, there's a fair bit of research to back them up. If you praise positive character traits, and treat kids as if they're responsible, there's a good chance you'll end up with responsible kids. You don't have complete control over your kids' temperament. But to some extent, you can shape who they are. That's why it's worth Shamu-ing them.

<hr>

THERE'S NO MAGIC MOMENT when a little kid becomes a responsible adult. It happens slowly, as they acquire new cognitive capacities. At the start—think Rex on his first night home from the hospital—you see your child through a purely objective lens. But as they grow, you begin to relate to them as people, and you find yourself feeling anger, resentment, and gratitude at the way they act. One day, you're playacting those emotions—pretending to be upset even as you struggle to suppress a laugh. The next day, you really are upset, since you think the kid could have done better. And then it's back the other way, because child development is a line with loops.

Rex took a leap forward around the time Hank learned to walk. He was four, and he would zoom around the house with wild abandon. It wasn't much of an issue when Hank wasn't mobile, since he was easily avoided. But once Hank was on the move, Rex started to run him down, mostly on accident. He'd crash into Hank. Hank would cry. And Rex would immediately launch a legal defense.

"I didn't mean that!" he'd say, if one of us happened to see.

He thought that exonerated him entirely. But he soon learned that it was only a defense against the worst charge he might face—battery. So I introduced him to the idea of negligence. I explained that he has to be careful around Hank. And I gave him a line I learned from a law school colleague, Margo Schlanger: "I'm glad you didn't mean to do it. But you need to mean *not* to do it."

That's a subtle lesson, but Rex quickly absorbed it. He still crashed into Hank. And Hank still cried. But Rex had a new theory of the case.

"I was trying to be careful!" he'd say.

So I taught him a bit more about negligence. Tort law doesn't care whether you're trying to be careful. It only cares whether you *were* careful. The law is interested in your conduct, not your mental state. There are many reasons for that, not least the fact that it's easy to pretend you were trying to be careful when you weren't, as was often the case with Rex.

"I'm glad you were trying," I would say. "But it's not enough to try. You have to *be* careful." And then I'd give Rex a time-out.

The time-outs felt like Rex's first serious punishments—for us and for him. They were serious for us because we were seriously punishing him, not just playing at it. We meant to condemn what he'd done—and convey that he ought to have done better. But there was more to it than that. We felt like we had to protect Hank—and make clear that Rex had to watch out for him.

The time-outs were serious for Rex too, since he could tell that we were really upset. He saw that we expected him to do better, and he felt awful about it. Sometimes he'd collapse into a heap, unable to bear the weight of our blame.

In vindicating Hank's right to have Rex watch out for him, we were doing a bit of corrective justice. Rex was acting like he didn't have to watch out for Hank. We made clear that he did. And we didn't just say it. We made his carelessness costly.

We were also doing a bit of retributive justice.

What's that? We've been putting the question off for a while now, but we're finally in a position to say—and to see why it sometimes makes sense to inflict suffering. If corrective justice is about vindicating victims, retributive justice is about condemning wrongdoers. It requires that we diminish their social standing, at least temporarily, as a way of rejecting what they did. Punishment signals that you've lost status, insofar as you're subject to harsh treatment that you ordinarily have a right to be free from.

It's easier to see with adults. So let's think about the sentence handed down to Brock Turner after he sexually assaulted Chanel Miller at a Stanford party. The prosecutor asked for a six-year sentence, but the judge gave Turner just six months. The sentence sparked outrage, and rightly so. But I want to ask: What was wrong with it? Was it flawed because it failed to balance some cosmic account book? If so, just how much suffering would be necessary to bring the book into balance? And how do we translate that into a term of years?

I think the sentence was flawed for more down-to-earth reasons. It sent the wrong messages about Miller and Turner. The sentence was too short to vindicate Miller. It seemed to suggest that what happened to her didn't matter much—or, worse yet, that *she* didn't matter much. (In California, you can be sentenced to six months in prison for petty theft—stealing less than $950.) That's a failure of corrective justice. And the sentence didn't do retributive justice either. It suggested that Turner hadn't acted all that badly—that he should be accepted back into society after a short time-out.

We imprison a shocking percentage of our population—more people per capita than any other country. And that's not an honor we should be happy to have. We should confine many fewer people. But I wouldn't abolish prisons altogether. When people abuse others, we should hold them accountable, and confinement can be a fine way to do it. Putting a person in prison signals that they are not, for now, fit to live with the rest of us. It signals that we don't trust them, that we need a break. It is, for some crimes, an apt punishment.

Or, rather, it would be if our prisons weren't such awful places. We are justified, sometimes, in separating people from the community. But there is no justification for packing people into overcrowded prisons, where they face serious risk of violence from inmates and guards, where their health needs are ignored, and they're treated in dehumanizing ways. A person who has acted badly, even egregiously, is still a person. When we fail to respect a wrongdoer's humanity, we fail to respect our own, since we imply that it's something easily lost.

Moreover, we should remember: in almost every case, we will live again with the people we confine. Punishment should hold open the possibility that we can do it harmoniously; indeed, it should promote it. If we treat people inhumanely, we should never be surprised when they return the favor. But the reverse is true too: if we treat people with respect, we are more likely to get it in return. Sometimes punishment is warranted, even harsh punishment—separation from friends and family. But we can condemn people without condemning them to the dangerous and desolate lives people live in our prisons.

Still, you might wonder: If the messages we send are what matter most—and if prisons tend to be terrible places—why can't we just condemn wrongdoers with words? Why do we have to send them away? The answer is: words can't convey every message. Actions speak louder, as we often say. Would you believe a person who said she loved you but never acted as if she did? I doubt it, and disapproval works the same way. You can say you're angry about what someone did, but if it doesn't affect the way you treat them, people won't take you seriously.

Why do we punish? We've seen lots of reasons: deterrence, rehabilitation, and incapacitation. But the primary reason *is* retribution. We punish to communicate condemnation. And retributive justice demands it whenever that condemnation is deserved.

THAT DOESN'T MEAN we always have to do it, though. Sometimes we can let justice slide. In fact, sometimes we should.

I was a law clerk for Ruth Bader Ginsburg. I learned a lot about law from her, but I also learned a lot about life. The Justice had a famously successful marriage with her husband, Marty. So people often asked her for relationship advice. She'd pass along guidance that her mother-in-law gave her right before her wedding. "In every good marriage," she'd say, "it helps sometimes to be a little deaf."

She meant: You don't have to take every slight seriously. In fact, your life will go better if you overlook some. Shifting to an objective perspective can help. Sutherland discovered that when she Shamu-ed her husband. "I used to take his faults personally," she explained, "his dirty clothes on the floor were an affront, a symbol of how he didn't care enough about me." But when she looked at him through an objective lens, she realized it wasn't really about her. Some habits, she came to see, are just "too entrenched, too instinctive to train away."

Strawson would not have been surprised that the objective attitude helped Sutherland release her resentment. It's dangerous to take the objective attitude to others all the time; it threatens their humanity—and yours. If you don't see others as responsible, you can't see yourself as a bearer of rights, since they are two sides of the same coin. But even Strawson thought that the objective attitude could be helpful on occasion. We can embrace it, he said, "as a refuge from the strains of involvement; as an aid to policy; or simply out of intellectual curiosity."

I stand by what I said before: you shouldn't Shamu your spouse. But there's a lot to be said for adopting an objective attitude on occasion. We're not fully rational creatures. We can recognize and act on reasons. But we cannot recognize all reasons. Or even act on all those that we recognize. We should do our best to make space—and find grace—for the bits of each other's personalities that are deeply ingrained and difficult to change.

That's not really the issue with kids, since they aren't set in their ways. But exhaustion, hunger, and stress also compromise our ability to respond to reasons. That's true for adults. (Do not get in Julie's way when she's hangry.) And it could not be more true for kids. They're at their worst whenever they are tired or hungry. That caused some tension in our house. Julie was often willing to write off bad behavior. "Let's just get him to bed," she'd say. I wanted to respond, lest the kid get the idea that exhaustion was an all-purpose excuse. Looking back, I think we were both right. Or, rather, the Justice was. You can cut kids slack. Sometimes.

We can scale these observations up. Our society is extraordinarily punitive. We lock away lots of people who commit low-level offenses when they are tired, hungry, or stressed. We need to work on the world outside prison so that fewer people are worn thin in that way. But while we work on that, we should remember: We don't have to condemn all the wrongdoing we see. We can let things slide. Sometimes. Indeed, letting things slide can be a way of doing a different, deeper sort of justice.

⁘ ⌇ ·

OCCASIONALLY, WE ALL PILE into bed together and read before the boys' bedtime. One night, when Hank was eight, he was reading a book about *Minecraft*. He didn't want to stop when it was his turn to peel away for lights out.

"Hank, it's time to close your book," Julie said, after issuing several warnings.

"No," he said sharply.

"It wasn't a question, Hank. It's late, and it's time for bed."

"I'm not stopping," he said, as he turned another page.

"If you don't stop, you won't be able to play *Minecraft* tomorrow."

That was a serious threat—we were mid-pandemic and *Minecraft* was Hank's main form of social contact.

"You can't tell me to stop reading," Hank said. "I don't have to do what you say."

"Yes, you do," Julie said, as she reached to take the book away from him. "And you better stop talking to me that way."

"I will talk to you however I want," Hank said.

That was ill-considered. The next day's *Minecraft* was quickly canceled.

I wandered into Hank's room a few minutes later to say good night, after Julie had tucked him in. He was distraught, curled up in a ball, crying against the wall.

I sat down next to him. "It sounds like you were having a hard time being respectful tonight."

"I was," he wailed, "and I can't believe you're blaming me for it."

"Well, you weren't respectful," I said.

"I know. But it's not fair to blame me. *I was having a hard time.*"

I swallowed my laugh. Hank is a good lawyer, constantly in search of an excuse. I couldn't credit that one, though. His sedition was too brazen to ignore, even though he was, indeed, having a hard time.

But I gave him a hug anyway. And I told him that I loved him. And I made silly jokes until he smiled.

Hank got the message "no *Minecraft*" sent. He knew he'd acted badly. But I didn't want that to be the last message he heard. He's one of us, and he always will be, no matter how badly he acts.

4

AUTHORITY

Y ou are not the boss of me," Rex said.

"Yes, I am."

"No, you're not."

"Fuck you."

～～～

THAT'S IT. That's the whole story. Except I didn't say "Fuck you."
Except in my head. And my dreams. Because *nothing* is more frustrating
than a kid who won't put on his shoes when it's time to leave the house.

"Put on your shoes."

Silence.

"Put on your shoes."

Maddening silence.

"Rex, you need shoes."

"No shoes."

"Rex, you have to wear shoes. Put them on."

"No shoes."

"*Put on your shoes.*"

"Why?"

Because they protect your feet. Because they keep you clean. Because the whole world has a sign that says NO SHOES, NO SERVICE.

But also: *Because I said so.*

"No shoes."

"*Fine.* We'll put them on when we get there."

When did this conversation happen? I don't know. When didn't it happen?

Rex learned *you're not the boss of me* in preschool. He was three or four. But he'd lived *you're not the boss of me* for longer than that. It's the creed of little kids.

They may do what you say. But only when it suits them.

————— ~ —————

WAS I THE BOSS of Rex? That depends on what it means to be the boss of someone.

I did boss Rex around, in the sense that I told him what to do. But as the story suggests, I didn't have much success.

Philosophers draw a distinction between power and authority. *Power* is the ability to bend the world to your will—to make the world be the way you want it to be. You have power over a person when you can make him do what you want him to do.

And I had power over Rex. In a pinch, I could simply put the shoes on him. And I did. But I had other ways of getting my way. I could withhold what Rex wanted until he did as I said. Or give him a reward. Or persuade him. (Not really.) Or better yet, trick him. (A well-placed *whatever you do, don't put on your shoes* was, for a long time, the fastest way to get them on his feet.)

Rex also had power over me. Indeed, if you were keeping score, it would be hard to say which one of us had more success bending the other to his will. Rex couldn't push me around. But he could throw himself on the floor, go boneless, or just generally resist until he got his way. He could also be cute in a calculated effort to control me. That often worked. And there's a lesson here: even in the most asymmetrical relationships, power is rarely one-sided.

But authority typically is. To differing degrees, Rex and I had power over each other. But only I had authority over him. What's authority? It's a kind of power. But it's not power over a person, at least not directly. Rather, *authority* is power over a person's rights and responsibilities. You have authority over another person when you can *obligate* him to do something simply by commanding him to do it. That doesn't mean that he will do it. People don't always do what they are obligated to do. But it does mean that he'll have breached his duty if he doesn't.

When I tell Rex to put on his shoes or, more recently, wash the dishes, I'm making it his responsibility to do so. Until I tell him to do the dishes, it's not his job to wash them. It would be awesome if he did! But I'm not in a position to get mad if he doesn't. Once I've told him to wash the dishes, that script flips. It's no longer awesome if he washes them; it's what's expected. And I'll be angry if he doesn't do it.

Philosophers illustrate the difference between power and authority with a stickup. You're walking down the street when a guy with a gun demands all your money. Does he have power over you? For sure, you're gonna cough up the cash. Does he have authority? No. You weren't obligated to give him money before he demanded it, and you're not obligated to give it to him now. In fact, you'd be within your rights to tell him to get lost (though I wouldn't recommend it).

Contrast the stickup with the tax bill that comes each year. The government also demands money. And it'll put you in prison if it doesn't get what it wants. So it has power. Does it have authority? Well, it certainly says it does. In the government's view, you are obligated to pay your taxes. Are you actually obligated? In a democracy, many people would say yes—you're obligated to pay what the government says you owe.

But not Robert Paul Wolff. He didn't think the government could obligate you to do anything. Indeed, he doubted that anyone could obligate you to do anything simply by saying that you had to do it.

Over the course of his career (which started in the 1960s), Wolff taught at Harvard, Chicago, Columbia, and UMass—an impressive set of institutions for an avowed anarchist. That's because Wolff isn't the sort of anarchist who takes to the street seeking mischief and mayhem. (At least, I don't think he is.) Instead, Wolff is a *philosophical anarchist*, which is just a fancy way of saying that he's skeptical about all claims to authority.

Why? Wolff argues that our ability to reason makes us responsible for what we do. More than that, Wolff says, we're obligated to *take responsibility* for what we do, by thinking it through. According to Wolff, a responsible person aims to act *autonomously*—according to decisions that she makes, as a result of her own deliberations. She won't think herself free to do whatever she wants; she'll recognize that she has responsibilities to others. But she insists that she, and she alone, is the judge of those responsibilities.

Wolff argues that autonomy and authority are incompatible. To be autonomous, you have to make your own decisions, not defer to someone else's. But deference is just what authority demands.

It may be okay, Wolff says, to do what someone else tells you to do. But you should never do it just because you were told to do it. You should do it only if you think it the right thing to do.

Wolff's conclusion is more radical than it might seem. He's not just saying that you should think before you follow an authority's orders. He's saying that those orders don't make a difference—that no one can require you to do something simply by saying you should do it—not the police, not your parents, not your coach, not your boss, not anybody.*

That's surprising. And it didn't take long before philosophers spotted problems with Wolff's argument. The leading critic was a character named Joseph Raz, who was, for a long time, the Professor of the Philosophy of Law at Oxford.

Raz argued that Wolff had missed something important about the way that reasons work. Sometimes when you think about what you should do, you discover that you have reason to defer to someone else—reason to do as they direct, rather than decide on your own.

To see what Raz means, suppose that you'd like to learn to bake, so you sign up for a class. Your instructor is a whiz-bang baker. And now she's barking orders. *Measure this, mix that. Knead the dough. Not that much.* Should you do as she directs?

Wolff would have you second-guess every order. Each time, he'd have you ask: Is this *really* what I should do? But how could *you* possibly answer that question? You don't know anything about baking. That's why you're in the class! Your cluelessness gives you a good reason to do as you're told.

And: You don't lose your autonomy when you do. Sure, you'll be doing as someone else directs. But only because *you* decided that you ought to defer to her judgment. Of course, if you do that too often, your autonomy will be compromised. But deferring on occasion—when you judge it the right thing to do—is consistent with governing yourself.

MY FATHER IS ENDLESSLY AMUSED by the ways in which Rex and Hank challenge my authority, since he sees it as comeuppance.

---

*At least, if you're an adult. Kids, Wolff says, have responsibility in proportion to their capacity to reason.

My mother had a strong dictatorial streak. She liked to lay down the law. And I did not like to follow it. We were locked in combat from the time I was little.

She'd issue an order, and I'd immediately want to know: "Why?"

"Because I said so," she'd say.

"*That is not a reason*," I'd insist. I was a four-year-old philosophical anarchist.

"That's all the reason you're going to get," she'd say. And she was stubborn. So she was right.

Whenever I looked to my father for help, he'd say, "Just make your mother happy," a sentence I found every bit as infuriating as *because I said so*.

"Why are we living under the tyranny of this woman?" I would wonder. Well, not at four. But certainly by fourteen.

Now I'm the one who says *because I said so*.

I don't like to say it. And it's rarely my first move. I like to explain what I'm thinking when the boys ask why. But there isn't always time. And I'm not always up for a full conversation—in part because they re-litigate issues endlessly.

But also: Even if I explain myself, they might not see the issue my way. And that's fine. They can attempt to persuade me. Sometimes they succeed. But if they fail, my view wins out. Which means that *because I said so* is often the final reason I offer, even if it's not the first.

* ⌒ *

BUT LET'S BE HONEST: *Because I said so* isn't *really* a reason. It's just what parents say when they run out of actual reasons. Or don't want to give them. I was right when I was four.

Except: I wasn't. Raz helped people see that *because I said so* could, in a way, be a reason—indeed, a conclusive one. In the right circumstances, one person *can* determine what another should do, simply by commanding him to do it.

When? Building on cases like the baking class, Raz argued that you're obligated to follow someone else's orders whenever doing so will help you do a better job at whatever it is you should be doing. If you're baking, and there's an expert baker on hand, you should do what she says; otherwise, your cake won't come out as well as it could. If you're playing basketball and your coach calls a play, you should play your part in the play called; otherwise, you'll be out of sync with your teammates.

In Raz's view, the point of authority is to provide a service to its subjects. Indeed, he named his view the *service conception of authority*. An authority, he said, should consider all the reasons that its subjects have. And then it should issue orders that will help them do what those reasons require. If the subjects would do a better job by following the orders than by deciding what to do themselves, then the orders are binding, and the subjects are obligated to follow them.

There are lots of ways an authority might provide that sort of service, and indeed, we've seen two ways already.

First, an authority might know better than its subjects. That is, it might have greater expertise. Your whiz-bang baking instructor has authority for just that reason. So too with the senior surgeon telling the new doctor what to do. Her experience means that she can make better judgments about what needs to be done.

Second, an authority might be able to help a group accomplish a goal that the individuals involved couldn't achieve on their own. Typically, an authority does this by getting the group in sync. Philosophers call these situations *coordination problems*. The classic example crops up in your car. We need to drive on the same side of the road as everyone else; otherwise, we'll crash into each other. But it doesn't matter whether we drive on the left or right; we just need to pick a side. By setting the rules of the road, a traffic authority coordinates everyone's conduct, helping us to avoid the chaos we'd encounter if we each decided for ourselves.

The question which side of the road to drive on is a *pure coordination problem*, since the answer doesn't matter—we just need to settle on one. But not all coordination problems are pure, since sometimes some solutions are better than others. Think again about basketball. It matters what plays the team runs, since some are more likely to succeed than others. But it matters much more that every player runs the same play, even if there might have been a better play to run.

The need to get players on the same page is part of what justifies a basketball coach's authority. If she can get her players in sync, then *because I said so* is a reason for her players to do what she says. After the game, they might second-guess the coach's calls. But if they fail to follow her instructions during the game, they'll almost surely play worse than they would if they went along.

But it's important to see: *Because I said so* is a reason for the players, not the coach. A coach should be able to explain why she made the choices she did. Her authority doesn't give her the right to act on whatever whims she happens to have. She should try to call the best play she can. Her job is to help her players do what *they* have reason to do—win the game, presumably. And her authority rests on her ability to do it well.*

Raz would say the same about parents. If they have the right to boss their kids around, it's because they can help their kids do better than they could on their own. As decision-makers, parents have lots of advantages. To start, they know things kids don't. For instance, I know how much sleep kids need, and I've got a good sense of what happens when they don't get it. (There are horror movies less scary.) So I'm likely to set a better bedtime for my kids than they'd set for themselves.

But knowledge is not the only reason parents can make better deci-

---

*She may make mistakes, of course. Every coach has an off night. For Raz, the question is whether her orders, on the whole, help her players to do better than they could do on their own. An off night here or there won't call that into question. But a lot of them will.

sions than kids. Most parents have more self-control than little kids. Indeed, it would be hard to have less. Kids tend to care about what's happening now, now, now. But parents can take a longer view, which often redounds to their kids' benefit.

Also: Parents can solve coordination problems for kids. For instance, we might set a schedule for piano practice, so as to ensure that each boy gets a turn before it's time for bed. Or we might tell Hank to unload the dishwasher, so that it will be empty when Rex does the dishes. It never goes that smoothly, of course. But in principle, it could. So we keep trying.

In these ways and others, parents can help their kids to do better than they'd do on their own. And that means that *because I said so* can be a reason for kids. Of course, there are always further reasons lurking in the background—the reasons parents have for making the decisions they do. And that's what I desperately wanted to hear when I was little. I wanted my mom to tell me why she'd made a decision, so that I could argue with her.

She would have none of that. I'm slightly more accommodating. I want my kids to learn to make decisions, so that I'm not stuck with the job. I also want them to be the sort of people who think through problems. So I share my thinking as often as I can. But there can be good reasons to say *because I said so*. It can cut off an endless conversation. Or better yet, stop it before it starts.

It's a delicate balance to strike, and I don't always get it right. It's maddening when a kid won't do what you say and things need to get done quickly. Sometimes I hear my mother's sentences coming out of my mouth. "You don't need to ask why. You just need to listen." But I try to remind myself that it's reasonable for them to want to understand why. Indeed, they are owed explanations, if not now, then later. But also, I want them to learn: sometimes you have to accept that someone else has the authority to settle a question.

RAZ IS, PERHAPS, the world's leading authority on authority. Many people are attracted by his suggestion that authorities should serve their subjects. And his influence runs well beyond that. He has shaped the way that generations of philosophers think about law and morality too. But Raz's biggest impact on my life didn't come through his work; it came through an act of kindness.

I went to Oxford on a Rhodes Scholarship. After you win the scholarship, you have to apply to a program there. I submitted an application to the philosophy faculty, which was promptly rejected. They thought I should study politics instead. I wasn't much interested in that, so I applied to the law faculty, figuring I'd get a jump on my legal studies—and maybe end up as a jet-setting lawyer someday.

But I couldn't quit philosophy. Once I was in Oxford, I started to go to philosophy lectures, on top of my law lectures. I liked Raz's. He was terrifying. But the subject mixed my interests. The lectures were about the philosophy of law. And it turns out you can earn a doctorate in that subject at Oxford. So I asked if I could switch degrees. Several people told me no. It was too late. I wasn't properly qualified. Those things were true. But then I asked Raz. And he said yes. And even better, he took me on as his student. That was crazy kind—it meant more work for him—and I remain grateful.

How did I repay Raz? Well, remember that contrarian streak I had as a kid? It carried over to my academic career. As soon as I became Raz's student, I set out to show that his work on authority was wrong. And not a little bit wrong, in a let's-patch-things-up sort of way. Just flat-out wrong, in a we-need-to-start-over kind of way.

Raz didn't mind. Or if he did, he didn't tell me. But I doubt that he did. Because that's how philosophy works. You say something, and the world sets out to show that you're wrong. That can be frustrating, but it's far worse for people to ignore your work. If you haven't written something worth criticizing, you haven't written something worthwhile.

Gordon Ramsay—the famously rude chef—can help us see the problem with Raz's account of authority. Years ago, he had a show called *Kitchen Nightmares*. In every episode, Ramsay attempted to revive a failing restaurant. At some point, he'd be in the kitchen, watching some poor chap cook poorly. Ramsay would turn ever redder, and when his anger boiled over, he'd start barking orders, telling people how to do things properly. The whole thing was super disturbing, since there was no reason to be so nasty. But it was also super satisfying, since Ramsay was, in a way, raging about every meal you'd been served in a place that just didn't care to cook better.

Were the cooks in those kitchens obligated to follow Ramsay's orders? Ramsay has run Michelin-starred restaurants, so it's safe to assume he's a solid chef. Certainly, you'd expect him to be more talented than the cooks in those failing restaurants. So if Raz is right, those cooks should do exactly what Ramsay tells them to do. Indeed, they'd breach their duty if they didn't.

Now I want to shift the story slightly. Forget about the show. Just imagine that Ramsay is out to dinner with his family, an ordinary patron in an ordinary restaurant, no camera crew on hand. He's served soup, takes a taste, and it's terrible. Instantly, he's on his feet. He bursts in the kitchen and starts barking orders, just as he would on the show. The cooks are bewildered. But one of them recognizes Ramsay.

"It's Gordon Ramsay," he whispers to his confused colleagues.

Now everyone knows: The guy barking orders is *not* barking mad. In fact, he's the best cook in the kitchen. Is everyone obligated to do as he says? Or is it open to them to say, "Get out, Gordo."

I'm on Team Get-Out-Gordo. The fact that Ramsay's a better cook doesn't give him a right to boss anyone around. On *Kitchen Nightmares*, the cooks had agreed to appear on the show, so they might have been obligated to go along with its premise. But they were obligated, if they were, because they'd agreed to participate, not because Ramsay could cook better than them. Ramsay's talent doesn't give him a roaming mandate to burst into kitchens and bark orders.*

That means Raz is wrong; the fact that someone can help you do better than you could do on your own does *not* give him the right to boss you around. Of course, it might be smart to listen to him, since you'd do better that way. But you're not *obligated* to listen to him. In lots of life, you're free to make your own mistakes. If you want to make bad soup in your kitchen, that's your business. Gordon Ramsay doesn't get to demand you do it his way.

         • ——— •

So WE NEED A new approach to authority, and as usual, Hank can help. His first foray into political philosophy came at age seven, just after we'd seen a musical version of *Tangled*, Disney's adaptation of Rapunzel. He was trying to make sense of the idea that a king could order people around.

"Just because you're called *king* doesn't mean you're in charge," he ventured.

"In a lot of countries," I explained, "the king was the person in charge. But people didn't like that, so some countries got rid of their kings. And some kept them, but they're not in charge anymore."

"But the word *king* doesn't mean anything," Hank insisted. "Just because people call you *king*, you shouldn't get to tell anyone what to do. It's just a word."

"That's right," I said. "*King* is just a word. In some countries, they had other words for the person in charge, like *emperor* or *czar*."

---

*Ramsay would probably be trespassing if he burst into a random kitchen, but I don't think that's the reason he doesn't have authority. Sit him at the counter in a diner, barking orders to the short-order cook, and he's still out of line. It's not his place to boss anyone around.

"But it doesn't matter what people call you," Hank said. "Your name doesn't mean you're in charge."

"Yeah, but *king* isn't the name of a person. It's the name of a job. And it's having the job that puts you in charge."

"King is a job?" Hank asked.

"Yeah. It's like being a coach. Is Coach Bridgette in charge of your soccer team because her name is Bridgette? Or because she's the coach?"

"Because she's the coach," Hank said. "Coaches have lots of different names."

"Yeah. And so do kings. It's the job that matters, not what people call them."

———~———

IN THAT CONVERSATION, Hank and I got a start on a better theory of authority. Some jobs put people in positions of authority. They're easy to name: boss, parent, coach, teacher, traffic cop, and so on. The people in all these roles claim to be able to obligate (at least some) others simply by commanding them to act. To decide whether they have that power, we should ask whether those roles are worthwhile—whether we want them in our lives, whether people ought to have the power associated with them. But we shouldn't think about that power in isolation. We should think about it in relation to the rest of the role.

Let me show you what I mean. To be a parent is to occupy a role, which has many features. If you were going to explain the role to someone, it would be natural to start with the responsibilities of parenthood. You need to feed your kid, keep him safe, and so on. And it's your obligation to see to it that the kid becomes a competent adult. Which means that you need to teach the kid how to think and act in lots of contexts.

It would be hard to do all that if you didn't have the right to set requirements for your kid. For instance, we require our kids to do chores in part so that they will be capable of caring for themselves someday. We also want them to see it as their responsibility to pitch in to collective projects, like keeping a house clean. In addition, we set bedtimes for our children so that they'll get sufficient sleep.

Why do parents have authority over their kids? Because they have responsibility for them. Parental rights and responsibilities are a package deal. We could arrange to care for children in different ways. We could have the village do it instead of parents. And to some extent, we do. But there are good reasons to assign parents primary responsibility, not least that they are likely to have special attachments to their kids.

You've probably heard the Peter Parker principle: *With great power comes great responsibility.* I'm offering you the Parker Peter principle: *With great responsibility comes great power.* It's not always true. But it applies to parental authority. You get to boss your kids around *because* it's your job to take care of them.

Notice how this story is different from Raz's. On his picture, a parent has authority because of her competence to command her kid. But there are lots of people who can command kids competently. When my kids were little, just about every adult they encountered could make better decisions for them than they could make for themselves. (Recall, Rex wouldn't even wear shoes.) But none of those adults had the authority to command my kids, unless they occupied some role of authority relative to them.*

The lesson here is that authority attaches to roles, not to people. I can set rules for my kids because I am their parent, not because I'm good at setting rules. That said, if I were truly terrible at the job, I should lose it.

---

*This is a bit too simple. Most of the people that can boss my kids around occupy roles of authority relative to them—like coach, teacher, or babysitter. But when our kids go to another kid's house, the parents present do have a right to boss them around a bit. Some of their authority is location-based: the owner of a house gets to decide what can be done there. (Owner is a role of authority, over a piece of property and others' relations to it.) But some of it owes to the fact that those parents are, for a time, standing in our shoes—temporarily occupying the role that we would play were we there. (The law says that they act *in loco parentis*—in the place of parents.) As soon as I show up, that bit of authority shifts back to me.

Competence matters. But competence doesn't confer authority. It's part of the package deal of parenthood.

—————

WHAT ABOUT OTHER AUTHORITIES? Could we tell similar stories about them? Perhaps, though we should expect different stories for different roles. Teachers, for instance, have much more limited responsibility for children than parents do, and that limits the scope of their authority. They are responsible for their students' well-being while they are at school, and for their education, more generally. They can issue orders to help discharge those responsibilities. But they don't get to decide how often a child snacks at home, or how much screen time he gets. If they have views on those questions, they make suggestions to parents; they don't issue orders.

But not all authority is grounded in responsibility. Workers are, for the most part, full-grown adults. Employers aren't parents. So why do bosses get to boss people around? Bosses do have responsibilities—to their bosses, to their customers, to shareholders, and so on—and hierarchical decision-making can help in meeting those responsibilities. In some respects, a boss is similar to a basketball coach, helping to coordinate conduct so that the group can achieve things no individual could on their own. But the fact that it's helpful for a boss to boss people around cannot explain why she gets to do it. After all, a boss can't boss just anyone around; just her employees.

Why employees? Well, they signed up for the job. That seems important. And they could quit if they wanted. That seems important too. We might sum it up by saying that employees consent to be bossed around. It's something they choose, presumably because they like the pay that comes with it.

The problem with this story is that it has little basis in reality. Most workers work out of economic necessity. They need to pay for food, housing, and a long list of other essentials. That means they are *not* free to leave their jobs, at least not without finding another. At best, they can choose their boss. But they can't choose to be free from bosses altogether. And when jobs are scarce, they have little latitude to choose their boss.

Worse yet, in America we give bosses near dictatorial powers. Most employees can be fired at will—for any reason, or no reason at all.* This gives employers almost limitless control over their employees' lives. Your boss can fire you for putting a political sign on your lawn. Or failing to wear your hair the way she prefers. Or doing such a good job that you show her up.

If you get the impression I think that's bad, I do. As a tenured professor, I'm one of the few Americans who is protected from the whims of my boss. I can't be fired, except for cause, which gives me the freedom to say what I want. And I don't have to worry about whether I'll be kept on from year to year. My job is mine until I don't want it anymore.

Some people think I shouldn't have those protections; they'd like to see tenure end. Why should professors get such a good deal when the rest of America lives with economic insecurity? Better, I think, to flip the question around: Why do we allow so many Americans to live with economic insecurity—and the power it confers on their employers?

If you're interested in that question—and I hope you are, whether you are a boss, an employee, or both—I've got a philosopher for you. My Michigan colleague Elizabeth Anderson is one of the most important thinkers in the world today. She's pushing people to see that the most oppressive government most people interact with is not associated with any political authority—it's their employer.

Retail stores routinely search employees' belongings without a warrant, let alone any reason to think they've done wrong. They schedule shifts on short notice. They set rules for hair and makeup. Workers in warehouses and factories are constantly surveilled; even their trips to

---

*The major exception is antidiscrimination law. You can't fire a person for their race, religion, sex, and so on.

the restroom are regulated. If you're lucky enough to work a white-collar job, you probably don't suffer those sorts of intrusions. But you too can be dismissed at any moment. And that leaves you seriously insecure.

Anderson's book *Private Government: How Employers Rule Our Lives (and Why We Don't Talk about It)* investigates how we came to accept this situation—and what we can do about it. Change won't come easy, but there are many ways to make things better. We could limit at-will employment. We could give workers a role in workplace governance, so that their interests are taken into account. We could also change the context in which we work, by guaranteeing a basic income and health care, so that no one feels forced to work for an abusive employer.

Somehow, lots of Americans have been convinced that government "handouts" hamper freedom. The truth is, providing for people's basic needs promotes freedom. It makes it possible for people to say no to a boss who would treat them badly.

Some also worry that the reforms I'm suggesting would reduce the dynamism of the American economy. I doubt that. But it's worth asking: Who does that dynamism benefit? If corporate profits are increased by keeping workers insecure, is that a trade we should be willing to make?

Americans talk a good game about freedom. We love our constitutional rights. But if you care about freedom, the American workplace should seriously disturb you. The government is powerful. But so is your employer. And as things stand now, you have nearly no rights in that relationship.

To be clear: I'm not saying you should be insubordinate at work. Often it's in your interest to go along. And if the work is important—if, say, people's health and safety are at stake—then you might even be obligated to follow orders while you're on the job.

But I won't defend the roles of employer and employee, at least not as currently constituted. For those on the lowest rungs of the economic ladder, they are relations of power, not legitimate authority. We can change that, though, and we should.

IF LIMITING THE AUTHORITY of employers sounds radical, it's worth remembering that limited government did once too. Not so long ago, kings and queens claimed absolute authority (and, of course, dictators still do). They had support from prominent philosophers, including the namesake of the greatest cartoon tiger ever—Thomas Hobbes.

We met Hobbes back in the introduction. He lived through a tumultuous century that included, among other conflicts, the English Civil War. Indeed, he spent years in exile in France. The political instability of the time may have contributed to Hobbes's interest in the conditions of political stability—and the price to be paid for failing to secure it.

As we learned earlier, Hobbes believed that, absent any government at all, society would devolve into a "war of every man against every man." Why? According to Hobbes, most of us are mostly selfish. So we're bound to come into conflict, especially when resources are scarce. In the state of nature, no one could feel the least bit secure, not even the strongest among us, because everyone is vulnerable to everyone else. "The weakest has strength enough to kill the strongest," Hobbes said, "either by secret machination, or by confederacy with others."

Because we'd be at war, we'd also be impoverished, Hobbes said. We wouldn't work much, since we wouldn't expect our work to work out. There would be no machines, no buildings, no culture, and little knowledge. In the state of nature, life would be "solitary, poor, nasty, brutish, and short."

But Hobbes saw a way out. He argued that everyone should agree to obey a sovereign, like a king, who could provide protection. To make it work, they'd have to give the sovereign all their rights. As a result, the sovereign would have absolute authority. No one could contest his actions. And there would be no limits on what he could do. Any attempt to constrain the sovereign, Hobbes argued, would lead to conflict over power.

And conflict means war (of just the sort Hobbes had lived through). Which was the thing to be avoided.

History has proven Hobbes wrong, at least about the last bit.

John Locke also had views about the sort of government people should institute to escape the state of nature. But he didn't think an absolute monarchy necessary, or even advisable. He argued for a separation of powers (not quite our legislative, executive, and judiciary, but close). He also supported (at least some) popular representation in the legislature.

Locke's ideas helped shape many of the world's constitutional democracies. The Framers of the U.S. Constitution divided the powers of government among three branches, believing that the best way to hold each in check. They also adopted a Bill of Rights, limiting the power of government—and giving people enforceable rights against it. That model has been copied by many of the world's constitutional democracies. And though they are far from perfect, their success shows that we can escape the state of nature without granting a single individual absolute authority over our lives.

~~~~~~

"EVERY KID WANTS A DEMOCRACY," Rex likes to say, "but every grown-up wants a dictatorship."

He's talking about families, of course. Rex wants one person, one vote, right at our kitchen table. I don't know what he envisions for 2–2 ties.

"What's so good about democracy?" I asked in one of those conversations. He was ten.

"If lots of people have a say," he said, "you can make better decisions."

"What if people are confused? Or just wrong?"

"Then you'd make bad decisions," he said.

"So we could get good or bad decisions. Are there other reasons to want democracy?"

"Well, if something might affect you, you should have a say in it," Rex said. He illustrated his point with a convoluted story about a utility company attempting to run a power line across our yard. "Wouldn't you want a say?" he asked.

"For sure," I said.

"Also, democracy's just fair," Rex added. "It's equal. Everyone counts the same."

That's a pretty pithy case for democracy. It gives people an opportunity to participate in important decisions. And it treats them as equals. Indeed, democracy *constitutes* people as equals, by creating a sense in which they are: one person, one vote.

But our family is *not* a democracy, and it won't be no matter how many times Rex asks. I've told you the reasons already. We are responsible for our kids, and to do our job, we often have to make decisions they don't like. We're *not* equals, not yet. And adopting procedures that constituted us as equals would be a serious mistake—for us and them.

But I try to remember: it's hard to be a kid, constantly told what to do by one adult or another. It makes you feel out of control, in a quite literal sense. So I try* to be patient when the kids seek control. It's never enough, though.

～

"I DECLARE INDEPENDENCE," Hank announced.

He was seven. We were taking a walk in a park. Or, rather, I was taking a walk. He was being pulled down a path while he protested the idea that we should get some exercise.

"Okay," I said. "Where do you plan to live?"

"At home."

"Whose home?"

"Our home."

---

*And mostly fail.

"You don't have a home."

He looked at me, puzzled.

"I have a home," he said. "Where we live."

"No, Hank. I have a home. And so do Rex and Mommy. But you just declared independence. So I'm afraid you don't have a home anymore."

Silence.

"Okay. I don't have a home," he said, grumpily.

"You could pay rent," I said.

"How much does it cost?"

"How much could you pay?"

"A dollar."

"Okay. We'll keep you around."*

---

*I never collected. When we got home, I offered Hank ice cream, and he ceded his independence. Which is good. He wouldn't have lasted long on his own.

5

LANGUAGE

Rex was alone in his room, reading Neil deGrasse Tyson's *Astrophysics for Young People in a Hurry.* This was a departure from our longtime bedtime ritual, which involved one of us curled up in bed reading with Rex. He'd recently gone to overnight camp for the first time, and at nine, he was asserting some independence. But I couldn't let go of the ritual. So I was reading too—on my own, in our guest room.

Then Rex bounded in, looking excited.

"It says there's an experiment we can do. Should we try it?"

"Sure," I said.

He read aloud from the book: "For a simple demonstration of gravity's constant pull, close this book, lift it a few inches off the nearest table, and then let it go. That is gravity at work. (If your book did not fall, please find your nearest astrophysicist and declare a cosmic emergency.)"

Rex closed the book and held it out. "Three . . . two . . . one."

It fell to the floor.

"Fuck!" Rex said as he shook his fists.

Then he looked at me with an impish grin. He was proud of himself. And I was proud of him too.

⁘

REX RETURNED FROM SUMMER CAMP CONFUSED—and slightly scandalized—by the frequency with which his bunkmates said bad words.

Outside our house, Rex is relentlessly well behaved. He had picked up several bad words by the time he went to camp, and occasionally he'd ask what they meant. But we'd rarely heard him use one.

As a kid, I was a lot like Rex—relentlessly well behaved, at least outside the house. But in my family, curse words were a common form of communication. In fact, my earliest memory might well be a parade of profanity emitted by my father as he attempted to assemble some furniture: *sonofamotherfuckingbitch*. At four, I thought it was all one word.

When Julie was pregnant with Rex, I worried that I'd give him a similar education. But as soon as he was born, a switch flipped and I stopped swearing, at least around him. Julie had a more difficult time than I did. But she got the hang of it before Rex could talk, leaving the boys to learn their bad words at school.

Or camp. We picked Rex up, hoping to hear tales of adventure. But first he wanted to talk about bad words.

"The kids say *so* many, and the counselors don't care," he reported.

"How about you?"

"I said some. But not as much as the other kids."

"That's okay," I said. "Camp is the kind of place you can do that."

"Some kids say them all the time," Rex said.

"That's what kids do at camp. Just remember, there's a time and place. At camp, it's okay. At school, it's not."

"How about at home?" Rex asked.

"A little, as long as you don't say them in a way that's disrespectful or mean."

A few days later, Rex issued his first *fuck*, in response to his failed attempt to cause a cosmic catastrophe. And it was a fine *fuck*. Perfectly timed. As I said, I was proud.

◦————◦————◦

WHY ARE SOME WORDS BAD? The idea that they could be bothered me as a kid. Words are strings of sounds. How could sounds be bad?

But of course: Words aren't *just* strings of sound. They are strings of sound to which we attach meaning. And yet it's not the meaning of words that makes them bad either. Just consider this list: *poop, crap, manure, dung, feces, stool*. It's all the same shit. And yet, it's only *shit* we shouldn't say.

Why is that? Fuck if I know.

There are taboo words in every language—different ones in different places. But there are common themes. Some relate to taboo topics—like sex, defecation, or disease. Others are borderline blasphemous. But we can talk about these topics without swearing, so it's something of a mystery why certain words shouldn't be said.

Rebecca Roache suggests that the sounds of swear words might have something to do with it. She's a philosopher of language (among other things), and she studies swear words. They tend to be harsh, she observes, like the emotions they express. And she doesn't think that's an accident. Soft words, like *whiffy* and *slush*, can't convey anger. Swearing with them, she says, would be like "trying to slam a door fitted with a compressed air hinge."

But Roache says that sound can't be the whole story. And she's right. There are lots of short, harsh words that no one finds offensive, like *cat, cut,* and *kit*. And some swear words have homonyms that are A-OK to say, like *prick, cock,* and *Dick*. (I'm sensing a theme.) Also, the words that are offensive shift over time, suggesting that we need a social explanation.

Roache argues that swear words are born through a process she calls *offense escalation*. If, for whatever reason, people don't like the word *shit*, then they're apt to be bothered when people say it. If the dislike becomes widespread and well-known, then saying *shit* will seem like a slight. And as the cycle repeats, the offense escalates. Once it's established that a word is offensive, it will seem extra offensive to say it.

But offense escalation can't be the whole story either, since people dislike all sorts of words. I can't stand *rhombus*. And now you know that, so if you say *rhombus* to me repeatedly, I'll be annoyed. But *rhombus* almost certainly won't become a swear word, since that preference is idiosyncratic to me.

Roache suggests that swear words tend to relate to taboo topics, because we know that those topics will cause discomfort, especially if discussed in disfavored ways. For instance, I know that I can upset you by calling you an asshole, even though I've never met you. I might be able to upset you by calling you trashy or posh instead. But to know that, I'd have to know a bit about you. Maybe you'd be bothered by those words; maybe you wouldn't. But *asshole*? Almost certainly.

Roache's explanation still leaves open the question how and why some words come to be disfavored in the first place. Why *shit* and not some other scatological term? Surely there's a story. But those aren't the sorts of stories that philosophers tell. (Historians have given it a go.) The question I want to ask is: Is it really wrong to swear?

⌇

I PUT THAT QUESTION to Rex recently. We were taking a walk.

"Is it okay to swear?" I asked.

"Sometimes," he said.

"When?"

"Well, you shouldn't be mean to people."

That's a good place to start. And Rex is, of course, right to worry that bad words are often used to say bad things. As Roache taught us, they're tools for doing just that. Indeed, if her story about offense escalation is right, bad words are bad because they are commonly used to say bad things.

But bad words aren't the only way to say bad things. And if your words are demeaning or degrading, I don't think it matters whether they're words that are commonly used for that purpose or ones that you tailored to the task. The wrong is the insult, not the words through which it's issued.

"Is it okay to swear when you aren't being mean?" I asked Rex. "What if you're just saying bad words, but they're not about anyone?"

"Sometimes it's okay, and sometimes it's not," Rex said.

"When is it okay?"

"You shouldn't swear if you are someplace civilized."

"What makes a place civilized?" I asked.

He paused. "I don't actually know what *civilized* means. It just sounded like a fancy thing to say."

"I think you know what it means," I said. "Is school civilized?"

"Yeah, mostly."

"What about camp?"

"Definitely not."

"How about our house?"

"Sometimes. But not when Hank and I take our shirts off and dance."

That is true. And I have the videos to prove it. In the best, Hank, barely four and barely clothed, asks: "Is this good booty shaking?" (It was.) In another, he's riding Rex like a horse, singing "Stayin' Alive." Both were filmed when Julie was on a business trip. We're deeply uncivilized without her.*

---

*I let the kids stay up late for that dance party. Hank kept shouting, "No Mommy, no bedtimey!" He was wrong about that, and he soon lost his enthusiasm for my solo parenting. When I put him to bed, he said, "I want she to come back."

But back to Rex—and his answer. Why is it wrong to say swear words in civilized places?

You can disrespect a place as much as a person.

If you swear in church, you disrespect the place. And the people in it. But the people will be upset because that's not the place. Down at the bar, they might say bad words with you. But church is different.

Indeed, rules for different places help make places different. Camp wouldn't be the place it is if kids had to act the way they do at church. And church wouldn't be the place it is if kids were permitted to act the way they do at camp. And we want both sorts of places in our lives. So Rex is right—it's okay to swear in some places but not others.

And there's an important lesson about morality lurking here. Some wrongs are wrongs regardless of what people think about them. Murder and rape, for instance, are not wrong because we think they are. They are wrong because they are deeply disrespectful of the dignity of human beings. But some wrongs *are* wrong because we think they are. And swearing in church is that sort of wrong.*

Ronald Dworkin (whom we met earlier) called this *conventional morality*. And he illustrated the idea by talking about what you can wear in church. In many places, it's customary for men to take off their hats when they enter a house of worship. Wearing a hat is seen as disrespectful. And because it's seen that way, it *is* disrespectful, at least when done by someone who knows how others will see it. But the custom could easily work the other way around. In fact, when I go to synagogue, I cover my head. Because that's how my people show respect.

Conventional morality often has an element of arbitrariness. It doesn't matter whether you show respect by covering your head or uncovering it. What matters is that the community has an agreed-upon sign of respect. Indeed, you can't really have formal spaces, let alone sacred ones,

---

*Or, at least, some swearing in church is—the scatological sort. Blasphemous swearing may be wrong because it's disrespectful to God.

without some rules that restrict what can be done there. It's those rules that set the place apart and make it feel formal or sacred.

The rules aren't always arbitrary. In libraries, you're supposed to talk softly, if at all. And that helps to make libraries a good place to study. But some rules serve little purpose beyond separating a space from others in our lives. Rules about whether you cover your head in church—or what words you may say while you're there—are those sorts of rules. They signal that we're somewhere special.

And, for the most part, we should follow those rules, so that we can have special places. We've debased an awful lot in our society, as an air of informality extends to ever more spaces. Sometimes that's good—better to fly in comfy clothes than return to the days when travelers dressed to the nines. But often it's bad, because we can elevate ourselves by elevating the places we spend time.

⌐~⌐

THAT SAID, we shouldn't always be elevated; we need downtime too. And that leaves lots of room for swearing. Rex's first *fuck* wasn't disrespectful—to a person or a place. It was funny. And an awful lot of swearing is like that. Is *that* sort of swearing wrong? The degree to which many parents police their kids' language suggests that it is. But I think those parents are making a mistake.

The problem with swear words is not the words themselves; it's what they signal. So if, on some occasion, they don't signal anything bad, there's no reason not to say them. That's why we set the rules we did for Rex. Don't be mean or disrespectful—to people or places. But beyond that, the occasional swear is okay.

Why just occasional? I suppose you might worry that in the same way you can debase a place, you can debase yourself. If you act crudely, you might become crude—consistently. But I don't have that worry about my kids. They're more than capable of code switching—acting differently in different contexts. I see them do it all the time.

But I do have a practical worry. Lots of people take swearing seriously, even when there is nothing serious at stake. That drove me crazy as a kid. And it still does. But to navigate the world, you need to know how others will react, even if you think it unwarranted. And as things stand in our society, lots of people won't think well of you if they think you swear too much.

But wait: If people think swearing is wrong, doesn't that make it wrong? Isn't that how conventional morality works? No. For people's views about what's wrong to matter, there has to be some reason to take them seriously. In the church case, the value in maintaining a sacred space gives people the power to mark off the space as sacred, in part by setting rules for what one can say and do in the space. In contrast, the fact that some busybodies might care how kids talk at camp or on the street does not give them the power to set standards for those kids' speech, since there's little value in policing speech in those places.

Parents are a special case. As we saw in the last chapter, they've got the power to set standards for their kids, at least within reason. But they shouldn't use that power to prohibit swearing, at least not altogether. Swearing is good. In fact, it's a skill all kids should master.

***

"WHAT'S GOOD ABOUT SWEARING?" I asked Rex on that walk.

"It feels good," he said.

"What do you mean?"

"When you're mad, it makes you feel better."

"Do you swear when you're mad?" I asked. I had never heard him do it.

"Yeah, under my breath. I mutter to myself."

Good for Rex! He should belt it out a bit louder.

In a famous study, Richard Stevens asked undergraduates to submerge one of their hands in a bucket of ice-cold water. Twice. Once they were allowed to swear; the other time, they weren't. When they swore, they could keep their hands submerged nearly 50 percent longer—and they perceived less pain too. Moreover, follow-up studies suggest that stronger swear words (think *fuck*, not *shit*) give more substantial relief. I'd bet that swearing loudly does too, at least to a point.

More important: Swearing soothes more than physical pain. Michael Phillip and Laura Lombardo showed that it helps with the pain caused by social exclusion too. They had people recall a time they felt left out. Some were told to swear afterward; others said ordinary words instead. The ones who got to swear reported substantially less social pain than the ones who didn't. Which is just what Rex—and every other kid ever—discovered all on his own.

I encountered these studies in Emma Byrne's *Swearing Is Good for You: The Amazing Science of Bad Language.* The science *is* amazing. (Chimps that learn sign language invent their own swear words. I shit you not.) Byrne makes some suggestions about why swearing makes us feel better; it has to do with the parts of the brain that process emotionally laden language. But that science is still in progress, and the details don't really matter. What's important for us is that swearing is excellent stress relief.

But wait, there's more! As Byrne explains, swearing can be "good for group bonding." She recounts research into the lighthearted banter that smooths social interaction. She tells tales of people who found social acceptance through swearing. And she illustrates the many ways in which it helps people communicate effectively. The research is cool. But I doubt you need to read it to know what she means. Find any group that gets along well, and you'll almost surely hear some swearing.

The social dimension of swearing is why I want my kids to master the skill. It's not enough to know when and where you can swear. Swearing is something you can be good at. And it's *not* easy. To start, you have to learn new ways to use words. Sometimes *fuck* is a verb, sometimes it's a noun. But often it doesn't function as any familiar part of speech. Consider the phrase *fuck you.* It sort of sounds like a command. But it doesn't work like one. Contrast it with *close the door*. I can embed that phrase in all sorts of sentences:

> Please close the door.
>
> Go close the door.
>
> I said to close the door.

But *fuck you* doesn't work like that. These sentences make no sense:

> Please fuck you.
>
> Go fuck you.
>
> I said to fuck you.

That tells you that the *fuck* in *fuck you* is not a verb. It's a special sort of word, designed to communicate disapproval.*

But it gets weirder, because the *fuck* in *fuck you* does function as a verb sometimes:

> I'll fuck you tomorrow.
>
> Don't let him fuck you.

And we're not done yet, since *fuck* acts funny in other contexts too. This pair of sentences makes sense:

> Turn down the loud television.
>
> Turn down the television that is loud.

---

*This observation traces to an article with a title that doesn't tip its topic: "English Sentences without Overt Grammatical Subject." In the 1960s, it circulated as a pamphlet, attributed to Quang Phuc Dong, of the South Hanoi Institute for Technology. (Go ahead, work out the acronym.) It was actually written by a linguist named James D. McCawley, who taught at the University of Chicago. It was serious work, which inspired further research on swear words. But it mocks Asian names in a way that now looks racist.

But this pair doesn't:

> Turn down the fucking television.
>
> Turn down the television that is fucking.

In the first pair, *loud* is an adjective. In the second, it looks like *fucking* is playing the same role, but it's not, since you can't move it around the same way.

I could do this all fuckin' day. Some of you would think that fan-fuckin-tastic. But not one of you would find it fanta-fuckin-stic. Because there are rules that govern the insertion of *fuck* into other words, *and you know them*, even though you've never read John J. McCarthy's epic paper "Prosodic Structure and Expletive Infixation."

Fuck might be the most versatile word in the English language. It's certainly the most fun, since it lets you do things nearly no other word can. But when it comes to swearing, there's more to master than grammar. As Byrne explains, you need a sophisticated model of other people's emotions in order to predict how they'll react when you swear. There are so many subtle variations. You can say *fuck off* in a way that ends a friendship. You can say it in a way that preserves one. You can say it in a way that's funny. And you can say it in a way that's anything but.

It's all about context, timing, and tone. And the norms that govern good swearing are constantly in flux, as people sort them out together. So I won't even attempt to teach my boys to swear well. They'll learn on their own, by trial, error, and observation, just like the rest of us. But I'll give them space to practice. Someday they'll thank me. By telling me to . . .

• ⌒⌒⌒ •

REX HAS COME a long way from that first *fuck*. Just a year later, he's a seriously good swearer. We discovered that the same night that I taught Hank his first bad word.

I was telling the boys stories about my maternal grandparents. They weren't good people; they were mean and selfish. The boys were shocked to learn that my grandfather didn't like kids. They couldn't make sense of it. To help, I told them that I could recall only one occasion when my grandfather played with me. I was five, and they were visiting for a few nights. He got down on the floor and taught me to shoot craps. Why? I don't know. It's not a skill a kid needs. But it might have been the best interaction we ever had.

At this point in the story, I paused, because I realized that I was about to say a word Hank didn't know. I told him I was going to say a bad word. His eyes lit up. So I carried on.

The next time I saw my grandparents, we went out to dinner. I was hoping to shoot craps again. So I asked: "When we get home, can we shoot the shit?"

He was furious. At me. And my parents. Who could not stop laughing. He grumbled about my bad language for days. But he seriously undersold me. *Shit* didn't scratch the surface of what I knew. He never heard me shout my father's anthem: *sonofamotherfuckingbitch*. If only he'd gotten to know me, I think he would have loved me.*

Not a chance, actually. And that's what I was trying to convey to the kids. As a result, Hank now knew the word *shit*, and it required some explanation. We told him it's a synonym for *poop*, and that *crap* is too, which is part of what makes the story go. And we told him it was okay to say it, subject to the same rules we'd given Rex.

Then Julie suggested Hank try it out. "When you discover something bad, you can say, 'Oh shit!'" she said. "Do you want to try?"

---

*Before you judge me, or my parents, too harshly, I should say: I wasn't at all aberrational. Lots of kids swear by three or four, some even younger. And research suggests that by five or six, kids have learned substantial numbers of swear words, including many of the most taboo. It's *my* kids who are aberrational; we so effectively limited our swearing that it took them longer than normal to pick it up. That actually made me worry a bit about them—as I said, I want my kids to be competent in lots of social situations, including ones that call for swearing. But as the story I'm telling indicates, my worry was misplaced.

Hank looked a little leery. Then he said, "Oh shit" so softly you could hardly hear it.

We laughed, and he sank below the table, slightly embarrassed. Then he popped up again, a bit bolder, and a bit louder: "Oh shit."

Now we were really laughing, and he was getting into it. "Oh shit. Oh Shit! OH SHIT!"

Meanwhile, Rex was losing his shit. He had spent years shielding his brother from bad words. They were part of what separated him from Hank—made him seem more adult.

But Julie and I were joining in, because we're good parents. The three of us had a chorus going: "Oh shit. Oh Shit! OH SHIT!"

Then Julie asked Rex to join in. "C'mon, Rex, everyone's doing it!" Did I mention we're good parents?

Rex turned red and sank under the table. He sat there for a second. Then just as the chorus reached its crescendo, he popped out to shout, *"There's no fucking way I'm saying 'Oh shit!' "*

———

JULIE HAS NEVER LAUGHED so hard. And I was impressed. In part, because the joke rests on a distinction we're going to need a little later.

Rex said he wasn't going to say *Oh shit*. But in saying that, he said it. Or at least, he sort of did.

Philosophers draw a distinction between using a word and mentioning it. Take these two sentences:

1. I'm going to the store.

2. *Store* rhymes with *snore*.

The first sentence uses the word *store* to refer to a place you go shopping. The second mentions the word *store* without using it. It invokes the word itself, rather than the place the word denotes.

Here's another example:

1. Shit, I spilled the milk.

2. You shouldn't say *shit* around the kids.

The first uses the word *shit*. But it doesn't refer to shit. Rather, it uses the word to express an emotion. In contrast, the second sentence doesn't use the word *shit* at all. It simply mentions it.

The distinction between using a word and mentioning it is foundational in philosophy. Philosophers are interested in the world *and* in the words we use to describe it. So they need a way to signal what they're talking about. The standard practice is to put words that you are merely mentioning in quotation marks, as in:

The word "shit" has four letters.

I think that looks ugly, especially if you have to do it a lot. So I adopted a different practice here. When I mention words, I put them in italics. Of course, italics are also used for emphasis, so I'm risking confusion. But I suspect you've been able to sort it out.

Rex's joke exploited the use/mention distinction. He said, *"There's no fucking way I'm saying 'Oh shit!'"* What he said was false, in a sense, since he did say it. And it was true, in a different sense, since he didn't use the phrase; he merely mentioned it. That tension is part of what makes the joke funny, alongside the fact that the phrase he did use (*no fucking way*) is much stronger than the phrase he merely mentioned.

That's a sophisticated sense of humor. And it's a large part of what I love about present-day Rex.

━━━━━◦〜〜◦━━━━━

I'm a lot older, and people still police my language. My editor says I say *fuck* too much. I'm not saying that's the reason I wrote this chapter. But I'm not *not* saying it either. (Hi, Ginny!)

Why do I swear so much? For two reasons. First, it's a way of establishing intimacy. Different relationships have different rules. When I say *fuck* around you, I reveal what I take the rules of our relationship to be. We're more like camp friends than colleagues or, worse yet, strangers.

Second, I swear because I want to signal something about philosophy. You can do it in a way that's fussy and formal. Or you can do it in a way that's fun. And I pick fun.

But the fun is meant to make a serious point. Philosophy should address every aspect of our lives—the sacred, the profane, and even the mundane. It's partly out of that conviction that I came to write this book. I want you to see that philosophical questions are present in the most prosaic experiences. I want you to know that philosophy is too important to leave to philosophers. And I want you to think that philosophy is fun. Because it can be, and it should be, and it is, when done well.

I'm not the only philosopher who thinks profanity fair game for philosophy. Harry Frankfurt's book *On Bullshit* was an unlikely bestseller. The slim volume aims to explain what bullshit is—and why we're knee-deep in it. The book is fun.* But I'm a bigger fan of another bestseller, Aaron James's *Assholes: A Theory*. It's just what it sounds like—an attempt to explain what assholes are and why we find them so bothersome. It is, I think, essential reading for our age.

Philosophers can be stodgy. I've heard more than a few grumble about Frankfurt, James—and me. We're just in it for the shock value, they say. But that's not it at all. Sure, I think philosophy should be fun and funny. But I also think it should help us make sense of ourselves. *We* are sacred and profane. Philosophy can be too.

---

*But I should warn you: it's bullshit. Frankfurt purports to explain bullshit's essence. But the sort he describes—speaking without caring whether what you say is true—is just one among many. Here are a few more: Flopping in soccer is bullshit. So are bad calls by refs. Most meetings are bullshit. And even if we stick to speech: An awful lot of bullshit comes from people who are flaunting the fact that they're not telling the truth. They're feeding you bullshit, and it's further bullshit that you have to take it. Buy me a beer sometime, and we'll work out a better theory of bullshit.

So I'm pro-swear, at least in some circumstances. But there *are* some words we shouldn't say. In our society, slurs are the words that are really taboo. We pay lip service to the prohibition on F-bombs—then drop them. That's because the F-word doesn't bother us much anymore. We protest for show, but we're not scandalized. The N-word, on the other hand, is a scandal.

Slurs are a trendy topic to study. Philosophers (and linguists) debate the way they work, just at the level of language. For instance, it's not clear what a slur *means*. Consider the following sentence:

A kike wrote this book.

Is that true? *Kike* is a derogatory term for Jews. And I'm Jewish. So some philosophers would say that the sentence is true—and yet shouldn't be said, given the contempt expressed by choosing that word rather than a less objectionable synonym. Other philosophers would say that the sentence is false, insisting that there's no such thing as a kike. But that raises the question what a kike is, if not just a Jew.

I don't want to take up those debates, as it's really a moral question that interests me: When, if ever, is it okay to say a slur? But it turns out that the linguistic and moral questions are linked. You can't answer the moral question without seeing how slurs work—at the level of language.

I learned that from my Michigan colleague Eric Swanson. He's a professor of philosophy and linguistics—and a kickass kayaker. According to Swanson, the key to understanding slurs is to appreciate their connection to ideologies. An *ideology* is an interlocking set of ideas, concepts, and attitudes that inform the way we interact with the world, or some part of it.

There are ideologies associated with economic systems, like capitalism and socialism. There are ideologies associated with different positions on the political spectrum, like liberal and conservative. But there are also ideologies associated with activities, like sports ("Winning isn't everything; it's the only thing") and theater ("The show must go on"). And there are ideologies associated with oppression: racism, sexism, anti-Semitism, and so on.

As that list indicates, there's nothing good or bad in the idea of an ideology. Indeed, anti-racism is itself an ideology, structured by ideas, concepts, and attitudes, which it uses to make sense of the world (think: white supremacy, privilege, and mass incarceration). But some ideologies *are* bad. American racism led to slavery, segregation, and lynching, among many other evils. Indeed, it's impossible to imagine those evils without some supporting ideology—one that casts Black people as inferior, such that they warrant that sort of treatment.

Swanson argues that slurs *cue* ideologies—they call them to mind, make them available to think about and act on. The difference between saying "A Jewish person wrote this book" and "A kike wrote this book" is that the second cues the ideology of anti-Semitism. It invites you to think in those terms—to entertain the idea that Jews are dirty, money-grubbing creatures out to control the world. Because that's the ideology in which the word *kike* plays a part.

When you use a slur like *kike*, you don't just call those ideas to mind. You also imply that it's okay to use the word—to operate within the ideology. You invite others to see the world in an anti-Semitic way. And that way of seeing the world is harmful. It led to the Holocaust and pogroms, and it remains the source of many hate crimes.

Some ideologies should be off-limits. No one should want to cue them, at least not in ways that suggest they are acceptable. And that means there are some words that simply should not be said.

—————

UNLESS YOU HAVE A really good reason. And sometimes you do. For instance, you can't critique an ideology—or resist it—without cueing it.

The N-word appears in James Baldwin's letter to his nephew in *The Fire Next Time*, in Martin Luther King Jr.'s *Letter from the Birmingham Jail*, and in Ta-Nehisi Coates's letter to his son in *Between the World and Me*. In each case, the word is called on to convey the full force of the hate-filled ideology it represents. Speaking less bluntly would blunt the message.

But let me be clear: I'm not saying you may say that slur whenever you aim to critique or resist the racist ideology it reflects. Whether you can depends, in part, on who you are.

Some people find that odd, but it's not really. As a Jew, I can say *kike*. When I do, I cue an anti-Semitic ideology. But no one will take me to embrace that ideology or encourage others to adopt it. A non-Jew who says *kike* might not endorse the ideology either. But it can be hard for others to tell. So it makes sense for non-Jews to avoid the word, at least as much as possible.

That means I can say *kike* and you can't. (Unless you're Jewish, or have some good reason—like teaching the history of anti-Semitism.) But the fact that I can say *kike* doesn't mean that I should, since it cues an anti-Semitic ideology whether I wish it to or not.

That's true even when people use slurs to communicate affection, as they sometimes do. Oppressed groups often attempt to reclaim slurs. *Queer* is the most successful case. It is embraced, and even preferred, by many who would have once been its targets. For most, it no longer cues an anti-gay ideology; quite the opposite.

But many reclamation projects are more limited. Women who call their female friends *bitches* do not envision an end point when men will do the same. For the foreseeable future, men's use of the word will continue to cue a sexist ideology, which means that women's use will too, even if it also cues an inversion of it. The same is true with the N-word. Among Black people, it's often a term of endearment. But it cues a racist ideology, along with its inversion, especially when said within earshot of unsympathetic Whites.

That doesn't make reclamation wrong. There are good reasons for oppressed groups to reclaim the words associated with their oppression. It saps some of their power. And it's no accident that slurs are often turned into terms of endearment. The fact that a woman can call a close friend her *bitch* signals just how close they are; so close, they can shift the significance of words.

Do the costs of reclamation projects outweigh their benefits? That's not for me to say. I'm an outsider to most of these communities, so I'm not in a good position to assess all the costs and benefits. (Except when it comes to *kike*. Anti-Semites can keep it.) It's a question for the people most affected. I just want you to see why, even among the targeted groups, these questions are often controversial.

•~~•

SOME PEOPLE THINK WHITES should have a little more leeway to say the N-word than I've suggested. (To be clear, I am suggesting Whites have none, or nearly so.) They point to the use/mention distinction we learned earlier. The idea is that you shouldn't *use* a slur to refer to someone, but it's okay merely to *mention* it.

For a long time, I thought that was a sensible line to draw, and I continue to think it morally meaningful. When you use a slur, you endorse an oppressive ideology—and demean whoever it is directed at. When you merely mention a slur, you don't do either of those things. And that matters. Using a slur can be seriously wrong.* Mentioning one rarely is.

But mentioning a slur is not completely benign, because you cue the ideology it represents merely by mentioning it. To be sure, there can be good reasons to mention slurs—even the most offensive ones. As I said, authors like Baldwin, King, and Coates could not communicate as ef-

---

*Swanson argues that the moral seriousness of a slur is a function of the harm that the relevant ideology causes. That's why the N-word is worse than *honky* or *cracker* (which refer to Whites) and far worse than *nerd* and *geek*.

fectively as they did if they talked around the word. Sparing mention of slurs is okay when there's a good reason to do it. But *sparing* is the key word in that sentence, since good reasons are rare.

Indeed, Swanson can help us see why Whites ought to welcome the chance to say *the N-word* rather than the N-word, in all but the most exceptional cases. It's not about what they can't do; it's about what they can do. When you talk around the word, you put your opposition to it— and the ideology it represents—front and center. Saying *the N-word* rather than the slur itself strikes a small blow against racism by signaling dissent from it.*

SWANSON'S THEORY OF SLURS can also help us understand why words that aren't taboo are sometimes harmful. He reports that a stranger, who saw him taking care of his young son, once said, "It's great that you help his mom so much." There are no slurs there. And yet, in choosing the word *help*, the stranger cued an ideology that assigns mothers primary caregiving responsibility and sees men as helpers, not as full parents. In saying what she did, the stranger endorsed that ideology and subtly encouraged Swanson to see himself that way too. No doubt, she thought she was being nice. And she *was* being nice. But she was nice in a way that undermined Swanson and his spouse.

Indeed, Swanson's theory of slurs illuminates more than language. It can help us understand why our actions are sometimes objectionable even when we don't intend them to be. Men opening doors for women cues an ideology that sees men as strong, chivalrous types coming to the aid of weak or meek women. Within that ideology, the action is well-

---

*At least that's true most of the time. If you say the circumlocution too ostentatiously, or too often, then it seems that you are really trying to cue the racist ideology rather than the antiracist one. You can abuse talking around a word, just as you can abuse mentioning it. Communication is complicated. Bright-line rules can't capture the relevant ethical lines, which are constantly in flux as social meaning shifts.

intentioned. So men are sometimes mystified when women object. But women who object are seeking a different sort of respect, one rooted in an ideology of equality.

There's a general lesson here: we should pay more attention to the ideologies that shape what we say and do. Often actions that are well-intentioned reflect and support ideologies we should reject.

⁘ ⸺ ⸺ ⸺ ⁘

"DO YOU KNOW ANY SLURS?" I asked Rex as I was writing this chapter.

"I know one. You taught it to me."

Uh-oh, I thought.

"Which one?"

"*Redskins*. Like the football team."

I was relieved. I remembered that conversation. We had talked about the Atlanta Braves—our favorite baseball team. I told Rex that I thought the Braves should change their name too. The team says it intends to honor Native Americans, and maybe that's true. But the problem is not what the Braves intend. It's what their name cues—an ideology that sees Native Americans as savages—which, for many decades, the team embraced in its imagery. Also: there's a better name. The team should be called The Traffic.

Then Rex added: "I think I learned another slur from *March*."

March is a series of graphic novels, which tell the story of John Lewis, the civil rights superhero–cum–congressman. If you've got a preteen, pick it up. Or grab a copy for yourself; it's great.

"It's a word that White people called Black people," Rex said.

Then he said the word.

I asked what he knew about it.

He said it was a really mean thing to say, maybe the meanest.

And we talked about why that is. He'd learned a lot of the history already, from *March* and other books. So we talked about why the word hurts—how it calls forth that history, and all the ugly associations that come with it. And we talked about how disrespectful it is to say the word, given its history.

For all those reasons, I told Rex he should never say the word again.

"I'm sorry," he said, looking concerned. "I didn't know."

"Don't be sorry," I said. "I wanted you to know. That's why I asked."

PART II

MAKING SENSE
OF OURSELVES

6

SEX, GENDER, AND SPORTS

Rex and his friend James ran their first 5K in second grade. They finished in just over thirty-four minutes. Among eight-year-old boys, that was good for ninth and tenth place. We greeted them at the finish line, just proud to see them run.

As we celebrated, I said, "Did you guys see what Suzie did?" Rex, James, and Suzie were inseparable in second grade—constant companions, in school and out.

"No, what did she do?" asked Rex.

"She came in first," I said. "And she was fast! She finished in twenty-five minutes." Just under, actually.

"She started before us," Rex said, as if that explained why Suzie finished a full nine minutes in front.

"I don't think she was *that* far ahead of you," I said.

"Yeah, she was," James said. "We couldn't see her when we started."

"I could see her," I said. "And there's a chip in your bib that records your start time. So it doesn't matter who starts first."

"I know," Rex said, "but we got stuck in the crowd."

"For nine minutes?" I asked.

"We weren't trying to run our fastest," James said defiantly.

"Yeah," Rex said. "We were taking our time."

"Okay," I said, annoyed at their unwillingness to celebrate Suzie. "But even if you ran your fastest, you wouldn't go as fast as Suzie. She's *really* fast."

WHY WERE THE BOYS making excuses? Because they lost to a girl. And boys aren't supposed to lose to girls. This is bad for girls. But it's also bad for boys. And actually, it's bad for girls in part *because* it's bad for boys.

The thought that boys should be better than girls at sports is bad for girls in obvious ways. It's an echo of the idea that girls aren't suited for sports, which was long the justification for excluding them entirely. But even the milder supposition that boys should be better limits opportunities for girls. If people don't expect girls to be good at sports, they'll get less encouragement and fewer chances to play. And that makes it something of a self-fulfilling prophecy. Boys turn out to be better at sports, not because they are inherently better, but because we've invested more in their athletic performance.

Why is that bad for boys? The idea that they should be better than girls at sports makes a boy's masculinity conditional on his athletic ability. If a boy loses to a girl, he's apt to be seen as less of a boy, or not a boy at all. And he may well take that message to heart, seeing himself as somehow defective.

That's bad for boys. But it turns out to be bad for girls too, because boys feel like they must defend their masculinity. Sometimes they exclude girls, so that they don't risk losing to them. Or they denigrate girls' achievements so that they can hold on to their sense of themselves as superior. That's what I thought Rex and James were up to at the 5K—minimizing Suzie's accomplishment so that it didn't pose a threat to them.

But don't blame the boys. They didn't set up this system. And though they defend their position within it, that position is not all privilege. It's pressure to come up to a standard that many boys can't (or don't want to) meet. And failure is not simply a matter of slipping to the less privileged position that girls already occupy. A boy who can't hack it as a boy is not welcome as a girl; he's simply not welcome, by boys or girls.

· ⌇⌇ ·

THESE ISSUES ARE NOT abstract for me. I was the smallest boy in my class, which is a serious problem when it comes to sports. I'd like to say that I made up for it with grit, determination, and impressive coordination. But I move like a motley collection of Mr. Potato Head parts.

Or at least I do whenever I attempt anything athletic. I'm not clumsy. I've got good balance and quick reflexes. I'm reasonably fit. But my mind does not have full control of my body. It's like the marionette strings got tangled, so every move slightly misses. And the more I try to make it work, the more tangled up I get.

I spent my childhood teetering on the edge of acceptable athletic performance—for a boy. I was the kid consumed by anxiety every time someone suggested we choose sides, since we were about to get ranked with ruthless efficiency. (Seriously, seven-year-olds should run the NBA draft.)

One summer, my mother signed me up for a week of sports camp. Which was fine. I liked sports. I just wasn't good at them. The last day, the counselors divided the campers into two teams for a full day of competition. At lunch, I heard two counselors talking about how they'd split the kids.

"You picked Scott?" one said, in a way that suggested it was a slightly worse idea than setting yourself on fire.

"Well, it was down to him and [name redacted]." [Name redacted] was the only girl in camp. But she was no Suzie. She was bigger and stronger than me, for sure. But she was new to most sports. And she was not a natural athlete.

"Tough call," the other guy said.

"Well, I figured I'd go with the boy. It's gotta count for something."

Boom, baby! Check my privilege. But also: check hers. It couldn't have been easy to be the only girl at sports camp. And I'm sure it would have hurt to know she was picked last. But [name redacted]'s femininity wasn't at risk. No one shamed her for her struggles or suggested that they made her less of a girl. Because a girl doesn't have to be good at sports, not even at sports camp.*

A boy does. And I wasn't. But that counselor let me be a boy anyway. And I was grateful. That no one heard him. Because the other kids would not have been so kind.

<hr />

REX DOESN'T REMEMBER the 5K conversation the way I do. And I owe his version a hearing.

"That's not what happened," he said when I shared my recollection.

"How do you remember it?"

"When we finished the race, you started making fun of us because Suzie was faster," Rex said.

"Do you really think I'd make fun of you for losing to Suzie?" I asked.

"Well, it sounded like you were."

---

*To be clear, I'm not saying that girls don't feel pressure to be good at sports. Of course they do, in some contexts. The difference is that failure at sports does not cast doubt on their femininity. Indeed, girls often have the opposite problem. Success in sports leads people to question their femininity. I haven't noticed this among younger kids. But it becomes an issue in adolescence, and it only gets worse as women ascend to the top of their sports.

I want to be clear: I would never make fun of my son for losing to a girl. (As you can see, I have some sensitivity on this issue.)

But I see why Rex heard me that way. Even pointing out how well Suzie had done was sufficient to stoke his anxiety. And I didn't drop it, because I thought it important that he celebrate Suzie.

So we talked about it, and I started the way I started here. I suggested that boys are taught that they shouldn't lose to girls.

"No one teaches us that," Rex said.

"You don't think so?"

"Well, no grown-up ever says it," Rex said thoughtfully. "But I guess we are supposed to think it."

"Why are you supposed to think it?"

"I'm not sure," Rex said. "I guess it's just the way people react when a girl beats a boy. And the way that teams are set up. I think everyone just understands that boys are supposed to be better."

"Are boys better?"

"No," Rex said without hesitation. "Some of the girls are really good at soccer."

"Do kids make fun of boys for losing to girls?"

"Yeah," Rex said. "My friends are pretty good about not making fun of anyone. But some boys do."

"What about girls?"

"Yeah, girls would make fun of you for losing to a girl too."

⁘

SEXISM IS COMPLICATED.

It's mostly bad for women and girls. But it can also be bad for men and boys. And if we want to help girls, we have to help boys too, because girls often suffer when boys feel threatened.

Also: Sexism is not just something that boys do to girls. It's something that girls do to boys. And that girls do to girls. And that boys do to boys.

We all participate in sexism, because we are all steeped in roles that are structured by sex stereotypes. And we all suffer from sexism, because we all feel pressure to conform to those roles.

We'll return to the roles in a while. But first, a bit more about the 5K.

I told you that Suzie finished first. But so did Blake, even though Suzie beat Blake by almost a minute.

Wait, what? How can you finish first when you finish second?

The answer is: Blake is a boy. And the 5K was sex-segregated. All the kids ran together. But there were two races going on: one for girls and one for boys.

Which raises a question: Why do we segregate sports by sex? Suzie did not need help. She was the fastest girl in her class. But she was also just the fastest, full stop. And we might wonder: Was it a good idea for Blake to get a first place medal too? Maybe second place would have taught Blake—and all the other boys—a lesson. A girl can stand atop the podium even when she competes with boys.

That sounds like a lesson worth learning. And if the 5K wasn't sex-segregated, the boys would have gotten schooled again the following year. Suzie doubled her lead, beating the fastest boy by two full minutes. And she wasn't the only girl who finished before him. He came in third. And yet he went home a champion—of the decidedly lesser sex, at least in that competition.

⁂

SO WHY WAS THE 5K sex-segregated? Honestly, I'm not sure that it should have been. I don't see any reason that boys and girls as young as Rex and Suzie shouldn't compete against each other. In fact, I think it would be good for both boys and girls to see that the girls are every bit as good, and often better, at athletic endeavors.

But that approach has a short shelf life. Before too long, boys will start to pass Suzie by. Not my boys. Not most boys. But some boys. Because the tail end of men's athletic performance is a bit longer than the tail end of women's athletic performance, at least in most sports.

At the top, the separation can be stark. Take the 100-meter dash. Florence Griffith Joyner holds the women's world record at 10.49 seconds.* Which is crazy fast. And yet it's nearly a second slower than Usain Bolt ran when he set the men's record at 9.58 seconds.

To put the difference in context, a man who ran as fast as Flo Jo would be so slow by the standards of the fastest men that he would have finished the 2019 track season ranked 801st. Indeed, he'd hardly stand out among high schoolers; in 2019, more than a dozen boys under eighteen ran faster than the fastest woman ever.

To be sure, there are sports in which women outcompete men all the way through adulthood. And we'll see some of them in a bit. But as things stand now, they are few in number. So if we did not segregate sports by sex, women would rarely win the marquee competitions. Worse yet, they'd be absent from them almost entirely, since they'd rarely qualify to compete.

⁘ ⸻ ⸱

So what? you might wonder.

That's not a stupid question. All sorts of people are excluded from elite sports. There are amazing basketball players who are too short for the NBA. There are amazing football players who are too small for the NFL. There are amazing soccer players who are too slow to play in the Premier League.

Some sports have ways of solving these problems. My grandmother's youngest brother was a boxer back in the 1930s. He fought under the

---

*That time is disputed, as it seems likely that the anemometer—which measures wind speed—was broken at the time of the race. It registered no wind. But subsequent investigation suggested that the wind present well exceeded the wind allowed. If you took that race off the record books, Elaine Thompson-Herah would have the top time at 10.54.

name Benny "Irish" Cohen. He wasn't Irish. But his manager was. And an Irish Cohen doubled the gate.

Benny was a terrific boxer. At his peak, he ranked third in the world—for his weight class.

You see, Benny fought as a bantamweight. He was five foot two and weighed 118 pounds. I'd tower over him, which is a sentence I've never gotten to say before. (So far as boxing's concerned, I'm a super light-weight. Which feels fitting.) If Benny had stepped in the ring with a heavyweight, he would have gotten himself killed. But boxing divides participants into weight classes precisely to make it possible for boxers like Benny to excel.

And the sport is better for it. The little guys are fun to watch. They're quicker than the big guys, and some are more technically adept. Boxing fans debate the best *pound-for-pound* fighters. The phrase signals that the best boxer in any pair might not be the one who would win a heads-up match. Indeed, many regard Sugar Ray Robinson as the best pound-for-pound fighter, period. He was a welterweight (147 pounds), then a middle-weight (160). Top heavyweights, like Muhammad Ali, would have destroyed him. But weight classes let Robinson set the standard for the sport.

Some make similar arguments for sex segregation. If Wimbledon didn't have separate draws for men and women, we wouldn't have witnessed the brilliance of the Williams sisters.

That's not my opinion. It's Serena's. When asked about playing an exhibition against Andy Murray, she responded, "For me, men's tennis and women's tennis are completely, almost, two separate sports. If I were to play Andy Murray, I would lose 6–0, 6–0 in five to six minutes, maybe 10 minutes. . . . The men are a lot faster and they serve harder, they hit harder, it's just a different game."

Of course, different does *not* mean worse. Indeed, the women's ver-sions of some sports are arguably better than the men's. Some basketball fans enjoy watching the WNBA more than its male counterpart, because the women show off different skills. They rely less on individual athleticism and work together more as a team, running set plays and structured defenses. Indeed, some say the WNBA has restored an older version of the game, which they enjoy more than the superstar-driven play in today's NBA. (Sidebar: Rex recently asked why it's not called the MNBA, and he's got a point.)

Discovering different athletes—or distinct styles of play—are without doubt upsides of sex-segregating sports. But they cannot be the whole story, or even the most significant bit of it. First, we can get these benefits in all sorts of ways, not just through sex segregation. Boxing proves that. And we could copy the approach, adopting height classes for basketball, speed classes for soccer, or strength classes for tennis. With every cut, we might discover new athletes and new ways of play. But no one clamors to see short guys play basketball, even though it would surely be fun to watch.

And that's not the only problem with this explanation for sex segregation. It doesn't apply to all sports. Elite men and women play somewhat different styles of basketball. But when it comes to running, sex segregation doesn't spotlight distinct ways to play. Running fast is running fast, regardless who does it.* That's the lesson Suzie might have taught the boys, had the 5K not been sex-segregated.

Finally, it feels like sex segregation in sports must have something to do with equality. It's not an accident that no one clamors to see short guys play basketball, even though their game might also rely more on teamwork than individual athleticism. It doesn't strike us as important to see short guys play, in the way we think it important that women compete.

---

*There do appear to be biomechanical differences in the way that men and women run. But it takes sophisticated observers to see them. And our interest in seeing women run does not rest on the ways in which their biomechanics might differ from men's.

BUT WHY IS IT IMPORTANT? To answer that question, it will help to think about why sports are important. Jane English was a philosopher—and an impressive amateur athlete. She died tragically young (just thirty-one), while climbing the Matterhorn. Just before she died, she published an article called "Sex Equality in Sports."

According to English, participation in sports provides two sorts of benefits. First up are the *basic benefits*. These include things like health, self-respect, and "just plain fun." English argued that we all have a right to the basic benefits of sports. She imagined a boy named Walter, who's a better wrestler than a girl named Matilda. Walter's superiority, she said, is "no reason to deny Matilda an equal chance to wrestle for health, self-respect, and fun." Indeed, English said that it would be unjust to discourage Matilda from wrestling simply on the ground that Walter is better.

English argued that we should make recreational athletics "available to people of all ages, sexes, income levels, and abilities," so that everyone could enjoy the basic benefits of sports. And she lived what she preached. She was an avid swimmer, runner, and tennis player. Several months before her death, she set a 10K record for her age group at a local track meet.

In setting that record, English secured one of the *scarce benefits* of sports. These include things like fame, fortune, and first place. We can't all be entitled to fan mail, English said, let alone first place in the race. When it comes to scarce benefits, skill matters.

But equality does too. Indeed, English suggested that men and women ought to have an equal chance to capture fame and fortune through sports.

But she insisted that no *individual* woman has a right to fame or fortune—or even to a competition she has a chance to win. Rather, the right to an equal share of sports' scarce benefits is held by women *collectively*, because it's important for women to have a prominent role in sports.

Why? I think that question was best answered by another philosopher—who was also an awesome athlete. In 1984, Angela Schneider represented Canada as a rower in the Summer Olympics. She won a silver medal in the coxed four. After she retired from rowing, she became a philosopher of sport. Which is just about the coolest job ever. Schneider writes about topics like doping, amateurism, and the relationship between sports and play.

As Schneider points out, we live in a world that's profoundly unequal. Women are "systematically denied positions of power and public attention." And their "aptitudes and achievements" often go "unrecognized and unheralded."

Sports are a major part of the problem. In our society, we celebrate athletes more than most anyone else. But we pay attention to a small set of sports, and most of them privilege male bodies. That's a problem in at least two ways.

First, representation matters. Young girls need to see women excel at sports. Otherwise, they might conclude that sports are not for them. And then they'll lose out on sports' basic benefits.

Second, we accord immense power and influence to people who excel in sports. Michael Jordan amassed a fortune, which he used to purchase an NBA team. Recently he pledged $100 million to fight racial inequality. Colin Kaepernick is part of that fight too. He accelerated the movement against police brutality simply by kneeling during the national anthem. He called attention to the issue in a way that no one else could, since he commanded the attention of NFL camera crews every Sunday. And Kaepernick and Jordan are far from the only athletes working for change. Muhammad Ali, Magic Johnson, Greg Louganis, Jesse Owens, Jackie Robinson—the list of athletes who have shifted attitudes is super long.

Thanks to sex segregation, the list includes lots of women too. In recent times, Serena Williams, Megan Rapinoe, and Maya Moore. Before them, Babe Didrikson Zaharias, Martina Navratilova, and Billie Jean King.

That list alone is a powerful argument for sex-segregating sports. The world would be worse without the inspiration those women—and so many others—provide. For girls, for sure. But for the rest of us too.

We don't watch sports just to find out who can run the fastest or jump the highest. As Schneider says, sports "shape and define our images of who we are and what is possible for human beings." The athletes we lift up lift us up in return. They model grit, determination, and perseverance. They fight through adversity. They succeed. And they fail. With grace and without. We learn from watching, and it's important to have our eyes on women as well as men.

<hr>

Though Schneider defends sex segregation, she thinks we wouldn't need it if the world were truly equal. Men and women could compete against each other in all sports, and they'd excel, equally.

For that to work, boys and girls would have to get equal encouragement to engage in sports. And equal support throughout their careers. And we'd need a wider range of sports, so as to fully realize women's athletic potential.

We already have some sports that privilege female bodies. Women's gymnastics is, perhaps, the most prominent. Men don't bother with the balance beam, but Simone Biles would likely destroy them if they did, as the apparatus rewards a lower center of gravity.

And Biles is not the only woman capable of outcompeting men. Have you heard of Fiona Kolbinger? In 2019, she competed in the Transcontinental Race, a cycling event that stretches more than two thousand miles across Europe. The race is grueling; it lasts more than a week. Athletes are completely on their own. They don't get assistance from anyone. And the clock never stops, so they have to strategize about when and where to sleep and eat. Kolbinger? She crushed the competition, beating the man who finished second by more than ten hours.

Jasmin Paris might be even more impressive. She set the record in the Montane Spine Race, completing the 268-mile course in just over eighty-three hours. *She stopped to express breast milk along the way so that she wouldn't get mastitis.* And still, she finished twelve hours faster than any man had ever run the race.

The fact that Kolbinger and Paris aren't household names is indicative of injustice. As Schneider says, women's accomplishments are often overlooked. But their victories are proof that women don't have less athletic potential than men; they just have different potential.

Men run faster. Until you ask them to run for three straight days. Then Jasmin Paris passes them by.

⌒‿⌒

MY BOYS LOVE WOMEN'S SPORTS. Because they are sports. Give them a score or a clock and they're all in to watch any competition.

And some of their heroes are heroines. We spent serious time looking for kid-sized Rapinoe jerseys in the midst of the Women's World Cup. And though we were traveling at the time, we did everything we could to track down a television to watch the games.

In the middle of one, Rex asked a question that complicates the story I've just told you.

"Can a trans woman play women's soccer?" he wondered.

"I'm not sure what the rules are," Julie said. "People argue about that."

"Why?"

"Some people think they might have an unfair advantage."

"I think they should be allowed to play," Rex said. And the rest of us agreed.

But lots of people aren't so sure. In fact, some say that permitting trans women to play women's sports would undermine the purposes of sex segregation.

~

I THINK THAT'S WRONG, and I want to explain why. But to think about the question clearly, we need a short primer on sex and gender. (If you were a gender studies major, now's a good time to get some popcorn—or just skim ahead.)

Sex is about biology; it's determined by the physical features of people's bodies. And it's not as simple as you were taught when you were a kid, as there's no single feature that sorts people into the categories male and female. Rather, there's a cluster of characteristics that typify males (XY chromosomes, testes, and external genitalia among them) and a cluster that typify females (XX chromosomes, ovaries, and internal genitalia among them). But some people have features from both clusters. Or features that don't fit in either of them. So not everyone is male or female; some are intersex.*

Some people use *sex* and *gender* as synonyms, but they're not really. Because gender is about social roles, not biology. A woman is subject to a set of expectations—about how she'll look, how she'll dress, how she'll walk, how she'll talk, what work she'll do, what feels she'll feel, what thinks she'll think, and so on, *endlessly*. Men are subject to the same deal; it's just different expectations. And the same goes for being a boy or a girl; they're junior varsity versions of these roles.

Many parents' first brush with all this, at least in relation to their kid, comes at an ultrasound, roughly eighteen weeks into pregnancy. I re-

---

*How many? It's hard to say, since it depends on what traits researchers count as intersex. On stricter definitions, about 1 in 4,500 people qualify. On more expansive ones, it could be as many as 1 in 100.

member Hank's well. The ultrasound tech put the wand on Julie's belly and immediately pulled it back.

"Are you sure you want to know?" she asked.

"Yeah, we're sure," Julie said.

"Okay. Because it's not hard to see."

She put the wand back, and the image came into focus. There was Hank, legs splayed, as if to say, "Have you *seen* my penis?"

We put that line on the picture and forwarded it to our family.

No, we didn't. But we did tell them we were having a boy. We hadn't told them when Julie was pregnant with Rex, even though we knew then too. We didn't want a house full of boy things. But we'd lost that battle long ago, so we told them about Hank.

Some parents now share this news at a "gender reveal" party. I'm not sure how this works, since it wasn't a thing when we had kids. But I think you need a special operations agent to pull it off. The parents—who were in the room for the ultrasound—somehow lack the relevant information. But it has been passed to a friend. And that friend obtains a cake, which is iced to obscure the fact that the cake itself is blue (for a boy) or pink (for a girl). Throughout the party, the tension builds. Until the moment arrives, and the parents cut the cake. The color is revealed, and the crowd cheers, as if they are thrilled at the result. Except: the other color would have elicited exactly the same cheer.

At least, that's how the staid version goes. Some parents are so excited about gender they set off explosions. At least two started wildfires. One person was killed by a cannon at a gender reveal party, another by a homemade pipe bomb. I don't love off-color cake; dessert should be chocolate. But make no mistake: pink or blue cake is better than pyrotechnics.

———

QUICK QUIZ: Are gender reveal parties properly named?

The answer is: no, no they are not. The only information revealed by

an ultrasound is whether a fetus has a penis or vagina. Or perhaps ovaries or testes. The screen just shows physical features of the future kid.

So really, they're sex parties.

But you can see why the marketing guys spurned that. Just picture
the invitations:

PLEASE JOIN

KAREN AND CARTER

FOR A

SEX PARTY!

Grandma's *not* going to buy the right sort of gift.

But actually, these gatherings aren't just sex parties. They're also *gender assignment* parties.

As soon as the cake is cut, everyone tacitly agrees to treat the kid
(who hasn't even been born yet) as if they occupy a certain social role. If
it's blue, we're gonna buy that boy bats and balls. If it's pink, we're gonna
buy that girl dolls and dresses—and pay her less than men who do the
same job.

That's just what the cheer means.

As the kids say: There ain't no party like a sex par-tay!

⌇

I'M PLAYING THIS FOR LAUGHS, but there's a serious issue here. We
assign kids roles before we even meet them. And the roles we assign
them structure much of their lives. They can also be constricting. Just
think about all the things that, through history, a woman could not do,
simply because she was a woman.

To justify the limitations, people would often point to women's bodies. They'd say they weren't suited to sport, or physically demanding work, because [mumble something about pregnancy or periods here]. But that's inane. Serena Williams could be pregnant, with a broken left arm and a serious case of the flu, and her body would still be better suited to tennis than mine. But also: there's nothing about being a woman that precludes participation in sport or physically demanding work.

The connection between gender roles and our bodies is just not that tight. And the connection between gender roles and our brains doesn't seem so strong either. The link between girls and pink, for instance, is completely cultural. Just ask a 1918 article in the classic rag *Earnshaw's Infants' Department*:

> The generally accepted rule is pink for the boys, and blue for
> the girls. The reason is that pink, being a more decided and
> stronger color, is more suitable for the boy, while blue, which
> is more delicate and dainty, is prettier for the girl.

Want to mess with people's minds? At your next gender assignment party, follow *Earnshaw's Infants'* rules.

I don't mean to say that there are *no* connections between bodies, brains, and gender roles. Certainly, as parents, we've seen our boys develop stereotypical interests with what seemed like little encouragement from us. But it's really hard to know what signals you send your kids. Or what they pick up from friends. And science has trouble here too, since it's not possible to run controlled experiments where kids are systematically introduced to different gender norms. But we can at least say this: the rapid pace of social change over the last several decades suggests that culture plays a far larger role in shaping gender roles than any facts about brains or bodies.

And for that reason, feminists have long argued for relaxing gender roles, or even abolishing them altogether. The effort to relax them has been enormously successful, as the list of amazing female athletes attests. The change has not been limited to sports: women are now leaders in every field they have entered. They still face barriers, of course. And they are not leaders in large enough numbers. But it's clear that the barriers are social, not biological.

REX'S QUESTION ABOUT trans women points to another worry about assigning rigid gender roles to kids. Some kids don't identify with the roles that we assign them—and even feel alienated from the features of their bodies that led us to assign them those roles.* As they get older, some kids transition, raising Rex's question: In a world that segregates sports, where do trans athletes fit?

Few people worry about trans men playing men's sports, even though some have been successful. But there's a lot of controversy about trans women playing women's sports, in part because people worry that they have an advantage.

And they might. Joanna Harper is a scientist who studies the performance of trans athletes. She believes that trans women do have an advantage in some sports—unless and until they take hormone therapy. The issue is testosterone. Men typically have more than women, and the difference is believed (at least by some) to be responsible for much of the edge that they have in strength and speed.

Harper can speak to the question from personal experience, since she's a trans athlete. For more than three decades, she ran men's marathons. Then she transitioned, started hormone therapy, and began competing as a woman. Harper reports that the drugs reduced her speed by

---

*In a recent Gallup poll, 1.8 percent of Gen Z (born between 1997 and 2002) identified as trans. For Gen X (1965–1980) and the Baby Boomers (1946–1964), just 0.2 percent did, so there's been a substantial uptick.

12 percent. But her new competition was slower too, so Harper stayed at roughly the same spot in the pack. Harper has gathered data that suggests her experience is not atypical. But her study is controversial, since it was small, and other factors, like age and training, could have affected the results.

The science is more murky than you might guess. To laypeople, it seems like testosterone must matter a lot, since we know that athletes who dope with it often see significant gains. But as Rebecca M. Jordan-Young and Katrina Karkazis explain in their book *Testosterone: An Unauthorized Biography*, there's no consistent relationship between testosterone and athletic performance. Indeed, successful male athletes sometimes have low levels. And the fact that doping with testosterone enhances performance does not imply that the naturally occurring stuff does the same, since an athlete's body may already be accustomed to it.

Still, many suspect that testosterone confers an edge on trans women, at least in some contexts. And since testosterone is thought to be the issue, the concern is not limited to them. Some intersex women also have testosterone levels more typical of men. And their participation in women's sports has become controversial too.

Sports officials haven't handled the controversy well. Over the years, they've stigmatized athletes by calling their sex and gender into question. And they've subjected them to degrading physical exams. I won't detail what they've done, because I think it mostly shameful. And for the same reason, I'm not going to name athletes they've subjected to scrutiny.

But here's the question I want to ask: Suppose that trans and intersex women do have an advantage. Does that matter? Harper says yes, and presumably sports officials agree, or they wouldn't scrutinize these athletes' bodies.

But why would it matter? Harper says that the point of women's sports is "to provide women athletes with meaningful competition." In her view, trans and intersex women should be allowed to participate only if they do "not unduly alter the playing field for other women." And sports officials seem to agree, since they are moving toward the system Harper suggests, which would key eligibility for women's sports to testosterone levels.

Testosterone can be checked with a simple blood test, so that's a better approach than one that requires invasive exams. But I still think it's a bad idea. Some women will be excluded—and stigmatized. Worse yet, some will feel pressure to take drugs they might not otherwise choose, just to get their testosterone levels down. And the drugs aren't benign. As Jordan-Young and Karkazis point out, lowering testosterone can cause "depression, fatigue, osteoporosis, muscle weakness, low libido, and metabolic problems."

Also: We should remember what we learned from Jane English. When it comes to the scarce benefits of sports, no individual athlete has a right to meaningful competition or anything like a level playing field. I'm sure the men who raced Usain Bolt didn't feel like they had much of a chance. I doubt those who raced Michael Phelps at the peak of his powers did either. And yet no one suggested that Bolt or Phelps stop racing so the rest of the men could have meaningful competition.

For recreational athletes, meaningful competition *is* important. If you're perpetually behind the pack, you won't have fun—and you may not even develop your skills. To get the basic benefits of sports, you really do need to play with people on your level. But no elite athlete can insist on that. This is a point that Veronica Ivy has made. She's trans—and a world champion cyclist. In recent years, Ivy has set women's world records for her age group in sprint events. And . . . she's a philosopher.

Ivy notes that there's lots of variation in athletes' bodies—in height, weight, musculature, and so on. The woman who finished first in the high jump at the 2016 Olympics was eight inches taller than the woman who finished tenth. Surely that gave her a leg up. But no one thought the competition unfair for that reason. Why treat differences in trans bodies differently?

Ivy also points out that trans women often aren't eligible to compete in men's sports, especially after they've received legal recognition for their transition. To exclude them from women's sports is to exclude them from sports entirely. That's bad for the reasons English taught us. Everyone should get the basic benefits of sports. And it's bad for the reasons Schneider taught us too: trans athletes ought to have access to the power and influence that sports provide.

I think we should stop worrying about the physical features of people's bodies and segregate sports by gender, not sex. If a person sees herself as a woman, she should be eligible to participate in women's sports.*

<hr />

BUT WAIT: If you can compete as a woman simply on your say-so, won't men pretend to be women just to achieve athletic glory? No. Men can't capture the athletic glory they're interested in by competing *as women*. History has a few suspected cases. But in retrospect, it seems likely that the athletes involved were intersex. Men masquerading as women to win medals is just not a thing.

Unless that's how you see trans and intersex women—as men pretending to be women. And sadly, that *is* how many people see them. So I want to take a moment to explain why that's wrong.

There's a difference between performing a role and identifying with

<hr />

*Would I stick to this view if trans women came to dominate women's sports? I regard this concern as fanciful, so I've confined it to a footnote. There's little reason to think that trans women will crowd out cisgender women in sports; they participate already, and cis women are holding their own. But what if I'm wrong? I think it would be a problem, since it would suggest that success in sports is reserved for people born with certain body parts. That's an idea that we're trying to leave behind. If trans women crowd out cis women, we'll need to look for new ways to include everyone in sports. But I doubt we'll face that issue.

it. In the music video for "The Man," Taylor Swift performs as a man. She's dressed like a man, walks like a man, and even spreads her legs like a man on the subway. But Swift is *just* performing. She doesn't identify with the role.

I also perform masculinity, every day—in the way I dress, walk, talk, and so on, endlessly. (But not in the way I sit on the subway. I don't know what's up with that.) The difference is that, for me, it's *not* just a performance. I identify with the role. I see myself as a man, not as a person playing one.

Trans and intersex women aren't playing a role. They identify with it. They see themselves as women. And we should see them that way too.

To be sure, you can reserve the word *woman* for people born with certain body parts. But when you use the word that way, you limit people's life possibilities by insisting that they conform to roles that were selected for them (not by them) simply on the basis of their bodies. That's sexist. And the fact that the word *woman* has long been used that way is no reason to carry on with it.

Robin Dembroff helped me sort this out. Dembroff teaches philosophy at Yale. They write about gender—what it is and how it works. Dembroff says that conversations about gender are often confused. Many people assume that the word *woman* has a single meaning—and push their preferred take on it. In fact, there are many ways of marking out that category, since there are many conceptions of what a woman is.

Once you notice that, you can ask a new question. Instead of asking what a woman *is*, you can ask which conception of the category we should *use*. One that tracks body parts at birth? Or one that defers to self-identification?

There's a field in philosophy known as *conceptual ethics*. It asks: What categories should we use to make sense of the world? Think, for a moment, about marriage. It's common to hear opponents of same-sex marriage say that a marriage just *is* a union between a man and a woman.

And for sure, that's one way of thinking about it—the dominant way, for a very long time. But there's another way to construe the category, and it's more welcoming. You can see marriage as a committed relationship between two partners.

Once you see the options, you can ask: Which conception of marriage should we use? The answer may not be the same in all contexts. In a political community committed to sex equality, there are reasons to prefer the welcoming view. It allows people to choose a partner without sex-based limitations. In contrast, a church might have religious reasons for preferring the more traditional view.

If we argue about what marriage *is*, only one side can be right. But if we reframe the debate—so that the argument is about which concept to *use*—then it might be possible to satisfy both sides. Imagine, for instance, a political community committed to sex equality *and* religious freedom (which is to say, ours). It might insist that, for legal purposes, marriage will be understood in the welcoming way. At the same time, it could permit religious communities to construe marriage as they wish, in relation to their own rituals.

What about *women*? Again, there's a welcoming way to construe the category—and a restrictive one. We could ask what a woman really *is*. But that question misses the mark, because gender is what we make of it. It's a social category, not a biological one. So the better question is: Which conception of women should we use?

I think we should use the welcoming one. If we defer to self-identification, more people will have a chance to live lives that feel authentic—and fewer people will live lives that feel forced.

You've probably heard the slogan Trans Women Are Women. If you use the word *women* in the welcoming way, it states a fact. But the slogan is also an invitation—to people who are not yet sure—to use the word that way.

We should accept the invitation, in sports and out.

WE NEED TO COMPLICATE this story one last time. We've been thinking about men's and women's sports. But not everyone identifies as a
man or a woman. Among young people, especially, there's a small but
growing group that disclaims traditional gender roles. They call themselves *nonbinary*.*

People have different reasons for adopting that label. Many don't feel
like masculine or feminine roles fit. Some, like Dembroff, have an additional reason: they embrace the identity as a political statement. Dembroff objects to the ways that gender roles structure our lives. In refusing
to claim one, they hope to diminish the hold that the roles have on us.

Dembroff's project can help us understand why shifting gender roles
are a source of discomfort. There are many reasons, of course, including
hostility toward those that are different. But even well-intentioned people are often confused by the ways that gender has become complicated.
I think that has a lot to do with the way that roles structure our lives.

There are social roles everywhere. And we could not function without
them. They sort out who will do what in different contexts. They also
script our interactions. When I walk into a restaurant, I look for the host.
That's the person who can help me get a table. When I enter a classroom,
I identify the teacher. That's the person in charge. If I see someone
struggling at a pool, I tell the lifeguard. That's the person trained to help.

Gender roles play these functions too. Imagine that you're at a party
and you meet someone new. How does their gender affect your assump-
tions about their family responsibilities, their professional lives, their
interests, or even just the experience they're having in the room right at
that moment? Gender is not a perfect guide, of course. But it helps paint
a picture before you've even spoken.

---

*In a 2015 survey conducted by the National Center for Transgender Equality, just
under one-third of those who identified as trans called themselves nonbinary.

And gender has more subtle effects on the way we interact too. As Julie likes to point out, my voice is softer with women, deeper with men, and deeper still with a stranger on the phone (a practice I picked up as a preteen, when I hated being mistaken for my mom). I also hold my body differently around men and women. With men, I'm apt to stand my ground, literally as well as figuratively. I don't like to be pushed around. I give women more space, especially if I don't know them. I'm concerned about the signals I'd send if I stood too close.

When you can't read someone's gender, you hit a little hitch. It's a bit harder to interact, since some of the standard cues aren't there. Dembroff *wants* us to hit that hitch—to pause—and then question whether gender ought to play the role it does in organizing our social relations. It would be better, they think, to relate to each other as people, rather than as men or women.

What about sports? Should we compete *as people*, not as men or women? I don't think so, at least not yet. We live in a world structured by gender, and we will for the foreseeable future. As we've learned, we need women's sports so that women can secure sports' benefits.

But what about nonbinary athletes? Where do they fit in? That's a hard question. We could let nonbinary athletes choose which competition to enter. But that requires them to tick a gender box, and their aim is to avoid it. We could have a gender-neutral category. But as of now, there may not be enough athletes to sustain it.

I don't know that there's a good solution—yet. But I'm confident our kids will sort it out. On questions of gender, *society* is transitioning as we learn to see new possibilities. The younger set has an easier time, since they aren't set in their ways. I have faith that they will make the world more just and inclusive—in sports and out.

⁘

HANK WAS READING NEXT to me while I was finishing up this chapter.

"What are you writing about?" he asked.

"Boys, girls, and sports."

He looked puzzled. "Sports? I thought it was a philosophy book?"

"It is. There's philosophy about everything. I'm writing about whether boys and girls should play sports together. What do you think?"

"They should," Hank said. "Why is it taking so long?"

"I don't know how to end the chapter."

"I know how to end a chapter," Hank said.

"Oh yeah?"

"Yeah. You say something really interesting, and then you write, 'And then . . .' but you don't say anything else, so people have to turn the page."

And then . . .

7

RACE AND
RESPONSIBILITY

The Henry Ford Museum in Dearborn, Michigan, is awesome. Unless you are three. Then it is crazy awesome. Also, it sucks. Because it is full of cars, trucks, planes, and trains. But you cannot touch any of them. Except—for reasons I cannot fathom—the bus on which Rosa Parks mounted her legendary protest. Not only can you touch that bus, you can sit in it. Indeed, you can sit in the seat that Rosa Parks sat in. And if you are three, you *will* sit in that seat. And all the other ones too. And then, on the way home, you will sit in your seat and ask questions.

"Why Rosa Parks won't go to back of bus?"

"Why Rosa Parks not do what driver say?"

"Why Rosa Parks sit in middle of bus?"

Your father will explain that Rosa Parks was standing up for herself—and everyone who's Black. This will lead to more questions.

"Why Rosa Parks stand up on bus?"

"Why Rosa Parks not sit down?"

"Why Rosa Parks riding bus?"

As you get sleepy, your questions will start to sound existential.

"Why Rosa Parks?"

"Why Rosa?"

"Why?"

At that point, your father will stop at a bookstore and buy *I Am Rosa Parks*. Because it is important to talk to kids about race. And we were not off to a good start.

⌣

REX LIKED THAT BOOK. So we got *I Am Martin Luther King, Jr.* And then *I Am Jackie Robinson*. And then *When Jackie and Hank Met.* That one addresses racism *and* anti-Semitism. In baseball. That's a home run.

Those books got us on the right track. Rex learned about the history of racism in America and the heroes who fought against it. The lessons were well-timed. Renewed attention to police brutality brought forth Black Lives Matter, and Rex caught glimpses of protests in the paper and on the news. So he learned that the heroes are not done yet. And that we need more.

All of which brings us to breakfast many months later, when Rex had a big announcement.

"I wish I was Black," he said.

I asked why.

"Because White people do lots of mean things to Black people. And it makes me sad."

"There's a lot to be sad about," I said.

"I wish we didn't do those things."

⌣

REX'S ANNOUNCEMENT DIDN'T SURPRISE ME. We'd been reading lots of books with Black heroes—and White villains. So he wanted to be

Black. He also wanted to be a cat. He had lots of wishes that wouldn't work out.

But the last bit of what Rex said stopped me cold: *I wish we didn't do those things.*

It's a simple sentence. And a simple sentiment. But notice the subject: *we.*

With that one word, Rex signaled that he saw himself as part of the *we* responsible for the wrongs we'd been reading about, like slavery and segregation.

Many White people wouldn't say *we* when it comes to those wrongs. They'd say, "I wish *they* didn't do those things," if they'd say anything like that at all. But they wouldn't take ownership with the first-person plural. The bad things were done by other people, with the implication that it's other people's responsibility to fix it. Except those people are dead. So, sorry, it won't get fixed.

Rex, on the other hand, saw himself as part of the group that had acted badly. And the striking thing about that is that Rex was just four at the time. If anyone could argue that he had a clean moral slate, it was Rex.

But he didn't see it that way. His whiteness was tainted. So tainted, he wished he wasn't White.

. ———— .

Is REX RIGHT? Is whiteness tainted?

That's a hard question. To answer, we have to figure out what whiteness *is*. Rex is White, not Black. But what does it mean to be White? Or Black? Just what is race? We all have an intuitive understanding, which we employ every day. But it's difficult to say what race is. Indeed, some think it doesn't exist at all.

And on some conceptions, it clearly doesn't. Many people think that race is about biology. And that makes some sense, since physical features of people's bodies are often the way we identify race. We look at skin, hair, and the shape of certain facial features. We know that these are, to a large extent, inherited. And for a long time, people imagined that these superficial differences signaled deeper differences in constitution—that you could look at someone's skin color, for instance, and infer something about the person's cognitive ability or, perhaps, character. More than that, they imagined that these deeper differences were driven by biology rather than, say, social circumstances.

But biology doesn't work that way. There is little correlation between the superficial signifiers of race—skin, hair, facial features—and other characteristics. History is littered with attempts to prove otherwise. But it's all bunk. As Craig Venter, a leader of the Human Genome Project, once declared: "There is no basis in scientific fact or in the human genetic code for the notion that skin colour will be predictive of intelligence." You could say the same for character, of course.

And indeed, we can say something stronger. Race does not sort people into biologically significant subspecies. Some traits are more common among some races than others. But every racial group has lots of diversity too. Indeed, when it comes to genes, there's almost as much variation within racial groups as there is in humanity as a whole.

We're all part of the same family—or at least the same family tree. Research suggests that *everyone* alive today has a common ancestor who lived just a few thousand years ago. If that sounds weird, it's worth spending a bit of time thinking about how ancestry works. You have two parents, four grandparents, eight great-grandparents, and so on. You can keep going with that. But you'll soon hit a problem. The number is growing exponentially. If you go back, say, thirty-three generations (roughly eight hundred to a thousand years), the math says you'll have more than eight billion ancestors. But there weren't eight billion people back then; there aren't even eight billion people today.

The puzzle is simple to solve. Many people occupy multiple spots on your family tree. At first, the tree expands. But before too long, it has to contract. As geneticist Adam Rutherford explains, "Your great-great-

great-great-great-grandmother might have also been your great-great-great-great-aunt." Indeed, if you trace everyone's tree back far enough, you'll reach a point where everyone shares every ancestor in common.

That shouldn't come as a surprise. We're all descended from a single population that lived in East Africa around a hundred thousand years ago. But you don't have to go back nearly so far to reach the point where everyone alive today shares every ancestor in common. In fact, statisticians think the *genetic isopoint*, as they call it, was something like seven thousand years ago, maybe less.

In the intervening years, we've been spread across the globe, living in communities that didn't always mix much. As a result, scientists see populations where some traits cluster. But when they study our species, they don't see anything like a rigid division into a small number of races, which differ in the ways that people have imagined that races do.

Indeed, the groups that stand out as scientifically significant don't match up with our ordinary understandings of race. My crowd—Ashkenazi Jews—is well-known to genetic counselors, since certain diseases, like Tay-Sachs, occur at a higher rate within the community. But we don't count as our own race for that reason. Most of us are White—a designation that also encompasses the Amish and the Irish, two groups that strike geneticists as distinct populations. So why do we group all those groups together? Science has no answer to that question. Racial designations don't mark meaningful differences in biology.

<hr/>

DOES THAT MEAN THAT race isn't real? In a sense, it does. If your picture of race presupposes that human beings can be divided into a handful of biologically distinct groups, which differ in socially significant ways, you're simply mistaken. When philosophers discover that a category is empty, they say that we should be *error theorists* about it. That's a fancy way to say, *Oops, it was all a mistake*—and then they try to explain how the mistake got made. When it comes to race as biological concept, *oops* would be the order of the day—if the idea had not had such devastating consequences.

But it did, and it still does. And those consequences point toward a different way of thinking about race. Instead of seeing it as a biological concept, we can see it as a social one. In particular, we can see race as a concept that structures a hierarchy among groups of people. To be Black, on this way of thinking, is to occupy a certain social position—to be subject to certain forms of domination. Think: slavery, segregation, mass incarceration, and so on. The point was put most pithily by W. E. B. Du Bois. "The black man," he said, "is a person who must ride 'Jim Crow' in Georgia."

If Black people are the ones that have to ride Jim Crow, what are Whites? They are the people who don't. Or perhaps, the people who make them do it. Whiteness is, on this picture, the photographic negative of blackness. Indeed, you could say that whiteness exists because of blackness. The slave trade brought people from several different parts of Africa to the Americas. They had no common identity before they came. But they were given one here. They were Black. And their identity necessitated a new one, which stood in opposition to it. In making them Black, other people became White. And that was not a peaceful process. In the words of James Baldwin: "No one was white before he/she came to America. It took generations, and a vast amount of coercion, before this became a white country."

The social nature of these categories is further illustrated by the ways in which they shift. Immigrants from Europe were not always seen as White, at least not right away. Italian immigrants, for instance, were seen as something close to Black, especially if they came from southern Italy. Indeed, they were sometimes lynched for racist reasons. The establishment of Columbus Day was part of an effort to write Italians into American history in a way that would allow them to be seen as White. That worked. Today Italian immigrants and their descendants are, without doubt, White so far as race in contemporary America goes.

The social dynamics are, of course, much more complicated than this compressed history indicates. And I haven't said anything about Native Americans, Asians, Pacific Islanders—or any other group that might count as a distinct race in America.* But we don't need the full story to see the central point. The biological idea of race is bankrupt. But that has not kept race from playing a significant role in our social relations.

•~~•

SOMETIMES PEOPLE try to capture that fact by saying that race is *socially constructed*. That's a tricky idea, because all concepts are, in a sense, social constructions, even the scientific ones. Think about Pluto for a moment. When I was a kid, it was a planet. Then suddenly, it wasn't. What changed? Not Pluto. It's the same ball of ice and rock it always was, one-sixth the mass of the moon. What shifted was something about *us*. We decided to conceive planets in a way that excluded Pluto.

Why? Well, once we got a good look, we saw that there are other Pluto-sized objects on the outskirts of our solar system. That left us with a choice. We could consider them all planets, in which case it would turn out that there were several more than previously thought. Or we could revise our understanding of what a planet is. Scientists picked the latter path, labeling Pluto and its playmates dwarf planets. They did this in part to preserve the idea that planets are significant objects in the solar system. To qualify now, a celestial body has to "clear the neighborhood" around its orbit. And Pluto hasn't. There are lots of rocks rocking out with it, and they orbit the sun, not Pluto.

The idea of a planet was constructed by us. And as we learned more

---

*I've also been silent about the way race works in other parts of the world. As the philosopher Michael Root says, "Race does not travel. Some men who are black in New Orleans now would have been octoroons there some years ago or would be white in Brazil today. Socrates had no race in ancient Athens, though he would be a white man in Minnesota." The fact that race does not travel underscores just how arbitrary it is—and that it is, at root, a social phenomenon, not a scientific one.

about our solar system, we reconstructed it. But make no mistake. Planets are real. We didn't make them up. We created the category. But the things that fit in it exist independently of us.

Race is different. When people say it's socially constructed, they mean it wouldn't exist if we never invented it. But that's not all they mean, because that's true of basketballs, beer, and bridges too—and they exist independently of us. What makes race different is that it's *just* a social construction.

Does that mean that race isn't real? No. Race is definitely real. Compare it to debt. You might have a mortgage or a car loan. Those are social constructions. Our debt doesn't exist independently of us; if we snapped out of existence, it would too. Debt is an idea that organizes our social relations. And it's real. Indeed, it can be devastating.

The same is true with race. It's a way of organizing our social relations. And like debt, it can be devastating.

So it's worth asking: Could we give it up?

⸻

MANY PEOPLE THINK WE SHOULD. Indeed, some think they already did.

"I don't see color," they say.

But we all know that's not true. Even the littlest kids see color. And they often respond to it in ways that embarrass their parents.

"That man is dark," Hank said more than once when he was a toddler. And Rex did the same. Skin is a highly salient feature of human bodies. It would be hard not to notice that it comes in many shades. And Rex and Hank saw a lot of light-skinned people when they were little, since they split their time between our house and the Jewish Community Center day care. Seeing someone with different color skin was, for a while, somewhat novel. So they remarked on it. That's what kids do.*

⸻

*When these conversations first started, we hadn't yet read Beverly Daniel Tatum's classic *Why Are All the Black Kids Sitting Together in the Cafeteria?* I wish we had, as

When they did, we taught them several lessons. First, skin comes in lots of colors. In the moment, we'd leave that fact to stand on its own. But the labels caused some confusion. "My skin's not really white," Hank would tell us, as if we'd made a mistake. "It's kinda pink, with a little bit of brown."

Second, we taught them that color doesn't matter. We all have different bodies. Some are big, some are small. Some are short, some are tall. We have different eyes, different hair, different skin. But we never treat anybody differently because of those differences.

Third, we taught them that color does matter, *a lot*. When we say that color doesn't matter, we mean it doesn't matter *morally*. But for sure, it matters *socially*.

Let me give you a few data points.

The median Black family has less than 15 percent of the median White family's wealth. Black workers are unemployed at twice the rate of White workers, and they're less likely to have a job that matches their skills.

We spend more to teach kids in predominantly White school districts—about $2,200 more per student per year.

White people live longer than Black people—about 3.6 years at last tally. And they get better health care too.

Finally, Black men are far more likely to spend time in prison than White men. In 2015, 9.1 percent of young Black men were incarcerated; just 1.6 percent of young White men were.

All those facts are related. Indeed, they help sustain one another. But they all also reflect a long, shameful history, which started with slavery but did not end there.

For instance, the racial wealth gap is the result of redlining (which limited the ability of Black Americans to accrue wealth through home-ownership). It reflects violence, like the Tulsa Race Riot (which destroyed

---

there's a chapter called "The Early Years" that anticipates these sorts of conversations and provides helpful models for them.

a business district that was often called Black Wall Street). And it reflects day-to-day discrimination too.

The disparities in the criminal justice system reflect deliberate decisions to police and punish Black people more harshly than Whites. To take just one example, White and Black people use drugs at roughly similar rates. But Black people are nearly four times more likely to be arrested for drug offenses.

We didn't share these statistics with our kids when they were little. But we did tell them that our society has a long history of treating Black people poorly.* And we told them that the bad treatment is not just history; it's part of our present too.

Can we move past race? Maybe. But it's not as simple as saying we have. If we want to live in a world in which race doesn't matter, we have to do away with the disparities. We can't just declare that we don't see them.

• ⌇ •

SHOULD WE MOVE PAST RACE? For sure, we should end those disparities. But some see value in race, despite its sordid history.

Chike Jeffers is a philosopher who studies race. And he agrees that it has its origins in oppression. Absent slavery, we might not have labeled people Black or White. But that doesn't mean that those labels are significant only in the context of that oppression. In America, Black people endure "stigmatization, discrimination, marginalization, and disadvantage." But Jeffers reminds us: "There is also joy in blackness."

---

*If you don't feel like you have a clear picture of America's racial history beyond the basics—slavery and segregation—a simple place to start is Ta-Nehisi Coates's article "The Case for Reparations," which was published in *The Atlantic* in 2014. (We'll think about reparations shortly, so the article will do double duty.) It conveys the weight of our history—and the way it weighs Black Americans down—more effectively than anything I was ever assigned in Georgia public schools. When my kids are capable of reading it, I'll assign it to them.

The joy is present in Black culture—in Black art, Black music, and Black literature. It imbues Black religious traditions and rituals. It's on display in Black ways of speaking, dressing, and dancing. At this stage of history, being Black connects a person to a rich and distinctive cultural heritage. The identity has its roots in oppression, but its significance extends far beyond that.

Kathryn Sophia Belle presses the same point. She's the founding director of the Collegium of Black Women Philosophers, an organization that aims to lift the voices of a radically underrepresented group in philosophy. Like Jeffers, Belle maintains that "race is not just a negative category used for the purpose of oppression and exploitation." For Black people, she says, it's also a "positive category that encompasses a sense of membership or belonging, remembrance of struggle and overcoming, and the motivation to press forward and endeavor towards new ideals and achievements."

Jeffers and Belle want to see racism end. But they want to see Black culture survive and thrive. Relating as equals, they argue, does *not* require discarding racial identities.

WHAT ABOUT WHITENESS? Is there joy in that? Should we want to see White culture survive and thrive? I don't think so. And I want to take a moment to explain why.

The beauty in Black culture is partly a function of the way it responds to oppression—and transcends it. Black history brought forth jazz and hip-hop; Maya Angelou and James Baldwin; Sojourner Truth, Martin Luther King Jr.—and so much and so many more. When we celebrate authors, activists, and art forms *as Black*, we connect them to that history—the struggle and overcoming, as Belle says.

White culture has none of that beauty. It was born of the other side of oppression.

We can, without doubt, celebrate people who *are* White. And we do—authors, artists, athletes, and on and on. In their individual stories, there are struggles and outsize achievements. We can also celebrate the cultures of communities that happen to be White—Irish, Italian, German, Jewish, and the like. But the idea that we would celebrate them *as White* is atrocious.

Whiteness was forged through other people's pain. And it has little life beyond that. It's a source of privilege, for sure. But it's *not* a source of meaning.

Some people think otherwise. They take pride in their whiteness. But they're making a mistake. They are the worst of whiteness *because they embrace it*.

Whiteness *is* tainted. And we see here one important way in which it is. Unlike blackness, it cannot overcome its origins.

We are a long way off, but we should welcome the day when White is not a meaningful part of anyone's identity.

<hr />

REX DIDN'T GRASP ALL THAT when he was four. He had a simple thought, flowing from the civil rights stories we read. The Black characters were good. The White ones, mostly bad.* So he wanted to be Black.

As I said, that didn't surprise me. It was the second bit of what Rex said that caught my attention: "I wish we didn't do those things." In saying that, Rex signaled that he saw himself as part of the crowd that had acted badly, and he expressed regret for what had been done.

Does that make sense? As I said at the start, many Whites wouldn't use the word *we* the way Rex did. If they were to express regret for the

---

*In *Why Are All the Black Kids Sitting Together in the Cafeteria?* (pp. 119–20), Tatum stresses the importance of providing positive White role models to kids in the context of race conversations. For us, the first model was Hank Greenberg, who stars alongside Jackie Robinson in the book I mentioned earlier, *When Jackie and Hank Met*. We'll get back to it in a bit.

wrongs we'd been reading about—slavery and segregation—they'd do it in the third person. And it's easy to understand why. Those wrongs are long past, and they weren't personally involved.

Of course, many Whites alive today have their own sins to answer for. Racism is not history, even if many of its most awful manifestations are. There's still an enormous amount of discrimination in our society, and I don't want to discount that. People are responsible for their own actions.

But I want to ask: Are Whites today responsible for past wrongs, like slavery and segregation, simply in virtue of their whiteness? Are they responsible for present-day discrimination even if they aren't personally involved? In other words: Is race itself a ground of responsibility?

Here's an argument that it's not.

Moral responsibility is a personal affair. Each of us is responsible for our own sins, not the sins committed by others. As I mentioned in chapter 5, my maternal grandmother was not a good person. She treated her children poorly. And her siblings too. I inherited her genes. But not her wrongs. It wouldn't make sense to blame *me* for the way *she* acted. We blame people when their actions reveal defects in their character. And her actions don't reveal anything about my character.

The same is true when we think about historical wrongs, like slavery and segregation. They reflect poorly on the people who participated. But their actions cannot be the basis for blaming anyone else—including present-day Whites.

* ——— *

I THINK THAT ARGUMENT WORKS, so far as it goes. But we can't stop our inquiry there, since responsibility is not *just* a personal affair. Sometimes we blame groups, separate from the individuals who compose them. Think about Boeing. The company cut corners in the design of its 737 Max planes. Two crashed, killing hundreds. We can blame Boeing for that. The company was supposed to ensure that its airplanes were safe. It failed. And its failure revealed a defect in its character: it put profits above people.

Why should we blame Boeing rather than, say, the individuals who made the relevant decisions? If we can identify responsible individuals, we can blame them too, and we should. But Boeing is more than the sum of its parts. Boeing can build 737s; no individual can. And Boeing can ensure that its planes are safe; no single employee can do that either.

I'm pretty sure that the street I live on has more philosophers of law (per capita) than any other street in the world. There are nine full-time residents, and three are full-time philosophers of law (not counting Rex and Hank, who might add up to a fourth). Will Thomas is one of those philosophers. He lives across the street. The boys have him on call to play a game they call soccer-golf. But he's got a day job too. Thomas teaches in the business school at Michigan, and he studies the ways we punish corporations.

For a long time, we didn't. In early America, you could punish the individuals who worked for a company but not the company itself. That changed toward the end of the nineteenth century. Why? Thomas says corporations changed. They acquired new forms of internal organization, which made them more complex than they'd been before. If a mom-and-pop grocery store is cheating on its taxes, chances are it's mom or pop that's the problem. But Boeing employs over 100,000 people, and it distributes responsibility for complicated tasks, like designing and testing airplanes, across hundreds of them.

Because tasks are distributed, Boeing's failings may not trace back to the failings of any particular employee. They may be the result of many mistakes, each of which, on its own, wouldn't have mattered much if other employees had done their jobs. You can even imagine extreme cases where the company acts badly even though no individual does. The problem might lie in the way the company is staffed or organized. In cases like that, Thomas says, only the company will be to blame, not the individuals who work for it.

But even when employees do act badly, the company might still be to blame. That's because the company is an independent moral agent. Boeing is capable of responding to reasons, and we can judge its character according to how well it does.

Can we blame White people *as a group*, in the way that we blame Boeing? No. When we talk about Whites, we're talking about a collection of individuals, not a corporation. Racial groups are *not* more than the sum of their parts. They don't have an internal organization that allows them to make collective decisions. Individual Whites are responsible for what they do. But the group has no responsibility separate from its members.

* * *

ADD ALL THAT UP and the answer to our question is: No, race is not a ground of responsibility. We aren't to blame for the acts of others simply because we are members of the same racial group. And that means that few Whites alive today are responsible for past wrongs, like slavery and segregation.

But: Whites should *take* responsibility for them.

There's a difference between *being* responsible and *taking* responsibility. Surely you've known someone who acted badly but refused to acknowledge it, or do anything about it. That person wasn't taking responsibility for what they did, which is its own, separate sort of failing.*
That's why we teach our kids: When you're wrong, you say so, and you set it right as best you can. Otherwise, you're in the wrong again.

For the most part, you should take responsibility when you *are* re-

---

Taking responsibility means something different here than it did when we considered Robert Paul Wolff's objections to authority. He wanted people to take responsibility before they acted—by considering the reasons and deciding what to do. Here, we're talking about taking responsibility after you've acted—owning up to your wrongs.

sponsible. But it's possible to take responsibility when you *aren't*, and sometimes you should.

Or so says David Enoch. He's another philosopher of law. He teaches at Hebrew University, so he doesn't live on our street. But I wish he did, because he's one of my favorite people to argue with. We disagree about almost everything, and often he leaves me worried that I'm wrong. That's the best you can ask in an intellectual opponent.

But Enoch is right about this. (Don't tell him I said so.) You can take responsibility even when you aren't responsible, and sometimes you should. Parents often find themselves in this position. Suppose your kid plays at another kid's house and breaks something. It's possible that it's your fault. Maybe you didn't teach your kid to be careful with other people's things. But chances are, you did nothing wrong. No matter how well you parent, kids won't always be careful. Still, you might think that you should apologize and offer to fix what the kid broke. That is, you might think that you should take responsibility, even though you weren't responsible.

Why? I think that's an interesting question. As a parent, you don't want your kid to be a problem for other people. Partly, that's pragmatic. You want your kid to go on playdates, so you can have an empty house. (Or so that he'll have friends. Whatever.) If you don't fix what he breaks, or at least offer to do it, he might not get invited back. But I don't think that this is just about self-interest. Indeed, I think there's something off about a parent who refuses to take responsibility for problems her child caused.

I'm not sure exactly how to explain that, though. Here's my best guess: we don't want other people's generosity to be (unexpectedly) costly for them. You're incurring a burden when you agree to take care of my kid, and that's a nice thing to do. I'll need to reciprocate at some point. But if it turns out to be surprisingly costly for you—say, because my kid broke something—then merely reciprocating won't put us back in balance. In taking responsibility, I'm making sure you don't get more than you bargained for.*

This phenomenon—taking responsibility when you aren't responsible—is not limited to parents. Indeed, Enoch points to a case that's instructive when we think about race. He imagines a person who is put off by something her country has done—perhaps it has started a war she thinks unjustified. It might not be her fault. Maybe she voted against the people in charge. Maybe she even protested the war. Still, Enoch suggests, she ought to take responsibility for it. That might involve apologizing for the war or working to mitigate its effects. There's something off, he says, if she washes her hands of it just because she didn't support it.

I think Whites are in a similar spot. It doesn't matter whether we personally participated in segregation, protested against it, or weren't even born when it happened. We can't wash our hands of it just because we aren't responsible. We should take responsibility.

Why? There's an old common law formula: *Qui sentit commodum, sentire debet et onus.* It means: *He who enjoys the benefit ought also to bear the burden.* It's trotted out to resolve certain sorts of property disputes. But I think the principle applies here too. Whites occupy a position of privi-

---

*This gets even more complicated, because you probably ought to decline my offer to pay. Among friends, cash transfers are awkward. Indeed, one way you know you're friends is that you don't keep a strict account of who owes who what. If the item my kid broke is small, you should tell me not to worry about it, at least if you want to maintain the friendship (or forge one). I think the situation is different if the item is expensive, or if replacing it would pose a hardship for you. (But then you might have your own responsibility to worry about, since you left it accessible to the kids.) I find these kinds of cases—where one person is required to make an offer and another person is required to decline it—fascinating, because they show just how nuanced our relationships are. Here I have to attempt to take responsibility for something that I'm not responsible for, and you have to turn me down—all so we can show that we have the right sort of attitudes toward each other.

lege, atop a social hierarchy that shouldn't exist. They should do their part to take it apart.

The second reason is simpler, and it applies to everyone, regardless of race. It's spelled out by Isabel Wilkerson in her recent book *Caste: The Origins of Our Discontents*. Wilkerson imagines America as a house. It looks beautiful on the outside. But inside, it's got problems. There are "stress cracks and bowed walls, and fissures built into the foundation."

That's not the present resident's fault. As Wilkerson observes, "Many people may rightly say, '*I had nothing to do with how all this started. I have nothing to do with sins of the past. My ancestors never attacked indigenous people, never owned slaves.*'" They're not wrong. But it doesn't matter. We inherited the house, and "we are the heirs to whatever is right or wrong with it. We did not erect the uneven pillars or joists, but they are ours to deal with now."

We can let the house fall apart. Or . . . we can fix it.

• ⁓ •

WHAT SHOULD WE DO if we want to fix it? There's no simple answer to that question. But one of the most powerful things we can do is: Talk to our kids. Those of us who are White need to teach our kids about racism—and not just in the past, but the present too. When the boys first saw Black Lives Matter protests in the news, we talked about the fact that the police sometimes kill Black people—for no good reason, or no reason at all.

That lesson was hard to teach—and hard to learn. Hank, in particular, had trouble wrapping his head around the idea that the police might be the bad guys.

"If the police do something bad," he said, "other police arrest them." It was a question as much as a statement.

"The police that kill Black people rarely get punished," I said. And I could see him lose a little of his innocence.

Good guys are good. Bad guys get punished. That's how stories go. But not the world outside them.

As hard as we found those conversations, they can't compare to the challenges that Black parents face in talking to their kids about race. When Hank seeks reassurance that the police won't hurt him, I can give it. Black parents can't. They have to teach their kids how to stay safe. And they know that there's nothing they can say that will ward off all the risk.

Recently I was talking to my friend Ekow Yankah. He's another philosopher of law—an expert in, among other things, policing and punishment. We had a conversation about the challenges that we face—as White and Black parents, respectively—in talking to our kids about race. For me, the main task is to get my kids to see the advantages that come with whiteness—to see that it's unfair that they have those advantages—to see it as their responsibility to make the world more just.

For Yankah, the challenges are much more urgent. He has to prepare his kids for the hostility that they'll face. He has to help them cope with the fact that it's not fair. And he has to help them think about it all—to make sense of something that doesn't really make sense.

One question occupies a lot of his attention: How should Black people relate to a country that has treated them so badly, for so long?

Some answers are obvious: sadness and anger. Rejection might be warranted too. But Yankah stops short of that, and he doesn't want it for his kids either. The story of America is still being written, he says. It's been a bad story for Black Americans, at least so far—centuries of oppression that shifts in shape but never ends. But there *is* progress to build on—and the seed of something better.

Yankah takes his inspiration from Frederick Douglass's famous speech "What to the Slave Is the Fourth of July?" At the start of the speech, Douglass celebrates America—its founders and founding principles—in ways that are striking for a former slave:

> The signers of the Declaration of Independence were brave men. They were great men, too . . . statesmen, patriots and heroes, and for the good they did, and the principles they contended for, I will unite with you to honor their memory.

And Douglass is sincere about that—he extolls, at length, the virtues of those men and their fight for freedom.

But the country, he soon declares, has not lived up to its founding ideals. "The rich inheritance of justice, liberty, prosperity and independence, bequeathed by your fathers, is shared by you, not by me."

Douglass does not mince words. He calls slavery "the great sin and shame of America." And he answers the question that frames his speech with a damning indictment:

> What, to the American slave, is your 4th of July? I answer: a day that reveals to him, more than all other days in the year, the gross injustice and cruelty to which he is the constant victim. To him, your celebration is a sham; your boasted liberty, an unholy license; your national greatness, swelling vanity; your sounds of rejoicing are empty and heartless; your denunciations of tyrants, brass fronted impudence; your shouts of liberty and equality, hollow mockery; your prayers and hymns, your sermons and thanksgivings, with all your religious parade, and solemnity, are, to him, mere bombast, fraud, deception, impiety, and hypocrisy—a thin veil to cover up crimes which would disgrace a nation of savages.

And yet, at the end of the speech, Douglass says: "I do not despair of this country."

Why not? Douglass invokes the "great principles" contained in the Declaration of Independence—and holds open the possibility that America could yet live up to them.

When Yankah talks to his kids, he tries to walk the line that Douglass did. He does not mince words. He won't hide the enormity of the injustice, or seek to soften its blow. But he also wants his kids to know that progress is possible. The idea of equality is not alien to America. It's inscribed in our founding documents. We don't live up to the standard they set. But the story—and the struggle—is not over.

I asked Yankah what he wanted my kids to learn. "That's easy," he said. "Nice is not enough." It matters, of course, whether we're nice to each other. But if we let our kids think that's their only job, we'll leave most of our problems in place. Nice won't improve access to health care. Or reduce the wealth gap. Or equalize funding among schools. And nice won't let Black parents reassure their children the way I can reassure Hank when he's worried about the police.

The way we act toward each other matters. But the way we act as a community matters much more. If we want to fix our problems, we have to push our country to take responsibility for its wrongs—and right them.

━━━ ⌣ ━━━

THE UNITED STATES IS a moral agent, independent of its citizens— for just the same reasons that Boeing is. A country is not just a collection of people. Our government is organized in a way that allows it to respond to reasons, and that makes it responsible for what it does. On race, its record is awful. The United States is responsible for slavery, segregation, redlining, mass incarceration, and much else that ails us. And it's never taken responsibility for a bit of it. We should all use whatever influence we have to demand that it does.

What would that look like? Recently there's been a lot of interest in reparations. In 2014, Ta-Nehisi Coates published an article in *The Atlantic* called "The Case for Reparations." The article talks a bit about slavery, but it mostly addresses what came after; it's focused, especially, on the sins of the twentieth century. Coates explains how redlining worked, and he shows, in detail, how the policy impacted particular people—

right down to today, in foreclosure crises centered on segregated neighborhoods.

It's hard to read Coates without thinking: *We have to right these wrongs.* They are our present as much as our past. And they will be our future too, if we don't take responsibility now. How? An apology would help. We ought to repudiate our wrongs. But an apology would ring hollow if it wasn't accompanied by an effort to repair the damage done.*

There's no way to undo it all. Many of the people most affected aren't with us anymore. But we *can* build a society that treats people equally.

That's what reparations is really about. Daniel Fryer is the third philosopher of law who lives on my street. He studies reparations and racial justice more generally. And he rejects the idea that reparations should aim to put Black people in the position they would have been in had slavery and segregation not happened. That's not possible. There's no going back—to the way things were or the way they would have been. But that's not the right goal anyway, says Fryer. Reparations, he argues, should aim to repair our relationships. The goal should be to build a society in which Black people are treated as equals—and have the same freedoms that White people do.

How? That's a hard question. Money has a role to play. Cash payments can reduce the wealth gap, which puts lots of opportunities out of reach. We can also spend money to improve schools and increase access to health care. But cash can't buy us out of all our problems. Money won't solve mass incarceration or police brutality or voter suppression. Reparations should root out all the ways in which our society treats Black people like second-class citizens. It's a project, not a payment. It won't be easy. And we won't

---

*This is the inverse of the idea that harsh treatment has to be a part of punishment if it is to send the right message about the wrongdoer's misconduct. Again, actions speak louder than words.

be able to say that we've succeeded until we've built what Frederick Douglass demanded: a society that lives up to its founding ideals.

· ⸺ ·

EARLIER I MENTIONED THE BOOK *When Jackie and Hank Met.* It tells the stories of Jackie Robinson and Hank Greenberg. They were two of the best baseball players ever. But they absorbed astounding abuse—Greenberg because he was Jewish, and Robinson because he was Black.

Greenberg made it to the major leagues before Robinson. He was older. But also, baseball was segregated. Robinson played in the Negro Leagues before Branch Rickey signed him to play for the Brooklyn Dodgers. He debuted in 1947. By then, Greenberg was in the twilight of his career, playing for the Pittsburgh Pirates.

When the teams first met, the men crossed paths—literally. In his first at bat, Robinson bunted. A bad throw pulled Greenberg off first base. He collided with Robinson, knocking him down.

The next inning, Greenberg walked. As he got to first base, he asked Robinson whether he'd been hurt. Robinson said no, and Greenberg said he hadn't meant to knock him down. Then he said, "Listen, don't pay attention to these guys that are trying to make it hard for you. Stick in there. You're doing fine." Greenberg also invited Robinson to dinner. That was the first encouragement Robinson had ever received from an opposing player, and he made clear how much it meant to him.

Rex loved that story. We read it over and over. And he asked me to read it to his pre-K class. But he struggled to make sense of it. And so did all the other kids at the JCC preschool. They were full of questions.

"Why don't people like Jews?"

"Why don't people like Blacks?"

"What's a bunt?"

I was thrilled for the third question, because I struggled with the first two.

"Some people don't like people that are different from them," I said. Which is too simple. But also, too true.

When Jackie and Hank Met has stayed on our shelves, even as the boys leave picture books behind. It played too big a role in our lives to let it go. The book was the boys' first window into the idea that some people don't like Jews.

I didn't learn that lesson until first grade. I was the only Jewish kid in school (that remained true all the way through twelfth grade). I liked the girl who sat next to me, and I thought she might like me back. She showed me her belly button once, which seemed like a good sign. So I was excited one day when she turned to talk to me. Then she said: "Jews killed Jesus."

I had no idea what she was talking about. But I wanted to defend my people. I only had the dimmest sense who Jesus was, so I couldn't argue the merits of the case. Instead, I put on character evidence.

"I don't think so," I said. "We're really nice."

"My mom says you did."

(Take a minute and think about that *you* in the context of what we've learned about group responsibility.)

Her mom was wrong. Jews didn't kill Jesus. Romans did. But the accusation underwrites lots of anti-Semitism, and it has for centuries.

So Jews joke about it, in part to highlight the absurdity of holding people responsible for something they're said to have done (but didn't) two thousand years ago.

Most famously, Lenny Bruce: "Yes, we did. I did it. My family. I found a note in my basement: 'We killed him—signed, Morty.'"

Funnier still, Sarah Silverman: "Everybody blames the Jews for killing Christ. And then the Jews try to pass it off on the Romans. I'm one of the few people that believe it was the blacks."

Silverman's joke captures something important about the social status of Jews in the United States. It's a weird mix of privilege and precarity. The privilege stems from the fact that most Jews are White. That colors the way we're treated. We aren't followed in stores. We don't have difficulty hailing a cab. We don't expect the police to harass us, let alone hurt us. And on and on. And yet we're not full members of the club. The white supremacists that marched in Charlottesville chanted, "Jews will not replace us." And they revived old Nazi slogans—a stark reminder that things can go south, even in a society that seems to accept you.

Some Jews respond to the precarity by trying to shore up their whiteness. And few pastimes are whiter than blaming Black people for things they didn't do. Hence Silverman's joke. Which is funny, because it's absurd. But also tragic, because it points to something real. In jockeying for social status, marginalized groups often take aim at each other. In the case of Jewish and Black Americans, that goes in both directions. There are racist Jews and anti-Semitic Black people. That's not just about social positioning. Hatred has many handmaidens.* But it plays a part.

There's another path forward, though: the path in the parable. When Jackie met Hank, they stood in solidarity—at first base and beyond. Greenberg went on to become the general manager of the Cleveland Indians. He refused to let his team stay at hotels that wouldn't admit Black players. And he integrated the Texas League.

Robinson became a vocal opponent of anti-Semitism, especially in the Black community. He castigated other Black leaders for failing to support a Jewish businessman who was the object of anti-Semitic protests. In his autobiography, he wondered, "How could we stand against anti-black prejudice if we were willing to practice or condone a similar intolerance?"

Solidarity is the central message of *When Jackie and Hank Met*. Jackie's struggle wasn't Hank's. And Hank's struggle wasn't Jackie's. Jackie had

---

*And sometimes resentment is warranted. Every Jew in America should read James Baldwin's 1967 essay "Negroes Are Anti-Semitic Because They're Anti-White."

it far worse, and Hank knew that. But both knew that they had more to gain from helping each other than hating each other. And they thought it was the right thing to do too.

I want my kids to see things the same way. I want them to stand with people that are oppressed. I want them to stand up for people that have been wronged. Indeed, if you told me my kids would do that, I wouldn't need to know anything else about them. I'd feel like I succeeded as a parent.

PART III

MAKING SENSE
OF THE WORLD

8

KNOWLEDGE

I wonder if I'm dreaming my entire life," Rex said. He was four and already a fine philosopher, so the question didn't shock me. We were eating dinner, and the inquiry might have been a vegetable-avoidance strategy. If it was, it worked. Rex knew his audience well.

"What a cool idea, Rex! A guy named Descartes wondered the same thing. Do you think you are dreaming?"

"I don't know. Maybe."

"If you're dreaming, where do you think you really are right now?"

"Maybe I'm still in Mommy's belly. Maybe I haven't been born yet."

I wasn't buying it.

"Can babies that haven't been born yet talk?" I asked.

"No."

"So do you think they dream about conversations like this?"

"No," he admitted.

But it wasn't hard to make Rex's argument more plausible. "What if you're just dreaming today?" I asked. "What if you haven't woken up since you went to sleep last night? Would you be able to tell?"

"No!" he said, happy at the thought he might be hallucinating.

• ⌒ •

WE'RE ALL SKEPTICAL SOMETIMES. A friend shares news, but you don't believe it. Or you start to doubt something you thought you knew.

The hypothesis that Rex raised—that he was dreaming his entire life—is a recipe for radical skepticism, for doubting almost anything.

Descartes was not the first dream skeptic. The idea appeared in antiquity, many times over. My favorite formulation comes from the *Zhuangzi*, a Daoist text, written more than two thousand years ago:

> Once Zhuang Zhou dreamed he was a butterfly, a butterfly flitting and fluttering around, happy with himself and doing as he pleased. He didn't know he was Zhuang Zhou. Suddenly, he woke up, and there he was, solid and unmistakable Zhuang Zhou. But he didn't know if he were Zhuang Zhou who had dreamed he was a butterfly or a butterfly who was dreaming he was Zhuang Zhou.

I asked Hank (age eight) whether there was a way for Zhuang Zhou to figure it out. He thought hard and asked, "Is he tired? If not, then he just woke up, so he dreamed he was a butterfly."

That's clever. But not clever enough. As Hank would later concede, you can dream that you've woken up, feeling refreshed. He just didn't think it likely. And of course, it's not likely that you're dreaming your entire life—either as a baby in your mother's belly or as a butterfly. The reason to take dream skepticism seriously is not that it's a serious worry. It's what it shows us about the state of our knowledge—and our relationship to the world around us.

THAT'S WHAT DESCARTES WAS thinking about when he dreamt up dream skepticism. René Descartes lived in the 1600s, and yet he remains one of the most influential thinkers ever. That owes partly to his work on math—in particular, the algebraic analysis of geometry. (Fifth-grade flashback: plot $y = x + 2$ on Cartesian coordinates. I'll wait.) But it has more to do with Descartes's efforts to free himself from false beliefs.

Instead of doubting this or that, Descartes set out to doubt everything. Why? He wanted to put his knowledge on firm footing. And he decided the best way to do that would be to doubt everything that he thought he knew. If anything was left—if he found something he couldn't doubt—then he'd have a firm foundation on which to build back his knowledge.

Dream skepticism was a powerful source of doubt for Descartes. The possibility that he was dreaming—right now, or throughout his entire life—called into question most of what he thought he knew. Why? Ask yourself some simple questions: Where are you? What are you doing right now?

When Descartes wrote about dream skepticism, he was sitting in front of a fire, dressed, and holding a piece of paper. Or was he? He started to wonder whether he might be asleep, in bed. It didn't seem like he was. Indeed, he didn't think that any dream could be nearly as clear as his present experience. But then he reminded himself: many times, he'd been deluded by a dream into thinking he was awake. And there was no sure marker that would tell him, without fail, whether he was awake or dreaming.

You're in a similar position now. I'm sure it seems that you're awake. But like Descartes, I bet you've sometimes been surprised—even relieved—to discover that you were dreaming. That makes it hard to be sure that, right now, you're not. And if you can't be sure that you're awake right now, why think that you can be sure about anything you've ever experienced? Sure, you remember that time you [fill in a favorite memory here]. But are you sure you didn't dream it?

If you find that disorienting, you can take comfort in the fact that some knowledge is immune to dream skepticism. As Descartes observed, some things are true whether we're awake or asleep. A square has four sides even in a dream. And sleeping doesn't change the fact that $2 + 3 = 5$. So you can hold on to those truths even if you can't hold on to much else.

But don't hold on too tight, because Descartes had a way of calling those facts into question too. Once he discovered the limits of dream skepticism, he busted out an even stronger skeptical hypothesis, the most powerful that anyone has yet put forth. Descartes imagined that an evil genius—let's call him Dr. Doofenshmirtz, after the boys' favorite bad guy—might be controlling his thoughts.* Indeed, Doofenshmirtz might have set out to deceive Descartes, so that his head would be full of falsehoods.

Why? Descartes never explained why Doofenshmirtz would care to deceive him, and to be honest, it doesn't seem like a genius way to spend one's time. But the mere possibility that Doofenshmirtz was deceiving him posed a problem for Descartes. It meant he couldn't be confident in anything he believed, not even straightforward facts about math. For all he could tell, Doofenshmirtz might be duping him.

And for all you can tell, you're a dupe too. Maybe Doofenshmirtz removed your brain from your body, put it in a vat, and hooked it up to electrodes so that he could simulate every experience you've ever had. You'd be none the wiser.

I know. You think you're dressed, sitting down, or lying in bed, read-

_____

*If the reference is lost on you, grab a kid for cover and binge *Phineas and Ferb*. Hank recommends. 14/10.

ing this book. But you're not doing any of those things. You're not dressed. You're not even naked. You don't have a body. You're just a disembodied brain. And while it might seem like you're reading a book, there's no book for you to read. It's all in your head.

Or, rather, it might be. And you can't rule it out. For all you can tell, the external world is an elaborate illusion. Things would appear just the same to you whether it actually exists or not.

—————

AFTER HANK AND I talked about Zhuang Zhou, we talked about Descartes and Doofenshmirtz.

"Is there anything Descartes can know for sure, even if Doofenshmirtz is trying to trick him?" I asked.

Hank saw it instantly.

"He knows that he's thinking," he said.

"Why can't Doofenshmirtz trick him about that?"

"Well, Doofenshmirtz can make him think things," Hank said, "but if he thinks he's thinking, then he is."

That's right. And Descartes saw it too. There's a limit to even the most extreme skepticism. *I am thinking*, Descartes thought, *and I cannot be confused about that.* And that thought led him to another that could not be a Doofenshmirtz deception: *I exist.*

Together, this chain of reasoning is called the *cogito*, after its Latin formulation: *cogito ergo sum.* In English: *I think, therefore I am.*

When all else was in doubt, at least Descartes had that. He *knew* he existed.

—————

OKAY, THAT'S A COOL BIT of reasoning—from Hank, maybe more than Descartes. But is the *cogito* really all that you know?

No one acts as if it is. Consider the following questions:

Do you know when the movie starts?

Do you know how to get to High Street?

Do you know whether there's pasta in the pantry?

We ask questions like that constantly. And no one ever protests that they couldn't possibly know whether there's pasta in the pantry on account of the fact they might have dreamed its presence, let alone been deceived by some sort of demon.

I dream about responding to the boys that way, though.

"Do you know where my socks are?"

"Does anyone really know anything?"

"Dad!"

"I mean, I think I saw socks. But how could I be sure? It might have been a dream."

"Where did you see them!?"

"Are you sure that socks are real? Maybe you're after an apparition."

That would be fun. But it would drive them mad, because no one supposes that Cartesian skepticism crowds out knowledge in our everyday lives.

So was Descartes wrong about what it takes to know something? Or are we systematically confused, thinking we know things when, really, we don't?

⁘ ⌒⌒ ⁘

THE ANSWER DEPENDS ON what knowledge *is*. For a long time, we thought we knew. But it turns out, we don't.

I put the question to Rex recently.

"When do you know something?"

"What do you mean?" he asked.

"Well, we know that Mommy's at the store right now. But what do we mean when we say that we know that?"

"It's in our heads," Rex said.

"Do you know everything that's in your head?"

"No. It has to be right. If Mommy wasn't at the store, we wouldn't know that she was."

"So, if it's in your head and it's right, then you know it?"

"I think so," Rex said.

"I'm not sure. Suppose you think it's going to rain tomorrow. And suppose it *is* going to rain tomorrow. But you haven't looked at the weather. You just think it's going to rain because tomorrow's Tuesday and you think it rains every Tuesday. But that's not true. In fact, it's silly. Do you know it's going to rain tomorrow?"

"No," Rex said after double-checking the story. "Your reason for thinking it's gonna rain has to be reliable, or you don't really know."

My last question was a bit leading, but I got Rex where I wanted him to go. In just a few steps, he re-created the traditional view of knowledge. To know something, philosophers long thought, is to have a *justified true belief* about it.

Let's take that in reverse. First, to know something, it has to be in your head, as Rex said. But it has to be in there in the right way. It won't work to *want* something to be true. You have to *believe* it is.

Second, you can't know what ain't so. Your belief has to be true.

And third, your belief has to be justified. That is, you have to have adequate evidence for it. Just guessing won't do, and neither will relying on clearly erroneous information, like the idea that it rains every Tuesday.

That account of knowledge—justified true belief (or JTB, for short)—was widely taken to be true until a guy named Edmund Gettier had a problem.

<hr />

GETTIER TAUGHT AT WAYNE STATE, and he was coming up for tenure. But he hadn't written anything, so there was no chance he'd get it.

Publish or perish, as the saying goes. Gettier's colleagues told him that
he had to get something done or he wouldn't keep his job. So he wrote up
the only idea he had. The paper, published in 1963, was just three pages
long. The title posed a question: "Is Justified True Belief Knowledge?"

Gettier said no, and he gave two quick counterexamples. They were
complicated, so I'll give you a simple one, inspired by his. You believe
that there's a copy of *The Joy of Cooking* in your house. You bought it years
ago, and you've used it many times since. And it's true: there *is* a copy in
your house. But the copy in your house is *not* the one you bought. Your
partner loaned that one out, and it hasn't come back yet. As it happens, a
friend sent you the book for your birthday, not realizing that you already
had it. It's wrapped, in your living room, waiting to be opened.

Do you know that there's a copy of *The Joy of Cooking* in your house?
You believe that there is, and your belief is true. Moreover, you're justified in believing that you have a copy—you bought it yourself and you've
used it often. So if the JTB account of knowledge is right, you know that
you have a copy. But Gettier says that's wrong, and just about everyone
who encounters these sorts of cases agrees. You're just lucky that there's
a copy in your house. It's not something that you know.

Gettier's article shocked philosophers; it showed that they did not
know what knowledge was. And it triggered a frantic effort to supplement the JTB account—to say what else is necessary for knowledge—so
as to avoid what came to be called the Gettier Problem.* Philosophers
have proposed dozens of solutions. But none of them work.

And that's not an accident, says Linda Zagzebski. She dashed many
people's hopes of finding a solution to the Gettier Problem. Zagzebski
argues that so long as you start from the (sensible) premise that you can
be justified in believing something false, you can always create Gettier

---

*Gettier's other problem—getting tenure—disappeared with the publication of the
article.

cases, no matter how you supplement the JTB account. Indeed, she wrote a recipe for them.

To start, you tell a story about a belief that's justified. Then you add a bit of bad luck, so it turns out that the belief is false. But you don't stop there! To wrap up, you add a bit of good luck, so the belief turns out true anyway.

One of Zagzebski's stories went like this. Mary believes her husband is in the living room. Why? She just walked past, and she saw him there. But, bad luck! Mary's wrong. She didn't actually see her husband. She saw his long-lost twin, who showed up unexpectedly. But, good luck! Her husband is also in the living room; he was sitting out of view as Mary walked past.

Does Mary know that her husband is in the living room? Well, she believes he's there, and it's true, he is. Is she justified in believing it? Yes. She walked past and saw a person who looked exactly like her husband. Now, if Mary knows that her husband has a twin (she might not), she'll know that there's at least one other person who looks like him. But she's got no reason to expect his twin to be there tonight, given that he's long lost. So Mary's got a justified true belief that her husband's in the living room. Nevertheless, she doesn't *know* that he's there. It's just luck that she's right.

People still propose solutions to the Gettier Problem. We won't explore them here, since they can be quite complicated. But lots of philosophers have come to think Zagzebski right—the problem will never be solved. And some of those philosophers have suggested that all along it was a mistake to try to analyze knowledge in terms of simpler ideas, like justification, belief, and truth.

We can't always break ideas down into simpler ones.

Quick: What's a chair?

If you said, "It's something you can sit on," your bed would like a chat. So would lots of large rocks. And if you're now thinking, "With legs! It has to have legs," please go to The Google and search "chairs without legs." You'll see many clear counterexamples.

And yet you have no trouble identifying chairs, even though you can't explain what they are. So too, some think, with knowledge.

What does Gettier think? How would he solve his Problem? We don't know. Edmund Gettier is one of the most celebrated philosophers of the twentieth century, known to everyone who enters the field. But he was also a one-hit wonder. Gettier taught for decades after his article came out. But he never wrote another word.

Why? It's simple, really. He had "nothing more to say."

⋅ ⌇⌇⌇⌇ ⋅

THAT MIGHT BE THE best mic drop ever.

But I'll tell you a secret. Gettier wasn't the first to spot his Problem.

In the eighth century, an Indian philosopher named Dharmottara told a story that went like this: You're walking in the desert, and you need a drink. You see water up ahead. Alas, it's a mirage. But when you arrive, you find water under a rock. Did you know there was water before you got there? Dharmottara says no; you just got lucky.

Gettier didn't rip off Dharmottara. He just happened on the same idea, twelve hundred years later. In the interim, an Italian philosopher, Peter of Mantua, hit on the idea too. He lived in the fourteenth century. But Gettier didn't know that either. Old texts aren't always translated. And people lose track of what's in them.

This is a problem for philosophy. Or, rather, it's several problems wrapped into one. Philosophers from distant times and places are often ignored. And they're not the only ones. For far too long, the field excluded women too. Earlier I credited Descartes with the idea that an evil genius might have filled his head with falsehoods. Recent scholarship suggests that he was influenced by the work of a Spanish nun, Teresa of Ávila, who put demons to a different purpose in her own writings about knowledge.* But while Descartes is studied by every student, Teresa is studied by nearly none.

A new generation of philosophers is working to fix that. They're looking for new ideas in old traditions from all around the world. As a result, philosophers in the English-speaking world now know about Dharmottara. And there's a concerted effort to surface and celebrate the work of women who were written out of the history of philosophy—or given less prominence than they deserved. Teresa, it turns out, isn't the only woman who influenced Descartes—and the philosophical ideas of his age. Later we'll meet a princess that quarreled with him about consciousness.

Expanding the ambit of philosophy is hard, at least when we look to the past. Lots is lost to history. But we can make sure we don't make the same mistake again—by listening to a wider range of philosophers today.

━━━━━

WITH THAT IN MIND, it's time to leave Descartes behind. And I know just the woman to help us do it. Like Gettier, Gail Stine taught at Wayne State. She died too young, just thirty-seven, in 1977. She was an epistemologist: a philosopher who studies knowledge—what it is and how we get it.

Stine was puzzled by the discrepancy we noted earlier. In everyday conversation, our default assumption is that we know an awful lot. But when we talk philosophy, it feels like our knowledge starts to slip away. By the time we read Descartes, we're not sure we know anything at all.

What's up with that?

Stine had an idea, simple yet powerful. The meaning of some words

---

*Teresa's demons make her false beliefs extremely appealing, remind her of earthly delights, and try to dissuade her from continuing on her meditative path toward knowledge of herself and God.

shifts depending on the context. Often that's easy to see. I'm tall at home but not at work. Why? The comparison class shifts. The boys are shorter than me, and so is Julie, so I'm tall relative to them. But I'm shorter than the average American man, so no one thinks me tall at work.

At six foot three, my friend JJ is tall—at work. But he's not tall for pro basketball. And even the tallest guy in the world isn't tall in all contexts. Put him next to a giraffe and he's short.

It's obvious that *short* and *tall* shift meanings. So do *big* and *small*. But some words are surprisingly context-sensitive. For instance, *empty*.

If I say "The fridge is empty" on a random day, I mean "We don't have food for dinner." If you look in the fridge, you might see all sorts of things: soda, condiments, and so on. But if we've coordinated on the context of the conversation, you'll agree, it's empty, so long as there's nothing to make a meal.

Now shift the context: the movers are coming, and we're rushing to get ready. "Is the fridge empty?" I ask. *Empty* means something new now. If the soda's still there, it's *not* empty. We can't have things rattling around inside it, or we'll have a mess to clean when the move is done.

It's tempting to think that this is what *empty* really means—no food or drink—and that I was just speaking loosely in the first case. But we should resist that temptation, because even a fridge with no food or drink wouldn't count as empty in all contexts. If we're running an experiment and need to create a vacuum inside the fridge, it won't be empty until all the air is gone. But in most contexts, *empty* does not mean devoid of all matter. It means whatever it needs to mean, and that shifts with the situation.

Stine suggested that the word *know* is context-sensitive, in something like the way *empty* is. In different situations, different standards determine whether people know things. The standards, Stine said, depend on the *relevant alternatives*, which shift across situations.

A standard example runs like this. You're at the San Diego Zoo, and up ahead you see black-and-white-striped animals. "There are the ze-bras!" you say, and off you go to see them. Do you know you're looking at zebras? Of course you do. Assuming it's a clear day and your eyesight is good, it would be hard to mistake zebras for any other zoo animal.

But . . . can you rule out the possibility that you're looking at cleverly disguised donkeys? From where you're standing, no. You'd have to get a lot closer to assess whether what looks to be a zebra is actually a donkey that's seen a stylist. But, Stine says, you don't need to rule that out in order to know that you're looking at a zebra, since it's not a relevant al-ternative. You've got no reason to worry that the zoo disguises donkeys as zebras.

There are places where you'd have to worry about that. In Tijuana, Mexico, donkeys painted with zebra stripes have long been a tourist at-traction. So if you think you see a zebra there, you should be suspicious. You won't know that you've seen one until you determine that it's not a disguised donkey.*

How does this help us subdue skepticism? Well, imagine that you just went to the zoo, and you report to a friend that you enjoyed seeing the zebras.

"You don't know that you saw zebras," she says.

"Sure I do," you snip.

"They could've been cleverly disguised donkeys," she explains, sig-naling that she's either insane . . . or an epistemologist.

At that point, Stine says, you can go one of two ways. You can insist that you *know* you saw zebras, since there's no reason to think that dis-guised donkeys are a relevant alternative. Or you can allow your friend to shift the conversational context, so that disguised donkeys are rele-vant. What would put them in play? If your friend lacks evidence that

---

*Fun fact: Tijuana's disguised donkeys are called zonkeys. More fun fact: They're not actually zonkeys. A zonkey is a hybrid animal—the offspring of a zebra and a donkey. They look like donkeys in zebra leggings. And they are *awesome*.

zoos are disguising donkeys, then she's playing the skeptic's game—searching for sources for doubt. And that's a good game! It teaches us something about the limits we face in our efforts to gather information about the world. But you don't have to play it with her.

Roughly, Stine's idea is this. The skeptic's right—we don't know anything—*when we talk the skeptic's way*. But outside philosophy, we've got no reason to talk that way. Indeed, in everyday life, it would be silly to speak as the skeptic does. There's lots we know by ordinary standards, and we need to be able to communicate that.

YOU HAVE TO BE on the lookout for people playing the skeptic's game. They're more common than you might think. And while the game is fun in philosophy, it can be insidious outside it.

N. Ángel Pinillos recently made this point in the context of climate change. He's another epistemologist, interested in the ways that people sow doubts about science.

The evidence that our carbon emissions are responsible for climate change is overwhelming. We're wrecking the world in slow motion. And we're not taking sufficient steps to stop it. Why? There are many reasons. But a large part of the answer is that some people profit from putting carbon in the atmosphere, and they don't want to stop. They won't say that straight up, of course. It wouldn't sell well. Instead, they say we don't know enough to act.

Some politicians adopt the same strategy. In 2017, a constituent asked New Hampshire Governor Chris Sununu whether carbon emissions cause climate change. His answer:

> I don't know for sure. And I've studied this at MIT. I studied earth and atmospheric sciences with some of the best in the world. And I've looked at the data myself . . . I think we should keep looking at it. We have to keep studying it, un-

derstand all the impacts, whether they're to the environment,
social, economic, or other factors that might come into play.
Is carbon the leading reason why the earth has warmed up
pretty much continuously over the last 150 years, I'm not sure.
It could be.

That sounds so reasonable. Sununu has studied the question. Carbon
emissions could be responsible. He's not ruling that out. He just doesn't
know.

But notice how Sununu slips in the phrase *for sure* to set the standard
for knowledge high. Do we know *for sure* that carbon emissions are causing climate change? Maybe not. But here's something else we don't know
for sure—that we're not dreaming right now. The question is: Why would
we need to know *for sure*? The consequences from failing to act now
could be devastating. And we're pretty close to sure, even if we're not
completely there.

This is a deliberate strategy, and it's a longstanding one too. By the
1980s, Exxon had decided that it would "emphasize the uncertainty in
scientific conclusions," even though its own scientists were convinced
that man-made climate change posed a real threat. They didn't draft
this playbook, though. Tobacco companies did, questioning the link between smoking and cancer, even as their scientists confirmed it. An internal memo at Brown & Williamson once declared, "Doubt is our product."

What should we do about doubtmongers? It's a tricky question. As a
philosopher, I'm professionally committed to doubt, in something like
the way Descartes was.* I think it important to interrogate what you
know, to look for ways you might have gone wrong. Scientists share that

---

*But not in exactly the way he was. Descartes set out to doubt everything, all at
once. And I don't think we're capable of doing that—or that it would get us anywhere
if we did. Everything is open to doubt, but we can't doubt everything at once or we'd
have no way to decide whether our doubts were warranted. Doubt is more of a piece-
meal project.

inclination, so much so that they quantify their uncertainty. That makes them easy marks for doubtmongers.

Rex and I started to talk about this recently. I teach him to doubt—to ask questions. But I want him to recognize that not all questions are asked in good faith. So I've been teaching him to question questioners. Does this person really want to understand things? Are they interested in the evidence? If they learn their view is false, do I trust them to tell me? Or do I think they'll obscure that?

Pinillos suggests another strategy. In public, we should talk about probabilities, more so than what we know. Sure, there's *some* chance that the scientific consensus is wrong—that our carbon emissions aren't causing climate change. But scientists can quantify that, and it's small. Should we bet our children's future on the slim chance that the science is wrong? That's what the doubtmongers are asking us to do.

We don't need to *know* in order to act. We reason with probabilities all the time. Pinillos draws an analogy with the lottery. You don't *know* that you're going to lose. Sure, the odds are against you. But there's a relevant alternative you can't rule out—you might win! So you'll dream on that. But you'd never *plan* on it.

Climate skeptics insist that we don't *know* that carbon emissions are causing climate change. By any reasonable standard, they're wrong. We do know. But we don't need to get into a debate about what we know, since the skeptics can always insist on impossibly high standards. Instead, we should put the question back on them: Why are they willing to bet our future on the slim chance that the science is off? Maybe we'll win the lottery. But we shouldn't plan on it.

⁓

IT'S IMPORTANT TO PREPARE kids for propaganda—to teach them how to evaluate evidence and identify reliable sources of information. Rex is game for those conversations, sometimes. But he'd prefer to ponder a wild idea. The one that's gripped him lately shares a lot in common with the possibility that we're brains in vats. He wants to know whether we live in a computer simulation. Indeed, he's obsessed with the idea that everything in our world (including us) might simply be a set of operations inside a computer—that we live in a super-high-resolution version of *The Sims* (or something like it).

It's been a hot topic ever since an Oxford philosopher, Nick Bostrom, said that he thinks there's a decent chance that we *are* living in a computer simulation. Indeed, the argument has attracted lots of luminaries, including Elon Musk, who declared it likely that we're Sims.

Bostrom is the founding director of Oxford's Future of Humanity Institute, an interdisciplinary group that worries about ways the world might go wrong. The scariest items on the list include climate catastrophes, aliens, and artificial intelligence run amok. In other words, the institute is trying to keep us out of Keanu Reeves movies.

But Bostrom is best known for suggesting that we're already in one. He thinks we might live in a simulation, sort of like *The Matrix*. Why? Here's a rough version of his argument. If people are able to simulate worlds, they probably will. And if they do, they'll probably do it more than once. Indeed, they might simulate many worlds—hundreds, thousands, even millions—if it's enlightening (or entertaining) enough. In that case, there would be many more simulated worlds than actual worlds. So odds are, we're in one.

As I said, that's just a rough version of the argument. Bostrom doesn't fully embrace the conclusion, since there's room for doubt at every step.

To start, it might not be possible to simulate worlds like ours. Many people think it will be. They're impressed by the progress from *Pong* to the present day, and projecting it forward. But progress might halt.

Or it might take too much energy to run a realistic simulation. (By some reckonings, the computers could be as big as a planet.)

Or it might not be possible to create conscious creatures in a computer.

To those worries, we should add: Even if people could simulate worlds like ours, they might not bother. Bostrom suggests that scientists would run simulations to learn about their ancestors. But maybe they'd prefer to use their computing power for other purposes. Or maybe they'd have ethical reservations about creating creatures that would suffer in the ways that we do. Again, it's hard to say.

But Bostrom thinks there's something we *can* say, for sure. At least one of these propositions is true:

(A) It's not possible to simulate worlds like ours.

(B) It's possible, but people won't do it much.

(C) We're almost certainly Sims.

I asked Rex which one he accepts. He says it's either (A) or (C). He's got no patience for (B). "From what I know of people," he pronounced, "we'd do it if we could." Rex also thinks that we'll be able to do it. So he leans toward (C). He thinks we're Sims. In some more fundamental reality, people figured out how to simulate worlds and set up ours.

I'm more skeptical than Rex. Even if it's possible to simulate worlds like ours, I suspect the energy demands will be extreme—too much to do it much. It would certainly take too much energy to simulate the entire universe, all the way down to the quantum scale. So people would have to pick the bits they'd want to include—human brains, perhaps, and their immediate environments. And that poses another problem. They'd need a fine-grained understanding of the way our brains work, and we're not remotely close to that.*

Advances in artificial intelligence might help with any or all of these problems. But *might* is the key word at every step of the argument.

---

*In some ways, it would be easier to simulate an entire universe. You set the initial conditions, let it go, and see what happens.

THE SIMULATION ARGUMENT is speculative. But it's endlessly interesting.

It raises ethical questions. Would *you* create a world in which people would feel pain? What could count as a good enough reason to let people suffer slavery or the Holocaust? If the answer is (as I suppose) nothing, does that bear on the odds that we're in a simulation?

It raises theological questions. If the simulation argument is right, most worlds have creators—the engineers who designed them. And those creators are, relative to those worlds, omnipotent and omniscient. Are they gods?

It raises metaphysical questions. Do we have free will if the creators control the course of the story? Or are we, in some sense, enslaved if we exist only to serve their purposes—and only so long as they want us around?

It raises practical questions. If you think you're in a simulation, what should you do? Rex wants to write a message to the Almighty Engineers. He imagines carving it into a field, like a crop circle. "Hi! We know we're in a simulation. More Shake Shack, please." But that could be dangerous. What if they don't want you to know? They could end the entire world, or edit you out. Oops.

FINALLY, THE SIMULATION ARGUMENT raises questions about what we can know. Indeed, it looks like a teched-up version of the evil genius story. It's the brain in the vat, but this time, there's no vat, since your brain is simulated too.

And once again, it seems like everything you think you know is wrong. If you're in a simulation, you're not holding this book. There is no book. And you don't have hands to hold it. It's all an elaborate illusion.

Or maybe not.

David Chalmers is something of a rock star among philosophers. For a long time, he looked the part—leather jacket and long hair (trimmed now, as he's gone gray). He's the University Professor of Philosophy and Neural Science at NYU, and a leading expert on consciousness, among other topics.

Chalmers isn't worked up about the possibility that we live in a computer simulation. And he doesn't think it threatens our knowledge. You think you have hands, Chalmers says, and you do, even if we live in a simulation. Moreover, they're made of matter—electrons, quarks, and so on—just like you thought. It just turns out that matter is made of something surprising—computer bits!

Your hands are still real, though. They aren't fake, like movie props, or imaginary, like the hands of your favorite fictional character. Imaginary hands aren't good for much, except in imaginary worlds. But your hands are good for a lot. They can hold books, cook dinner, and do dozens of other things, dexterously. Without doubt, you'd miss them if they were gone. That's the mark of something real.

But my hands aren't real! you want to insist. They're just simulated. The Almighty Engineers might have real hands. But we're stuck with sad simulacrums. Indeed, *we* are sad simulacrums.

There's a subtle confusion here. We have hands, as we have always understood them. That doesn't change if we discover (or simply suppose) that we live in a simulated world. All we learn is that reality has a different character than we thought; it's fundamentally computational, not physical.

To see what I mean, think about Rex's hands. He knows he has them, and he has for a long time. He even knows a bit about them—that there are bones and muscles inside. And by now, he knows a bit more—that his bones are made of molecules, and that those molecules are made of atoms.

At some point, he'll learn that atoms are made of protons, neutrons, and electrons. And then he'll learn that protons and neutrons are made of quarks. And after that, he might learn that electrons aren't really little balls orbiting the nucleus of atoms, as they are often depicted in textbooks. They're spread out, sort of like clouds.

At every step, Rex will learn a little more about the nature of his hands. But at no point will it make sense for Rex to say, "Oh no! I don't have hands. Hands are made out of muscles and bones. But these things attached to the end of my arms are made out of electrons and quarks!" If he did say that, we'd tell him that his hands *are* made out of muscles and bones. It just turns out that muscles and bones are made out of electrons and quarks.

If it turns out that we live in a simulation, then we'll be able to extend that story an extra step. The fundamental physical stuff will be made of something computational, like computer bits. If Rex discovers that, he'll have learned more about the nature of his hands. He won't have discovered that they're not real, or that he doesn't have any.

It's easy to get confused about that, because it's tempting to take up the perspective of the Almighty Engineers. If *they* live in a world that is fundamentally physical, then they will think our world virtual—a simulated version of their reality. From their perspective, we'd be virtual people, with virtual hands. But from our perspective, we're just people with hands, same as we always were.

And actually, I'll go a step further than Chalmers and say: from the Almighty Engineers' perspective, we're *not* virtual people. We're people. To be a person is to have a certain moral status—to be a bearer of rights and responsibilities. And that moral status does not depend on whether one is ultimately made of matter or bits. It depends on whether one can recognize reasons, feel pain, and so on.

Anyone who proposes to simulate worlds with people in them faces serious moral questions, since those people will be objects of moral concern. These questions share something in common with the ones prospective parents face when choosing to have a child, since every human life involves some suffering. They also share something in common with the questions that God faces in choosing to create the world (if indeed there is a God). Simulation is an act of *creation*, not imagination. I'd hope that any society advanced enough to simulate worlds would recognize that.

Regardless, our reality is not threatened by the simulation argument, and neither are most of our beliefs. The simulation argument is not a *skeptical* hypothesis. It's a *metaphysical* one. It describes one way our world might work; it doesn't say we could never know.

—————

KIDS LOVE TO PRETEND—to suppose that the world is not what it seems. I suspect that's why they like skeptical arguments—and the simulation hypothesis.

For a while, dream skepticism was Rex's favorite bit of philosophy. And that made it mine too. In fact, one of my favorite moments as a father came courtesy of Descartes.

Rex was seven. He made me a card for my birthday. On the inside, he wrote: *I love you, therefore I am.*

I hereby propose that we replace the *cogito* with the *te amo*. It works just as well. Any mental state makes the point. So when you look inside, look for love.

But before you swoon at my relationship with Rex, let me assure you, he loves Julie more.

He confirmed that one day when we were walking home from school. Rex was in second grade, and we were talking about dream skepticism. Back then, we played a game. Rex would try to find a way to prove he wasn't dreaming. I would knock it down.

"Wouldn't it be weird," Rex said, "if you and I were having the same dream. And we *have* to be having the same dream if we're talking to each other."

"Yeah, that would be weird," I said. "But what if I'm not real. What if I'm just a character in your dream?"

That blew his little mind. He took time to process it. And repeat it. And extend it.

"So my friends might be characters too?" he said.

"Yeah, that's right."

We were rounding the corner into our driveway. Julie had just arrived home with Hank.

"What about Mommy?" Rex said, pointing ahead.

"She could be a character in your dream too."

Rex's face fell.

And he said, softly, "Then I don't want to wake up."

9

TRUTH

I learned about a new animal," Hank said.

"Which one?"

"It's called a du-o-brak-eee-um-spark-say." (I can't really capture the way a second grader says that.)

"That's cool," I said. "Did you know there was a *Duobrachium sparksae* in my first-grade class?"

"No there wasn't," Hank said. "They just discovered them. Scientists didn't even see one until 2015."

"They should have looked in Ms. Doseck's class," I said. "Because one of the kids was a *Duobrachium sparksae*. His name was Sparky."

"That's not true," Hank said.

"Sure it is," said Rex. "There were a lot of animals in Daddy's elementary school. He sat next to a penguin in kindergarten, and his best friend was a monkey."

I'd done this bit before. Rex had outgrown it, but I was glad for the assist.

"How big was it?" Hank asked.

"First-grade size," I said.

"They're not first-grade size," Hank said. "They're really small."

"I know," I said.* "I was just trying to keep Sparky's secret. He was actually three *Duobrachium sparksaes* stacked up in a trench coat. They took turns being on top."

"They live in water," Hank said, disdainfully. "They're like little jellyfish."

It would have been helpful to have that information at the start.

"Yeah," I said, "you could hear a lot of sloshing in the trench coat. Once Sparky let me look inside, and each one was in a fishbowl, holding the next one up."

"How did they walk?" Hank asked.

"You know, I could never figure that out. The trench coat was really long, so it dragged on the ground."

"I bet the bottom one used its tentacles," Rex said.

"Or maybe Sparky had a scooter," I said, getting a nod from Rex. "If I ever see him at a reunion, I'll ask."

"They don't have faces," Hank said sharply.

"Well, not in the ocean," I said. "But Sparky drew himself a face with a Sharpie."

Hank banged his fist on the table. "Lies!" he shouted. "STOP TELLING ME LIES!!!"

<hr/>

I feel bad when I push Hank too far. But I don't feel bad for pushing him. The bit was fun. And it gave Hank a chance to outsmart me. Instead of repeating what he'd learned, he put it to use to prove me wrong.

But it left him a little frustrated. He thought I'd lied. Was he right? I don't think so. For sure, I said things that weren't true—and I knew it.

<hr/>

*I did not know.

But I was just pretending, and Hank knew that. So I don't think I was lying. But the line here is harder to draw than you might think.

"What's the difference between lying and pretending?" I asked Rex a few days later.

"When you lie, you say something that's not true," Rex said.

"Don't you say things that aren't true when you're pretending?"

"Yeah, but when you lie, you're trying to trick someone."

"Can't you pretend in order to trick someone, like after a math test?" The surest sign that Rex crushed a math test is the sad face he makes before sharing his grade.

"I guess," Rex said slowly. He'd just realized how hard the question is.

In a sense, all lying is pretending. When you lie, you act like something is true—but it isn't. So there's pretense involved. And yet Rex was wrong. When you lie, you don't always say something false.

He realized that, all on his own, a few days later. At bedtime, he said, "I've been thinking about lying and that Gettier guy, and I've got a case for you."

"Go for it," I said.

"Okay, it's a Monday night, and you ask whether I put the trash out. I don't think I did, but I say yes anyways, because I don't want to get in trouble. But actually, I did put it out. I just forgot. Am I lying?"

"What do you think?"

"I said something true," Rex said. "But that was an accident. I thought it was false. So I think I lied."

"I think so too," I said. Then I realized it was Monday night. "Rex, did you put the trash out?"

"Maybe," he said with a smile. (He did.)

I thought it was cool that Rex drew a connection between lying and the Gettier Problem. On the surface, they don't have much to do with each other. The Gettier Problem is about what you know, not what you say. But there *is* a connection. In a Gettier case, you believe something that's true, but that's just luck for you, since your evidence isn't as good as you take it to be.* In Rex's case, he said something true, but that was just luck for him, since he believed his claim was false. (One reason Gettier gets so much attention is that his general strategy—things work out, but only by luck—is fruitful all over philosophy.)

Even more impressive: Rex was right. A lie can be true. But there *is* something false in every lie. It's the way you present yourself. When you lie, you claim to believe something you actually don't.

Typically, you do that to trick your audience. But as it happens, not all lies aim to deceive. I learned that from my friend Seana Shiffrin. She's another philosopher of law. Several years back, she blew my mind by introducing me to candlepin bowling, which is much better than the regular sort. (Shiffrin says she'll take me duckpin bowling too, but I refuse to believe that's a thing.) Bowling is just a sideline for Shiffrin, though. She studies promises, contracts, free speech, and . . . lying.

Most liars mean to deceive. But people can have other reasons for misrepresenting their mental states. Shiffrin imagines a witness at trial, perjuring himself, even though he knows that everyone knows his story is false. He has no prospect of deceiving anyone, and may not even mean to do it. Why lie, then? Perhaps he wants to avoid the truth. Telling it might implicate someone else. Or anger the mob. So he tells a tale, even though he knows no one will believe it.

When you couple Rex's trash story with Shiffrin's trial, it turns out that Rex's first attempt to say what a lie is (a false statement, made to deceive) was wrong on both counts. But a better theory is close by. According to Shiffrin, a person lies when they assert something they don't

---

*A quick refresher, so you don't have to flip back. In a Gettier case, you've got a justified true belief, but something's misfired, so your belief doesn't count as knowledge. Our illustration ran like this. You think there's a copy of *The Joy of Cooking* in your house, since you've owned it for years and used it many times. As it happens, your partner loaned that copy out. But a friend gifted you a new copy; it's wrapped in your living room, waiting for your birthday. Your belief is both justified and true. But you don't *know* that there's a copy of *The Joy of Cooking* in your house. It's just lucky that you're right.

believe in a situation in which sincerity is reasonably expected. That last bit is super important. We don't always expect sincerity. At an improv comedy show, I know the actors will say things they don't believe. There would be little point to the enterprise otherwise. So too, when I read a work of fiction, I don't expect an author to assert only what she takes to be true.

Shiffrin calls situations in which sincerity isn't expected *suspended contexts*. But we need to be careful about the idea that sincerity isn't expected. If you lie to me a lot, I won't expect you to tell me the truth. But that's not what Shiffrin has in mind. She's interested in situations where there's good reason to accept insincerity. She calls those *justified suspended contexts*. In those situations, she says, you don't owe anyone the truth. So your falsifications won't count as lies.

We're in justified suspended contexts more than you might think. When you see people you know, you offer up a series of pleasantries. *It's good to see you. Everything's great. I like your hair.* Those sorts of statements, Shiffrin says, are "demanded by the social context." Roughly, we need to acknowledge each other and affirm our relationship. But a "competent listener," Shiffrin says, knows that these sorts of statements "are not offered in order for their content to be absorbed as true." So it's okay to be insincere. You can say *everything is fine* when, actually, everything is awful. In fact, Shiffrin doesn't even think you're lying when you do.

That sounds odd to some people. They'd say it's a *white lie*. But presumably, they'd agree: it's okay to say. (You don't owe everyone an account of how your life is going, even if they ask how you are.) So we shouldn't get hung up on labels here. We can use the word *lie* in different ways. What matters is the moral point. In a justified suspended context, it's okay to say things you don't believe.

Back, then, to our question: What's the difference between lying and pretending? Before, we said that all lying is, in a sense, pretending. But lots of pretending takes place in justified suspended contexts. When you are playing with a kid, for instance—pretending to be superheroes or sorcerers—you suspend your expectation of sincerity, so that you can have the fun that comes with occupying imaginary worlds. That's what I wanted to start up with Hank when I told him there was a *Duobrachium sparksae* in my first-grade class.

The boys had long enjoyed the tall tales I'd tell. And they still tell tales of their own. But little by little, they're leaving those worlds behind. Which is, I think, the saddest part of watching them grow older.

• ⌒ •

I LEARNED THAT YOU shouldn't lie when I was three. My brother, Marc, was seven. My parents thought we were making too much noise, so they sent us outside. Marc wasn't willing to let them off that easy, though. He told me to stand at the front door and make as much noise as I could. That sounded fun. I screamed. I sang. I banged. And then my mother opened the door, and she screamed. We were summoned back inside.

"Marc told me to scream," I said as soon as I saw she was upset.

He blamed me, and then I understood why he didn't join in.

My memory of what happened next is hazy. We were interrogated in separate rooms. He stuck to his story for a while. But at some point, he snapped and acknowledged that he'd issued the order.

I don't recall what our punishment was, but I do recall that his was harsher than mine. And I remember the reason: *he lied*. (It was said in italics.) I wasn't sure why that mattered. But whatever he did wrong took the heat off me. So I made a mental note: don't do that.

But why not? That was never clearly explained. And philosophers aren't so clear on the answer either. At least, not the philosophers in my house.

"What's wrong with lying?" I asked Hank one night at dinner.

"You're not telling the truth."

"Right," I said. "But what's wrong with that?"

"You're lying," Hank said.

It seemed we were stuck in a circle.

"But what's wrong with that?"

"You're trying to make someone believe something that's not true."

That was progress. And it put Hank in league with lots of philosophers. Many think that lying is wrong because it's deceptive.

But wait a minute. What's wrong with that? A standard story runs like this. When you deceive someone, you're manipulating their mental states for your purposes. In doing so, you interfere with their ability to manifest their will in the world. It's an echo of the Kantian idea we encountered earlier: we should treat people as people, not as objects we can put to our own use.

That story is fine, so far as it goes. But it doesn't cover every case. As Shiffrin taught us, not all lies are deceptive. Her perjured witness didn't mean to mislead. But that doesn't let him off the hook. It's wrong to lie in court, whatever you intend. And that's not the only problem with the thought that lies are wrong because they're deceptive. Most people think that lying is worse than simply misleading someone. Indeed, people often avoid telling lies even as they dupe their audience.

Philosophers love to tell the story of Athanasius of Alexandria. He was set upon by people out to persecute or perhaps kill him. But they didn't realize who he was, so they asked: "Where is Athanasius?" He answered: "He is not far." And off they went to find him. We're supposed to think that Athanasius was clever. He misled his attackers without telling a lie! But what would be bad about lying to people who are looking to kill you? Why not say that Athanasius is days away, or that he's dead already?

"Just go ahead and lie," says Jennifer Saul. She's a philosopher of language. And she wrote a paper with that advice in the title. In it, she argues that lying isn't worse than merely misleading. She offers this example: Dave and Charla are about to have sex for the first time. Dave asks Charla whether she has AIDS. As it happens, Charla is HIV positive, and she knows that. But she also knows that she doesn't have AIDS yet. Not wanting to scare Dave off, she answers: "No, I don't have AIDS." Reassured, Dave agrees to have unprotected sex.

Charla didn't lie. She answered truthfully. But she did deceive Dave, in a pretty dreadful way. Of course, he could have been more careful in the way he phrased his question; there's a difference between HIV and AIDS. But Charla knew what he was getting at, and her answer was guaranteed to mislead. "It seems completely absurd," Saul says, "to suppose that Charla's deception was even a tiny bit better due to her avoidance of lying."

In Saul's view, lying is wrong because it's deceptive. And for the most part, the mode of deception doesn't matter. If you're going to deceive someone, Saul says, you might as well lie. If your deception is wrong, it won't be any worse for the fact that you said something false. And if your deception is justified—if you have good reasons for it—you won't have done anything wrong at all. Indeed, that's what she'd say about Athanasius. He didn't lie, but it would have been fine if he did.

I agree with that last bit. I don't think Athanasius owed his attackers the truth. But I'm not sold on the idea that lying is on a par with other forms of deception. For sure, a lie that aims to deceive is wrong so long as the deception is. But as Shiffrin has explained, lies are also wrong for another reason.

To see the reason, we have to take a step back—all the way to the Introduction, where we considered the shifted color spectrum. There, we worried about our lack of access to other people's minds. We don't have a direct connection to anyone else's mental states. And sometimes we need to know what they are. We could hardly live together, let alone work together, if we didn't have a way to find out what other people are thinking. Speech, Shiffrin says, is our best tool for overcoming the opacity of each other's minds. It helps us reach a deeper understanding than we ever could without it.

With that understanding, we can care for each other, learn from each other, and pursue joint projects and plans. Without it, we'd lead impoverished lives. So we have reasons to respect speech and preserve its capacity to render us intelligible to each other.

A lie is wrong, Shiffrin says, because it misrepresents the liar's mental states. In doing so, it undercuts the capacity of speech to do what only speech can do—help us to understand each other. Lying puts static on the channel, calling into question the reliability of future communication. If it became commonplace, Shiffrin says, we'd lose "reliable access to a crucial set of truths."

Shiffrin's explanation isn't exclusive. Lies can also be wrong for other reasons. They can be disrespectful. They can diminish trust. And they can deceive. In any given case, one of those other wrongs may overwhelm the one that Shiffrin highlights. Charla's deception exposed Dave to serious danger. That's already awful; a lie would hardly make it worse. But in many cases, misleading is a more modest wrong. (The boys have been known to obscure the amount of *Minecraft* they play.) And in those cases, there *is* something to be said for avoiding outright lies. It holds open the possibility of honest communication.

◦────◦

"HEY, GUYS, I've got a question for you. Someone wants to kill your friend, so you're hiding him in the attic."

"What's his name?" Hank asked.

"Jack," I said. "And then the guy who wants to kill him shows up and asks where he is."

"What's *his* name?" Hank asked.

"It doesn't matter."

"Let's call him Bob," Rex said.

"Okay. Bob wants to know where Jack is. What do you tell him?"

"Not here!" Rex said.

"So you're gonna lie?"

"That's not a lie."

"But he's in the attic."

"Yeah, but when I say he's not here, I mean he's not right here, where we're standing."

Apparently, we're raising the Athanasius of Ann Arbor. Two of them, actually.

"What would you say, Hank?"

"I'd say I saw him on the street earlier."

"Is that true?"

"Yeah, I saw him on the street when he came over, before he went up to the attic."

"Why not lie? You could say Jack left town."

"I don't think you need to lie," Rex said.

"Would it be okay to lie if it was helpful?"

"Yeah, I think so," said Rex. "I don't have to help Bob kill Jack."

Kant would have categorically rejected that suggestion. At least, according to the most common reading of his short essay "On a Supposed Right to Tell Lies from Benevolent Motives." In it, Kant considers the case I presented to my kids—a murderer at the door, asking where his intended victim is. And he seems to say that you may not lie, even to the murderer.

That's bonkers. No one thinks it's right, not even the most committed Kantians. And Kant probably didn't think it either. The story stems from an argument he had with the Swiss-French political theorist Benjamin Constant. Allen Wood, a leading Kant scholar, has traced the history, and he contends that both men were primarily interested in the "duty to speak truthfully . . . in *political contexts.*" Indeed, Wood thinks that Kant wasn't imagining just any old murderer at the door. He was picturing a police officer demanding information about the location of a suspect. Wood thinks that Constant disagreed with Kant in part because his experiences during the French Revolution left him leery about the line that separates the police from criminals.

Wood suggests that a better case for making Kant's point might have run like this. You're a witness at trial, under oath, and you're asked a question "the truthful answer to which will predictably result in the conviction of your friend . . . , whom you know to be innocent, on a charge of murder." That's an awful position to be in. But you have to tell the truth, Wood says, unless "the legal process is illegitimate, or a mere sham." Otherwise, you'd be the one "turning the process into a sham," by ensuring that it proceeds on the basis of a lie.

Kant might agree, but I'm not sure I do. I'm open to the idea that, in extreme cases, a lie might be justified; it depends how the details of the story get filled in. But set that aside. What should we make of the original case, the one that has attracted so much attention—and derision? Clearly, you can lie. And Shiffrin gave us the tools to explain why. You're in a justified suspended context. The murderer has no claim on your cooperation, since he's up to no good. As Rex said, you don't have to help Bob kill Jack.

⋅ —— ⋅

THE MURDERER AT THE DOOR gets more attention than he deserves. Few of us will confront him. And even Kant and Constant were primarily concerned with something else: "the duty of politicians and statesmen to be truthful."

Rex is interested in that too.

"I can't believe he lies so much," he said about Donald Trump, on several occasions. He liked to look at the list of lies that you'd see in the newspaper.

Of course, many politicians have a tenuous relationship with the truth. What was striking about Trump was his outright hostility to it. On his first day in office, he lied about the rain at his inauguration—and allowed his press secretary to lie about the size of the crowd. And the lies only grew from there. By the end of his term, he was insisting, against all evidence, that the election had been stolen, setting the stage for the storming of the Capitol by some of his supporters.

"Donald Trump is a bad president," Rex said one night at dinner, shortly after the insurrection.

"He's a bad president to us," Hank said. "But he's a good president to the people that like him."

"No, he's a bad president," Rex said.

"To us, he's bad," Hank insisted. "But he's good to the people that like him."

"Hank, do you mean that the people who like Donald Trump *think* he's good—but they're wrong?" I asked.

"No," he said, emphatically. "They think he's good, and we think he's bad, *and there's nothing in the middle that says who's right*."

"Doesn't someone have to be right?" I asked. "Either he's a good president or he's not."

"No," Hank said. "We're right to us, and they're right to them."

This is relativism—the idea that different people have different truths. And I was shocked to hear it in my house. It is not how I see the world—or talk to the boys about it.

And I wondered: Just how deep did Hank's relativism go? Many people are skeptical that there's a single truth about ethical issues—or evaluative judgments, like whether Donald Trump is a good president. Was that Hank's view? Or did his relativism run deeper?

"Hank," I said. "Suppose that we go outside and I say it's raining and you say it's not. Is one of us right?"

"I'm right to me," he said. "And you're right to you."

"But either drops are falling from the sky or they aren't," I said. "It's not up to us whether it's raining."

"They're falling for you but not for me," Hank said.

At first, I wasn't sure how serious Hank was. He likes to make mischief. For years, I couldn't tell whether he knew his ABCs. Each and every time I asked him to sing them, he'd get some letters out of order. I thought he was messing with me, since I used to mess with Rex that way. But he was so persistent—and so resistant to correction—that I started to wonder whether he knew the order was important.

Once he got to kindergarten, it was clear he was trolling me—and had been since he was three. In front of his teacher, he had clear command of the alphabet, and lots else we didn't know he knew.

So I'm suspicious of the guy—and always on the lookout for the little smile he gets when he's up to something. *This might be an epic troll*, I thought. *At eight, he's identified the idea that irks me most.* But over the course of the evening, it became clear that Hank really meant what he'd said. He'd thought it through and decided that each of us gets our own truth.

<hr>

WHY? THE KEY to his thinking was what he said to Rex: "They think he's good, and we think he's bad, *and there's nothing in the middle that says who's right.*"

As he said that last bit, Hank lined his hand up with his nose, and moved it up and down, to illustrate the idea that there was nothing in the middle. But what he really meant was that there's *nobody* in the middle—no neutral arbiter to settle the dispute.

Back in the chapter on rights, I told you that Hank likes to hear about the legal cases that I teach, and every time, he asks: "What did the judge decide?" He wants to know the right answer, and he thinks the judge settles the question. If there's no judge, there are just different answers for different people.

Many of my students are tempted by similar arguments—especially (but not only) the ones who were serious about sports. All their lives, referees have made calls: in or out, ball or strike, catch or not. And their decisions were final; they couldn't be appealed to anyone. What a ref says goes. If he says it was in, it was in. It sure seems like he has the power to make things true.

But no ref does, really. If anything, instant replay should have taught us that. In a tennis match, whether a ball was hit in or out depends on where it landed relative to the lines on the court, not on the call the umpire made. Ideally, the ump tracks the truth; he doesn't determine it.

It helps to remind people that you can play games without refs. We can go out and whack a tennis ball and decide for ourselves whether it's in or out. Much of the time, we'll agree. Sometimes we won't. We've got different points of view, and self-interest can shape the way we see things. That's a reason to have refs. But refs are just extra people, who can be right or wrong. Truth exists independently of them.

It's easy to get confused about that, because there *is* a sense in which what the ref says goes. If the ref in a football game says a player was offside, we carry on *as if* he was offside, whether or not he actually was. A ref has the power to determine what we will *treat as true* going forward. But there was a fact of the matter before the ref made the call, just as there would be if the game was played without refs. The absence of a neutral arbiter doesn't, in any way, imply the absence of truth.

<hr>

STILL, MANY PEOPLE are skeptical about the idea of objective truth. It's fashionable, in some circles, to say that truth is socially constructed. But as we learned in the chapter on race, the fact that our concepts are social constructions does not mean that the objects they pick out are. We get to decide what a planet is. But once we decide, Pluto's either in or out. And we could be mistaken about it, if we've misjudged the facts.

Hank aside, hardly anyone is a relativist about the rain. When it comes to the physical world, most of us are comfortable with the idea that there's truth full stop. If Hank insists it isn't raining in the midst of a downpour, I won't think he has his own truth. I'll think he's barking mad—or messing with me again.

But when it comes to evaluative judgments, Hank has many more friends. Was Donald Trump a good president? Is abortion wrong? Was Beethoven better than Bach? There are no right answers, some say. Just different strokes for different folks.

The people who say that don't reject truth entirely. Instead, they reject objective truth—truths that hold for all of us, no matter who we are. To rescue truth, they *relativize* it. There's no single answer to the question whether abortion is right or wrong, they say. But there *are* answers relative to different worldviews. For the feminist who prizes reproductive freedom, abortion is permissible. For the Catholic who follows the teaching of the church, abortion is off-limits. Which one of those worldviews is right? That's not a question you can ask, they say. The feminist has her truth; the Catholic has his.

This is a dark way to see the world—all of us sorted into separate camps. It's a world in which we can clash but not converse. On this picture, the feminist and the Catholic are, in an important sense, talking past each other. She's making claims relative to her worldview. He's making claims relative to his. They're each right, on their own moral framework. But according to the Hanks, there's nothing in the middle that makes one framework better than another. So there's little point in arguing about it. Any attempt to persuade can't really appeal to reason, since reasons too are relative to worldviews. (The feminist will be moved by different considerations than the Catholic. And there's nothing in the middle that says who's right.)

This way of thinking is more popular outside philosophy than in it. Indeed, most philosophers think thoroughgoing relativism (that is, relativism about absolutely everything) is incoherent. What sort of claim is *there is no objective truth* supposed to be? An objective claim, which holds true for all of us? If so, it's self-defeating. Or is it, instead, a subjective claim, true relative to the views of the person who asserts it? If so, it doesn't contradict the idea that there are objective truths. It just tells us something about the psychology of the person pushing the argument.

A more modest relativism wouldn't eat itself in that way. You can make sense of moral relativism. It's not self-defeating to say *there are no objective moral truths*. The question is whether that's true.

The standard argument starts with sensible observations. We diverge, sometimes wildly, in our moral views. That's true around here. But it's even starker if you look to distant places or the distant past. Moreover, the moral views that people hold are shaped, to a large extent, by the culture and community they grew up in. Had we been born in a different time and place, we would think differently about many moral questions. Indeed, some of our most deeply held moral beliefs weren't common in earlier ages. At many points in history, slavery was widely accepted. Now we think it abhorrent.

On top of that, many moral disagreements seem intractable. Think how long we've argued about abortion—and whether it should be legal. We're decades in—centuries, really—and people still march on both sides.

The relativist offers us an explanation—roughly Hank's. There's nothing in the middle that determines who's right. We've each got our own framework, none of them better than any other. But notice that comes at a cost. It means that there's no fact of the matter about whether slavery is wrong, except in relation to the moral views we happen to hold. So too with genocide. We could say to a Nazi, "We think you ought not kill Jews." But we couldn't give him a reason if he didn't accept our worldview. We'd have to concede: he has his own truth, just like us. What started off sensible now seems absurd.

So maybe we drew the wrong conclusion from the observations we started with. That's what Ronald Dworkin thought. He liked to point out that disagreement does not imply indeterminacy. Indeed, it suggests the opposite. If we're arguing about whether abortion is wrong, it's almost certainly because we think that there's a right answer—and that it matters. We may not reach agreement. But agreement doesn't establish truth. And disagreement doesn't imply its absence.

It's true: we might think differently had we been born in a different time or place. But it's not just our moral views that would have been different. Our scientific views have been different too. In an earlier era, we would have been sure the sun circles the earth. Now we know that the earth circles the sun. The fact that we once thought differently doesn't cast doubt on that judgment. We can explain where we went wrong and why the view we hold now is better supported. So too, I should think, with slavery.

The contingency of our moral views doesn't call their truth into question. Instead, it suggests that we should have some humility about them. We should wonder whether we're wrong. We should talk to people who think differently. And we should be open to revising our views in light of what we learn. But we shouldn't give up on the idea of truth or the search for it.

What exactly are we searching for, though? What makes moral truth? That is one of the trickiest questions in all philosophy. As Dworkin observed, no one thinks that "the universe houses, among its numerous particles of energy or matter, some special particles—morons—whose energy and momentum establish fields that . . . constitute the morality or immorality, or virtue or vice, of particular human acts or institutions." But if morons don't make morality, what does? I can't do justice to the debates about that here. But I can give you a window into the way I think about the problem. It's much like the way Dworkin did.

To my thinking, moral truth rests on the reasons we offer in support of moral claims. As Dworkin pointed out, if you ask a person why she thinks abortion is wrong, she won't tell you that its wrongness is woven into the fabric of the universe. Instead, she'll give you reasons. She might say that God forbids it. Or that it's disrespectful of the dignity inherent in human life. Or that it's wrong to kill the innocent. Once she's offered her reasons, we can ask: Are they any good? Are there any she's overlooked? Did she reason through the problem well? Ideally, we'd do that with her. That is, we'd reason together.

Now imagine that we're in the midst of that conversation when a skeptic intervenes. "You're wasting your words," he'd tell us. "Reasons aren't real." We'd ask why he thinks so. He'd give us his . . . reasons. And then we could ask: Are they any good? Are there any he's overlooked? Did he reason through the problem well?

There's no escaping reason. As Dworkin once said, "We can do no better for any claim, including the most sophisticated skeptical argument or thesis, than to see whether, after the best thought we find appropriate, we think it so." If we do, we'd best believe it—unless and until we see reason to think otherwise.

⁓

HANK'S RELATIVISM DIDN'T LAST LONG. I broke him at bedtime.

Some nights, instead of reading, we have what he calls a man-to-man chat. Mostly they are silly. Sometimes they are serious. That night, we were continuing the conversation about relativism. I was trying to argue Hank out of it, with little success. But I had a secret weapon, which I'd held back all night.

I turned out the light. I sang his lullaby. And as I was about to leave his room, I said, "Good night, Hank. You're the sweetest six-year-old I know."

"I'm not six," he said. "I'm eight."

"Oh?" I said. "To you, maybe. But to me, you're six."

"I'm eight," he said, getting agitated.

"That's not true for me," I said. "You're six, so far as I'm concerned."

"I'm eight," he said, sharply. "*Some things are just true.*"

⁓

AMEN TO THAT. But why do we have so much trouble agreeing on the truth? C. Thi Nguyen thinks a lot about that. He was a food writer for the *L.A. Times*, which is more or less my dream gig. (Note to food editors everywhere: Rex and I are available for taco truck reviews. Hank is all in for sushi.) Nguyen left food behind for philosophy, though. He writes about trust, games, and the ways that communities work.

The key to Nguyen's thinking is a distinction he draws between *epistemic bubbles* and *echo chambers*. An epistemic bubble, he says, is *"an informational network from which relevant voices have been excluded by omission."* Increasingly, we live in such bubbles. We've sorted ourselves geographically, so we're surrounded by people who are like-minded. Our social media feeds are populated by friends who share similar views. And algorithms tailor the internet to our preferences.

Epistemic bubbles are bad. They screen out information that contradicts our views, leaving us overconfident. They convince us that everyone thinks the way we do, even when that's far from true. And they can even hide entire issues from us. But for all that, Nguyen isn't worked up about epistemic bubbles. They are "easily shattered," he says; to pop one, all you have to do is expose people "to the information and arguments that they've missed."

Nguyen worries much more about *echo chambers*. The phrases sound similar. But there's an important difference. An echo chamber is *"a social structure from which other relevant voices have been actively discredited."* The problem with an echo chamber is not that it leaves information out; it's that reliable sources of information have been undermined.

Nguyen offers Rush Limbaugh as an example of someone who actively worked to create an echo chamber. For decades, Limbaugh hosted a popular radio show, which he used to advance his conservative views. His listeners had access to outside information. Many consumed other forms of media, so they weren't in an epistemic bubble. But Limbaugh taught his listeners not to trust anyone who disagreed with him. He painted a picture in which his opponents were out to get him and his audience. And he questioned their integrity, so they'd be seen as malicious, not just mistaken. Limbaugh is gone, but the right-wing echo chamber he helped create isn't. Indeed, it's dramatically expanded, spurred on by cable news and social media. The distrust that Limbaugh and his like sowed set the stage for the storming of the Capitol; a large set of people were ready to believe any lie they were told, so long as it came from the right side.

There are echo chambers on the left too (though none with near the reach that Limbaugh had). In her book *Nice Racism: How Progressive White People Perpetuate Racial Harm*, Robin DiAngelo offers up a list of actions and attitudes that are racist. Some of the items on the list are clear-cut cases—wearing blackface, for instance, or refusing to learn the proper pronunciation of people's names. Others aren't as obvious. There's room for doubt, for instance, that it's racist to include neurodiversity in your organization's "diversity work." (It's not a zero-sum game, after all; you can root out racism and make a workplace hospitable to people wired up in different ways.) But DiAngelo doesn't want to hear any doubts about the entries on her list. Indeed, she says it's racist to have them. The last item on her list is: "not understanding why something on this list is problematic." In saying that, DiAngelo is attempting to insulate her views from criticism—to discredit any dissent in advance, regardless of the reason for it. That's a good way to get an echo chamber going.

Our politics would, for sure, be in better shape if we had fewer echo chambers. But as Nguyen points out, not all echo chambers are political. The anti-vaccination community is an echo chamber. It teaches people to see conspiracies where there are none, undermining trust in doctors and scientists. There are also echo chambers related to diets, exercise, and multilevel marketing schemes. Nguyen says you can identify them with a simple question: "Does a community's belief system actively undermine the trustworthiness of any outsiders who don't subscribe to its central dogmas? Then it's probably an echo chamber."

Echo chambers are more resilient than epistemic bubbles. You can't just expose people to outside information, since they'll see it through the lens the echo chamber supplies. That said, there are ways out. People can free themselves from echo chambers, Nguyen says, if they take on something like Descartes's project: radical doubt. They need to suspend the beliefs they acquired in the echo chamber and build back up.

But Descartes's method doesn't work, Nguyen says. If you insist on certainty, you won't have anything to build on at all. Nguyen suggests a reboot of your epistemic operating system, in which you start by trusting your senses and trusting others, equally and openly. You expose yourself to the world, taking in lots of sources of information, without automatically assuming that any of it's untrustworthy. Eventually you'll have to decide what sources of information to trust. But if you encounter it all with an open mind, he suggests, you're more likely to trust what's trustworthy.

<hr />

NGUYEN AFFECTED THE WAY I think about parenting. Families are epistemic bubbles, at least for little kids. At first, kids get almost all their information from their parents and, perhaps, siblings. It's important to make sure kids get good information. But also: it's important not to create an echo chamber by teaching kids not to trust sources of information with which you might disagree.

There's a balance to be struck here. I want my kids to know that not everyone is trustworthy. I want them to be on the lookout for people that aren't. And I want them to know what sources of information I trust. But most of all: I want them to be able to assess sources of information for themselves.

Last chapter, I told you that I encourage Rex to question questioners: Does this person really want to understand things? Are they interested in the evidence? If they learn their view is false, do I trust them to tell me? Or do I think they'll obscure that? Those questions work just as well for evaluating news sources. And to those, we could add others: Are these trained journalists? Do they consult experts? Do they publish corrections? Are they trying to outrage me? Or inform me?

Rex has already left our epistemic bubble. He wanders the internet on his own. Hank is soon to follow. We hope that we've inoculated them against echo chambers by teaching them to be open-minded—and giving them the tools to think critically about whom to trust.

• ◦———◦ •

THE FACT THAT FAMILIES are epistemic bubbles is key to sustaining the magical beliefs of childhood. So long as you control information, Santa doesn't sound so implausible. It's when kids encounter kids who know—or have doubts—that they start to have doubts themselves.

We weren't into Santa. But we did feel obligated to sustain belief in him. We didn't want the boys to ruin Christmas for their friends. That led to many comical conversations in which Rex suggested schemes to get Santa to come to our house. He didn't succeed, but the tooth fairy did drop by. And the boys loved her. They looked forward to the note she wrote—and the dollar coin too. Rex and I once spent a ride home trying to figure out what the tooth fairy does with teeth. He suggested that they're a form of currency in fairyland. I tried to explain that a society of magical creatures would want to control its money supply. Mining for teeth is just like mining for gold: it's no way to run an advanced economy.

Hank started to have doubts about the tooth fairy well before he lost his first tooth. A friend told him the tooth fairy wasn't real—that mommies and daddies were doing the job. (See how easily epistemic bubbles are popped.) We didn't want Hank to miss out. So we lied. Indeed, we created a bit of an echo chamber.

"I don't know why he'd say that, Hank. I think he's confused. The tooth fairy visits Rex, and she visited Mommy and Daddy too."

That got us through a half-dozen teeth before doubts resurfaced. But looking back, I wonder: Was it okay to lie like that? Hank asked a direct question, and we didn't tell him the truth.

Perhaps we were in a suspended context. Earlier I suggested that pretending puts you in one. But in most cases, kids know that you're pretending. Here, we were actively trying to obscure that fact from Hank. We were playing with him in an entirely different sense. And maybe we shouldn't have been. Shiffrin suggests that you're not in a justified suspended context unless everyone knows that the presumption of truthfulness has been suspended—or can figure it out.

I think she's wrong about that, though. And not just in relation to kids. You're not lying when you lure someone to a surprise birthday party. Sure, you might say something that's not true—that you're going out for a quiet dinner, or need to rush home because there's an emergency. But within limits, we've all got a little leeway to tell untruths as a way of surprising or delighting someone. And that's what we were trying to do for Hank. We wanted him to enjoy the fantasy, at least for a little bit. So I don't think we lied to him, at least not in a morally significant sense.

⋅────∿────⋅

WEAVING FANTASY WORLDS for Hank is one of my favorite pastimes. Once I told him that Kirby Smart, the coach of the University of Georgia football team, wanted him to play in the next game.

"What position?" Hank asked.

"Running back," I said. "He thinks you'll be able to run through people's legs."

"I could also ride on someone's back," Hank said.

"Good idea. No one will see you there."

"Or I could stand on the quarterback's shoulders and throw."

"Be careful up there," I said. "Sounds dangerous."

That went on for a while. But Hank must have known it wasn't real. He was six, and he'd seen lots of football.

So I was surprised when he said: "This is just pretend, right?"

"What do you think?"

"Tell me," he said.

"Hank, you know."

"*Tell me*," he said.

So I did. And for years, I had to do that almost every time we pretended. At some point, Hank would say, "This is just pretend, right?" And if I didn't reassure him right away, he'd get frustrated, pleading for me to tell him what he already knew.

Shiffrin helped me understand Hank. We accept insincerity in justified suspended contexts. But Shiffrin notes that we need ways to exit those contexts—to lift the suspension and return to the assumption that everyone is being honest.

Suppose your friend asks whether you like her outfit. She might want your honest opinion. Or she might be seeking reassurance. If you know her well, you'll probably know which she wants. And if the answer is reassurance, you're in a justified suspended context. You can say, "Looks great!" even if you don't think so.

But suppose your friend follows up with: "No, really. Tell me what you think. I want to know." Then your answer should be honest. She's ended the suspended context.

Shiffrin thinks it's bad to lie. But she thinks it much worse to lie after assuring someone that you're telling the truth. She draws an analogy with the way the white flag is used in war. It signals surrender, or a cease-fire, and an invitation to negotiation. It's a war crime to abuse the white flag—to pretend to surrender for purposes of surprise or sabotage. Why? "Even when we are at each other's throats," Shiffrin says, "we must preserve an exit through which we can negotiate an end to conflict."

Of course, war is a different sort of suspended context. But Shiffrin's analogy helped me see what Hank was really after—he wanted to know that he had a way out. He loves to pretend. But he needs to know that we'll tell him the truth when he asks for it. He needs to know that his white flag will work.

One night at bedtime, Hank drove that point home—and ratified the choice we'd made about the tooth fairy. Julie was tucking him in, and he was talking about the tooth he'd lost that day.

Suddenly, he got serious. "Before I'm a daddy," he asked, "will you tell me if the tooth fairy is real?"

"Yes," Julie said. "I'll tell you before you're a daddy."

"Okay," Hank said. "If I'm supposed to do something, I want to know, so I don't mess it up." Then he went to sleep without asking whether the tooth fairy was real.

Hank wanted to know that he could know. But he didn't want to know—yet.

10

MIND

What is it like to be Bailey? We spend a lot of time talking about that in our house. Bailey, you might recall, is our mini goldendoodle.

Rex loves to narrate her life. But he doesn't do it like a sportscaster. It's not: "Bailey, hot in pursuit of Sammy Squirrel . . . will she get him . . . closer than ever. . . . No! A near miss for the millionth time."

Rather, he talks as if he's Bailey: "Ooh, a squirrel. Gonna get it. Go fast! Ooh, another squirrel . . . the chase is *on*. . . . Or maybe I'll just rest."

The bit is funny because we can be sure that Bailey doesn't have an inner monologue like that. She recognizes a few words, but just a few. It's also funny because it imagines that Bailey has human thoughts and motivations, when we can be sure her inner life is rather different. Why? She greets dogs by sniffing their butts. She eats rabbit poop. (She got a parasite from it.) And she barks at balloons, for no apparent reason.

Sometimes we can tell what Bailey's thinking. We know when she's hungry, needs to pee, or wants to play. We know that she doesn't like baths. She loves Julie and the boys. She's less sold on me, and that shows good judgment.

But we've got little idea what it's like to be Bailey. Even just perceptually, she must experience the world much differently than we do. She gathers lots of information through her nose—way more than we sniff out. Scientists think that a dog's nose is ten thousand to one hundred thousand times more acute than a human's. The part of a dog's brain dedicated to smell is (proportionally) about forty times larger than the similar bit of a human brain. And dogs have an organ we don't, dedicated to the detection of pheromones.

What would it be like to live with such a rich sense of smell? I can guess, but I don't have a good idea. If I could pop into Bailey's head— and perceive the world as she does—I'd bet I'd be surprised by how different things seemed. But even then, I wouldn't know what it's like to be Bailey. For that, I'd need more than doggy perceptions. I'd need doggy beliefs, doggy desires, and so on.

I asked Hank once. "What's it like to be Bailey?"

"It's pretty different," he said.

"How so?"

"She has different rules."

We weren't on the same wavelength yet. But I was curious. "What do you mean?"

"She has to pee outside. I don't. And I get to eat chocolate. She doesn't."

"Do you think she experiences the world differently than we do?"

"Yeah," Hank said. "She can't see all the colors we can."

That's true. Dogs see mostly blues, yellows, and grays.

"What do you think is going on in her head right now?"

Bailey was staring at us blankly while she gnawed on a toy.

"I don't know," Hank said. "You should ask her."

I did. She turned in my direction but didn't deign to respond.

Bailey is a key member of our family. But for the most part, her mind is a mystery.

THE BOYS' MINDS HAVE long been mysteries to us too. Less so now that they talk, since they sometimes share their thoughts. But when they were babies, they were even bigger mysteries than Bailey. She moves, so you often have an idea what she's thinking about. But babies just lie about, watching the world go by.

My mother was obsessed with the mystery of their minds. When they were new, her constant query was: "What is going on in his head?"

"He wants to know when you're going to stop asking," I'd say.

But of course, I had that question too. I think everyone who spends time with infants does. They gaze at the world so intently. But their thoughts are completely obscure to us.

Well, not *completely* obscure. Psychologists study the way that babies' minds work. But that's not an easy task, since they can't tell us. So psychologists watch them, as intently as the babies watch the world. They track where they look and how long they stay locked in. When they are a bit older, they give them games to play, so they can see what sort of cognitive abilities young kids have.

As limited as those methods are, they've revealed a lot. If you take a developmental psych course, you'll learn about how babies direct their attention, how their memory works, and how they work out what causes what. But you won't learn what it's like to *be* a baby—or even a toddler. No one knows. They're at least as foreign to us as dogs are, maybe more so.

It's tempting to think that little kids' minds are the same as adults', just less sophisticated. But that's not right. As Alison Gopnik, a leading developmental psychologist, explains:

> Children aren't just defective adults, primitive grown-ups gradually attaining perfection and complexity. . . . They have very different, though equally complex and powerful, minds, brains, and forms of consciousness, designed to serve differ-

ent evolutionary functions. Human development is more like
a metamorphosis, like caterpillars becoming butterflies, than
like simple growth—though it may seem like children are the
vibrant wandering butterflies who transform into caterpillars
inching along the grown-up path.

Kids' minds are capable of astounding feats that grown-up minds can't
match. Just watch a kid learn language, and you'll wish, wistfully, that you
still had the same skill.

And it's not just skills that set kids apart. Their imaginations are more
lively. They're constantly creating worlds. We're not like that any longer.
We have to work, which leaves little time for pretend and play. But it's not
just work that gets in the way. Our brains work differently. We're locked
in this world. We can imagine others, but we don't take the same joy in
taking them up.

When the boys were little and I'd play their pretend games, I'd mar-
vel at the pleasure they took in them. And I wished I could capture it
too. Sometimes I had fun—but it was mostly delight at their delight.
And often I was bored out of my mind, wishing the game would end so
I could get on with some sensible task.

I'm supposed to feel guilty about that.

"You'll miss these days," people say.

That's true. I miss my boys already. And I tell them that.

"How can you miss me?" Hank asks. "I'm still here."

"You're here," I say. "But the boy you were a minute ago just left, and
he won't come back."

But as much as I miss the boys, I also miss myself. I was a crazy kid
once, creating my own worlds, and I can't get that back. I can't even recall what it was like, except in bits and pieces. When you spend time
with little kids, you can't help but wish to see the world their way, to lose
yourself in play.

Even the scientists that know the most about kids share that same wish. John Flavell, another top developmental psychologist, told Gopnik that "he would trade all his degrees and honors for the chance to spend just five minutes inside the head of a young child—to genuinely experience the world as a two-year-old once more."

I love that image: an eminent scientist emigrating to the mind of a child, trying to recapture what we all once had. It shows how little we know about what it's like to be a little person. For all Gopnik, Flavell, and others have discovered about how babies' minds work, their inner lives are shrouded in secrecy. We were all babies once, but none of us knows what it's like to be a baby.

THE QUESTIONS WE'VE BEEN ASKING—What is it like to be Bailey? What is it like to be a baby?—are reminiscent of the title of one of the most famous papers in twentieth-century philosophy, Thomas Nagel's "What Is It Like to Be a Bat?"

Nagel has extraordinary range as a philosopher. He's written about altruism, objectivity, the nature of reasons, and . . . tax policy. But he's best known for asking what it's like to be a bat. It's an interesting question, because bats can do things we can't. They fly. And echolocate. Which is the bit that attracted Nagel's attention. Bats emit high-pitched shrieks, and they use the echoes to gather information about their surroundings. That sonar sense allows a bat to "make precise discriminations of distance, size, shape, motion, and texture comparable to those we make by vision."

What is it like to be a bat? We don't know. And it's not clear how we could find out. Nagel explains:

> It will not help to try to imagine that one has webbing on one's arms, which enables one to fly around at dusk and dawn catching insects in one's mouth; that one has very poor vision and perceives the surrounding world by a system of reflected

high-frequency sound signals; and that one spends the day
hanging upside down by one's feet in the attic.

Doing all that, Nagel says, would (at best) give him some insight into
what it would be like for a person to live as a bat does. But that's not
what he wants to know. He's curious "what it is like for a *bat* to be a bat."
And he doesn't see a way to figure that out, since he's limited to the
resources of his own mind.

Some philosophers think that Nagel is too pessimistic, in part because
some people *can* echolocate. The most famous might be Daniel Kish,
who's known as the real-life Batman. Kish is blind; he lost his vision at
thirteen months. But soon he started to click, and like a bat, he uses sonar
to gather information about his surroundings. He does it so well he can ride
a bike. Indeed, he says he can see. And scans of Kish's brain suggest that
the parts that process visual information are indeed active, making it plausible that his echolocation generates an experience something like sight.

So could Kish just *tell* us what it's like to be a bat? No, Nagel would
say. People who can echolocate might have a partial understanding of
what it's like to be a bat. They share more in common with bats than the
rest of us, so they're in a better position to take up a bat's perspective.
But they can't take it up completely. What Kish knows is what it's like
to be a human who can do something a bat can do. But he doesn't know
what it's like to be a bat doing it, any more than we know what it's like
to be a toddler doing things that we too can do.

The problem we're hitting here is the same one I discovered in kindergarten, when I realized that I didn't know what red looked like to my
mother. To put the point in the present idiom, I wanted to know what it
was like to be her, looking at something red. And I realized I had no way
to find out.

So what? you might wonder. There's lots we don't know about the
world. Why get worked up over the fact that we don't know what red
looks like to other people? We don't know whether there's life on other

planets, whether cold fusion is possible, or why people care about the Kardashians. The world is a perplexing place.

That's true. But we *could* know those other things if we had the time and resources to investigate. The fact that I don't know what red looks like to my mother stems from different—and seemingly insurmountable—problems. It's not clear that time or money would help. And neither will asking her, even though she knows. My mother can't tell me what red looks like to her, since we don't have words to describe the redness of red. In philosopher-speak, the experience is *ineffable*. And it's also *private*. Her experiences are hers; I can't get a glimpse of them.

We each have our own perspective on the world, and we cannot access anyone else's. It's not an accident that we can't pop into each other's heads. Indeed, when you think about it, the idea doesn't make sense. To experience the world as a toddler does, you'd have to *be* a toddler, while somehow staying yourself at the same time. But if you stay yourself, you can't be a toddler. You can't have experiences that aren't your own.

We shouldn't overestimate the problem. We are good at reading each other's minds. I can tell when Hank is happy or sad. I can tell when he's hungry or mad. He wears his feelings on his face:

And I recognize them, in part because I have similar emotions, which I express in similar ways. When mental states manifest in behavior, we're decent at detecting them.

But we make mistakes. And not all mental states get manifested. So we shouldn't underestimate the problem either. Indeed, our inability to access each other's minds affects the way we relate to one another, profoundly. It gives me a bit of privacy. I can keep my thoughts to myself. And it lets people surprise me, since I don't always know what they're thinking. That's good, for the most part. But there are downsides too. The fact that we can't feel each other's feels makes it easy to ignore others' pain.

$$\sim$$

OF COURSE, that assumes that other people have pain. And maybe we shouldn't assume that. All along, we've taken it for granted that there is something it's like to be a baby, a Bailey, a bat—or even just someone else. That is, we've taken it for granted that other creatures have inner lives. But why be so sure? I know that I am conscious. That is, I know that there's something it's like to be me. In fact, I know that more intimately than I know anything else. But why should I think that you're conscious too—that there's something it's like to be you?

Maybe Descartes's demon has filled my world with creatures that look to be thinking, feeling things but don't experience the world at all. Or maybe I'm the main character in a computer simulation, the only one the programmers endowed with a mind. Perhaps everyone else I encounter is an empty thing—just an appearance, like characters in a video game. (Notice that you've never wondered what it's like to *be* Mario, on an endless quest to save Princess Peach. Or Pac-Man, eating the same meal over and over again.)

When philosophers entertain worries like this, they think about zombies. But not the sorts of zombies that are part of pop culture. In philosophy, zombies don't want to eat your brain. They're disturbing in an entirely different way.

What's a philosophical zombie? The easiest way to get a grip on the idea is to think about my Zombie Twin. He's just like me, in every respect save one. He's the same height, same weight, same age—indeed, he's an exact duplicate, down to the last fundamental particle (electrons, quarks, etc.). And he acts just the way I do. He moves the same way, talks the same way, and even says the exact same things at exactly the same times. He's writing a book, which is word-for-word this one. He's my double, with just one difference: he's not conscious.

It's important to pin down what we mean by that, since consciousness is a slippery concept. Sometimes when we say someone is conscious, we mean that they are aware of the world around them. You're conscious in this sense when you're awake, not asleep or in a coma. And my Zombie Twin *is* conscious in this sense, at least much of the time. When he's awake, he's aware of what's happening around him, and he can respond to it; indeed, he responds exactly the way I would.

How's he different? He lacks what philosophers call *phenomenal consciousness*. He's all behavior, no experience. Think for a minute about what it's like to eat a taco—the medley of flavors in your mouth. Or what it's like to listen to Bach or Bachman-Turner Overdrive. Or feel the breeze in your hair. My Zombie Twin has none of those experiences. He acts like he does, since he acts like I do in all circumstances. But he's empty inside. Inputs yield outputs, just as they do with a calculator or computer. But there's no experience—no inner life—associated with any of it, not for him. He's dark inside.

So here's the question: I know that I'm not a zombie, since I know I experience the world.* But why should I think that anyone else does? I can't access anyone else's experiences, so I can't distinguish between a

---

*Of course, my Zombie Twin would say just the same.

world in which other people have inner lives and a world in which they don't. Everyone around me could be a zombie, and I'd have no way of knowing.

This is a skeptical hypothesis, similar to the ones we encountered when we thought about knowledge. And I think we put them in their proper place there. It's interesting to note that there's a possibility that I can't rule out, given my perspective on the world. But I'll carry on as if other people are conscious. Indeed, I'll believe it. With good reason.

As I said, I know that I'm conscious. To doubt that other people are requires me to think that I'm special. In a really astounding way. Why should *I* be the only person who experiences anything? I'm just some schmuck who was born in suburban Atlanta in 1976. The idea that the world exists for me, and just me, to enjoy is something I haven't thought since high school. It could be true. But it's hard to see how. And I shouldn't take the idea seriously, given what it says about you.

So no, I don't think you're a zombie. But the mere possibility that you might be presents a Hard Problem.

The problem is not deciding whether you're conscious. The problem is figuring out why. Why do we have inner lives? Why is there something it's like to be you? Or me? Or a baby, a bat, or Bailey? Why are any of us conscious? Why aren't we all zombies?

I asked Hank once, in a roundabout way. He was eight.

"Can you play a middle C on the piano?"

"Of course," he said. He'd been taking lessons for years.

He walked over and struck the key.

"How does it make that sound that we hear?" I asked.

Hank explained the way pianos work: the key moves the hammer, which hits a string, and the string vibrates to make the sound.

"Yeah," I said, "but how does *that* make something happen inside your head?"

"Mmmm . . . sound waves?"

"What are sound waves?"

"Wavy things," Hank said with a smile.

So I explained. "When the string vibrates, it bumps into some air molecules, which bump into some others, which bump into some others, and that keeps happening until the air molecules in your ear are getting bumped."

"Then they bump my eardrum," Hank said.

"Yeah. And that gets the nerves in your ear excited, and they send a signal to your brain."

"That makes sense," Hank said.

"Yeah, now here's my question: When your brain gets that signal, why do you experience it as the sound you hear?"

"I don't know," Hank said, with a shrug. "I'm not an expert or anything."

That's true. But as it happens, Hank knows the answer to this question as well as anyone, since *no one knows the answer.*

The point was made most vividly by Thomas Henry Huxley, a biologist who lived more than a hundred years ago. "How it is," he wrote, "that anything so remarkable as a state of consciousness comes about as the result of irritating nervous tissue, is just as unaccountable as the appearance of Djin when Aladdin rubbed his lamp in the story."

Let's pin down the mystery a bit more precisely. The signals carried from Hank's ear to his brain are processed in several different places, which have several different jobs. One part of the brain decodes the duration, intensity, and frequency of the sound. Another identifies its location. Still others sort the significance of the sounds—are they sirens or songs, wails or words? Scientists know a lot about how all that happens, and they're constantly learning more. What they don't know is why, when that happens, you experience the sound. That is, they don't know why there is something it's like to hear a middle C. They don't know why we aren't silent inside.

David Chalmers (who helped us think about the simulation hypothesis) calls this the Hard Problem of consciousness. He means to mark it off from other problems that are, in comparison, easy to solve (though we don't know all the answers yet). The easy problems relate to the way the brain processes information—identifies it, integrates it with other information, stores it, makes it available for further use, and so on. Those are the sorts of processes that neuroscientists study, and there's every reason to think that, as they continue to study them, they'll come to understand them. Indeed, they understand a great deal already.

The Hard Problem is figuring out why all that information processing has a sensation attached to it. Some system in my brain cannot only detect sound waves with a frequency of 262 Hz, but broadcast the fact that such waves have been detected to other parts of my brain so they can use that information too. But why does all that give me the sensation I get when I hear middle C? Why does it give me any sensation at all?

* ———— *

PHILOSOPHERS HAVE BEEN THINKING about the mind for a long time. Descartes believed that the mind and body were separate substances. (This is called *dualism*.) He could imagine a mind without a body—and a body without a mind—so they must be different sorts of things. The mind, he said, is a thing that thinks. The body is a thing that extends in space. They're related to each other, of course. But the question how turned out to be tricky. Descartes said the mind is not *in* the body, in the way that a sailor is in a ship. Rather, it's intermingled with the body so that they form a single unit. Descartes believed that the interaction happened in the pineal gland, a small structure that sits in the middle of your brain.

That is anatomically absurd. Now we know that the main function of the pineal gland is to make melatonin. But philosophers saw reasons to reject Descartes's view long before scientists discovered that. One of his earliest critics was a princess—Elisabeth of Bohemia, with whom he traded letters. Elisabeth pressed Descartes to explain how an immaterial substance, like the mind, could influence a material one, like the body. She doubted that he could.

To put Elisabeth's point in more modern terms, the body is physical, and so far as we can tell, the physical world is *causally closed*. Every physical event has a physical cause. That doesn't leave any space for a nonphysical mind to influence what a physical body does.

We can capture the critique with a question: Just what did Descartes imagine happened in the pineal gland? How did the ghost in the machine make the machine move?

Nowadays, nearly no one is a Cartesian dualist. The dominant view is the opposite. It holds that there's only one sort of stuff—roughly the stuff studied by physics—and everything in the world either is that stuff or is built up out of it. In short, on this view (commonly called *materialism*), the mind is the brain. And mental states (beliefs, desires, sensations) are brain states.*

This view has many virtues. It's science friendly, since it doesn't posit a ghost in the machine. To learn about the mind, all we have to do is study the brain. Moreover, we can clearly see that there are many connections between the mind and the brain. Damage to the brain often affects the mind. Many mental illnesses are rooted in the biology of the brain. And we're constantly learning about the ways brains do the things that minds do, like store memories.

That said, not everyone signs on to the materialist idea that the mind is the brain. To see why, we can get help from Rex . . . and a philosopher named Frank Jackson. Jackson is a leading philosopher of mind. And he's the author of one of the most influential stories in contemporary philosophy.

---

*Alternatively, some say mental states are the functions of brain states. The distinction is meant to hold open the possibility that creatures that are constituted differently than us—say, robots whose CPUs are made from silicon—could have the same sorts of mental states we do, like pain. This is probably the more plausible materialist view. But the one in the text is simpler, so I'll stick with that.

One night, I told the story to Rex.

"There's a scientist named Mary," I started, "and she lives in a room that's completely black and white. Those are the only colors in the room."

"Why?" Rex asked.

"Because Mary's the subject of an experiment. The people who put her in the room don't want her to see any colors other than black and white."

"What's she wearing?" Rex asked.

"Only black and white clothes. And they cover every bit of her skin. Also, there are no mirrors in the room, so she can't see herself."

"That's a really weird experiment," Rex said.

"Yeah, and it gets weirder. Because Mary studies colors and the way we perceive them. And it's really far in the future, so scientists know absolutely everything about colors and what happens in our brains when we see them. Mary has learned it all too—from her black-and-white books and her black-and-white television. She just hasn't seen any colors besides black and white."

"Okay," Rex said.

"Then one day, they decide it's time for Mary to see something red. So they give her an apple."

"She must think that's cool," Rex said, anticipating Jackson's point.

"Why?"

"Because she gets to find out what red looks like."

"Are you sure she didn't know before? Remember, I said Mary already knows absolutely everything that happens in a person's brain when she sees something red."

"Yeah," Rex said, "but she doesn't know what red *looks* like. She'd have to see it herself to know that."*

_____

*An aside about Mary: It takes a lot of work to set that thought experiment up, and

IF REX IS RIGHT, materialism is false. Mary knew all the physical facts—what the neurons in her brain would do when she saw something red. But still, she didn't know what it's like to see something red. That means there are facts that are not physical—for instance, what it's like to see red. Moreover, it means that there's more to the mind than the brain, because it turns out that you can know everything there is to know about the brain and still not know everything about the mind.

Is Rex right? Before we take that up, let me give you two more arguments against materialism.

First up is the argument I offered my mom when I said that I didn't know what red looked like to her. We can imagine two versions of my mother. They're physically the same in every respect. One experiences red the way I do. But the other experiences red the way I experience blue. If it's possible that both versions of my mother could exist—in some world, if not this one—then materialism is false, since the physical facts about her brain don't fully determine what she experiences.

For the second argument, imagine a third version of my mother. This one is physically identical to the first two. But she doesn't experience anything at all. She's a zombie. Again, if it's possible that this version could exist—in some world, if not this one—then materialism is false,

---

it's wholly implausible. You've got to shrink-wrap Mary in black and white, prevent her from seeing herself, and hope that she doesn't have any stray color experiences when she closes her eyes. For that reason, I think it better to imagine that Mary is an expert in human sexuality. She knows absolutely everything there is to know about our physical response to sexual stimulation. It just so happens that, for religious reasons, she's never had an orgasm herself. Then one day, she does. Does she learn anything? I think so. She learns what it's like to have an orgasm. Indeed, it's easy to imagine her being surprised by that experience—delighted (or disappointed) to discover the sensations that accompany the neural activity she's studied.

and for just the same reason. The physical facts about my mother's brain do not settle what she experiences.

A simple way to see the point is to ask: How much work does God have to do to create the world? (Assume, for the moment, that there is a God. We'll get back to that.) On the materialist picture, God is finished once he creates the physical world, since that's all that exists. The mind comes free, since the mind just is the brain. In contrast, the arguments we've been considering suggest that God still has work to do after he creates the physical facts. He has to decide whether any creatures should be conscious, and if so, what sorts of experiences they should have.

These arguments—and others like them—tug some philosophers back toward dualism. In recent years, David Chalmers has done more than anyone to reignite interest in it. But he doesn't embrace Cartesian dualism. He doesn't think there's a ghost in the machine. Rather, Chalmers suggests that the mind and the brain may be two different aspects of some deeper, more fundamental reality, which is neither physical nor phenomenal. He thinks that *information* might be the basic building block of the world, manifesting as both matter and mind. Indeed, he suggests that all matter may have experience associated with it—a view known as *panpsychism*. So in addition to worrying about whether your friends and family are conscious, you might want to worry about your bathroom scale too.

• ⁓ •

BEFORE YOU WORRY TOO MUCH, I should say: many philosophers reject the arguments against materialism just offered, none more fiercely than Daniel Dennett. Dennett is an avid sailor—and one of America's most prominent philosophers. He's written about free will, religion, and evolution. But he's best known for his work on consciousness.

Dennett thinks that Rex is wrong about Mary. He doesn't think she'll learn anything new when she gets to see the red apple. And he has fun extending the story. He imagines trying to trick Mary by giving her a blue apple instead of a red one. He says she'd recognize the ruse instantly, since she'd know that her brain was in the blue state when apples are supposed to be red.

How? Dennett insists that if Mary knew *all* the physical facts, she'd be able to identify subtle differences in the way she'd respond to blue or red. (For instance, blue might affect her mood in a way that red wouldn't.) That would clue her in to what sort of color experience she was having. I think Dennett's right about that. But I don't think it's enough to show Rex wrong. The question is not whether Mary could somehow figure out whether she was having the experience of seeing red; the question is whether she already knows what it's like to have that experience. And knowing some ways in which it would affect her is not enough. She'd have to know *every* way. Otherwise, she'd learn something new. And as Rex says, it's hard to see how she could anticipate the redness of red.

Except: Dennett denies that there's anything that answers to the description "the redness of red." Philosophers of mind talk about *qualia*. That's a fancy word for the qualities of our experiences: the redness of red, or the blueness of blue. Or the feels you feel when you're tired, hungry, or anxious. Or the pain you feel when you're hurt. In short, qualia are the stuff of your phenomenal consciousness. Or so say most people, but not Dennett, who denies that qualia exist.

What we think are qualia, Dennett says, are really just judgments and dispositions. We judge things to be red. And we're disposed to react to red things in certain ways. But there's no experience to seeing red beyond all that, and certainly no redness of red. We're just mistaken if we think we're having private, ineffable experiences.

What does Dennett make of the shifted color spectrum? It's nonsense. In fact, he calls it "one of philosophy's most virulent memes." We don't have private experiences of red or blue, so they can't get mixed up between us. Indeed, he says something bolder. When pondering the possibility of zombies, Dennett writes: "Are zombies possible? They're not just possible, they're actual. We're all zombies."

Wow. That's a wild claim. And it's hard to tell whether Dennett believes it. In one of the oddest footnotes in all philosophy, he declares that it would be an act of "desperate intellectual dishonesty" to quote that last sentence out of context. But to be honest, I'm not sure what context would make the claim less wild.* Philosophers joke that Dennett's book *Consciousness Explained* should really be called *Consciousness Explained Away.* But I'll say: If you read the book, and really grapple with what Dennett says, you might start to think he's right. He's got an acid tongue, but it's silver too. He'll teach you a ton about your brain. But by the end, you'll wonder whether you've lost your mind—or ever really had one in the first place.

Dennett's view has lots of adherents, but he hasn't persuaded everyone. Chalmers notes that, when he looks inward, he finds a rich set of mental states (sensations and emotions) that Dennett either disclaims or redescribes in ways that fail to capture what they're like. The sensation of seeing red, for instance, does not seem like a judgment or disposition. At one point, Chalmers wonders whether Dennett really is a zombie. (These guys are tough on each other.) More charitably, he suggests that Dennett has just grown accustomed to thinking about his mind from the outside (extrospecting rather than introspecting), since that facilitates a certain sort of scientific inquiry. But Chalmers insists that there's knowl-

---

*In the passage quoted, Dennett is rejecting the idea that we have *epiphenomenal* qualia. To say that something is epiphenomenal (in this sense) is to say that it doesn't have any causal consequences. If zombies are possible, that suggests that conscious experience is epiphenomenal—that it doesn't affect what happens in the world—since zombies are just like us, save consciousness. Dennett might be right to reject epiphenomenalism—it's controversial even among defenders of conscious experience. But his zombieism is on display elsewhere; earlier he suggests that qualia are just "the sum total of dispositions to react." Most of us think there's more to red than those dispositions. There's the redness of it. So too with the anxiety. The dispositions can be a problem, but the feeling is bothersome too.

edge to be gleaned from introspection, which cannot be accounted for on a materialist picture. Mary can study the brain all she wants; she won't know what it's like to see red until she does.

The controversy continues. Many materialists aren't moved by Chalmers or his clever arguments. And many neuroscientists doubt that his Hard Problem is any harder than the other problems they study. We may not be able to see how the physical stuff in the brain could give rise to phenomenal consciousness yet, they say, but give science time. It will figure it out.

—————

WHAT'S MY VIEW ON all this? I don't have one.

Jules Coleman has been a friend and mentor for decades. He was my teacher in law school. And he taught me one of the most important lessons I ever learned.

I saw him in the hall when I was a student, and we started to talk philosophy. I can't remember what the question was. But I do remember attempting to share my view.

"In my view . . ." I started.

He cut me off.

"You're too young to have views," he said. "You can have questions, curiosities, ideas . . . even inclinations. But not views. You're not ready for views."

He was making two points. First, it's dangerous to have views, because often you dig in to defend them. And that makes it hard to hear what other people have to say. One of Coleman's signal virtues as a philosopher is his willingness to change his views.* That's because he's more committed to questions than answers. He wants to understand,

---

*Frank Jackson has that virtue too. After decades of defending his story about Mary, he changed his mind and decided that she wouldn't, in fact, learn anything on seeing red. But he gets no deference on that question. The story stands on its own, and debate about it continues.

and he's willing to go wherever his understanding takes him, even if it requires him to backtrack from where he's been before.

Second, you have to earn your views. You shouldn't have a view unless you can defend it, make an argument for it, and explain where the arguments against it go wrong. When Coleman said I was too young for views, he wasn't really making a point about age. (I was twenty-six.) He was saying I was too new to philosophy. Decades on, I have lots of views. I can say why I hold them and where I think others go wrong. But I don't have views on every question, because I haven't done the work to earn them.

Philosophy of mind is a field in which I haven't done the work. I read a lot, since I've got questions. But when I read, I'm struck by the fact that brilliant people hold a bewildering array of views. And the arguments for and against pile up faster than I can assess them. If you pressed me to take a stand, I'd say, with Hank, "I'm not an expert or anything."

But that doesn't stop me from trying to figure out how consciousness fits in the world. The fact that someone else knows more than you—has read more, studied more, pondered more possibilities—in no way undermines your efforts to think through a problem. It's rewarding to work something out—to achieve insight on your own. You don't have to be the best pianist in the world to make it worth playing the piano. And you don't have to be the best philosopher in the world to make it worth thinking philosophically.

Indeed, it's wonderful to discover that there are philosophers who know more than you, since it gives you the chance to learn from them. But you won't learn by accepting what they say at face value. You want to work through the problem yourself, with the aid of people more expert than you, not just defer to their judgment. That's one reason that I never pull rank on my kids. I won't tell them what to think about a question, even if I tell them what I think about it. I'd rather they work their ways toward views of their own.

As I said, I'm still working my way toward views about consciousness. I may never get there. But this is my book, so I'll share my inclination. The person whose work I find most intriguing in this terrain is Galen Strawson. In the chapter on punishment, we learned a bit about Peter Strawson, Galen's father. (Philosophy runs deep in some families.) Galen is a phenomenal philosopher in his own right, a leading thinker about free will, personal identity, and the nature of consciousness, among other topics. I like his work because it emphasizes just how ignorant we are.

Strawson has no patience for Dennett's zombieism. He calls it "the silliest claim that has ever been made," since it denies what's most manifest: that we experience the world. If science turns out to be incompatible with that, it's science that has to go. But it's *not* incompatible, Strawson says. Indeed, he's a straight-up materialist, convinced that everything in the world is physical, including the mind.

How could that be? Strawson says the problem is the way we think of physical stuff. We start from the assumption that physical stuff (like matter and energy) doesn't experience the world, and then we wonder why certain arrangements of it (a baby, Bailey, a bat) *do* experience the world. Strawson wants to flip our perspective. You know, for sure, he says, that physical stuff experiences the world, since *you* are physical stuff that experiences the world. The problem is not explaining consciousness; we know exactly what that is, he says. Indeed, you know that more intimately than you know anything else. The problem is that we don't understand the physical stuff well enough to know how consciousness fits in.

Strawson suggests that the simplest hypothesis is that all matter experiences the world. Which brings us back to panpsychism. Strawson posits that experience is a part of the world, even at the smallest scale.

What's it like to be an electron? He has no idea. Maybe it's just a constant "bzzzz."

What's it like to be a kitchen table? Likely, nothing. To say that all matter experiences the world is not to say that all arrangements of it do. The electrons in the table might experience the world, but the table might not be a separate subject.

How about your bathroom scale? It's hard to say. It does sense your weight. But you don't need to worry that it's judging you. Panpsychism is *not* the idea that everything thinks; it's the idea that experience is woven into the fabric of the world.

This is all speculative, wildly so. But as Chalmers has emphasized, we need to speculate, since there's so much we don't understand. We're at the stage where we need ideas, so we can ponder possibilities.

Will we ever understand how consciousness fits in the world? There are some philosophers who say we won't. Bailey will never understand general relativity. It's beyond her cognitive capacity. Perhaps consciousness is beyond ours. That would be a bummer. But there's only one way to find out. We have to think it through.

———

WHEN HANK WAS LITTLE—four or five—we'd play a game as he got ready for his bath. I'd tell him to take off his clothes, and he would. Then I'd tell him to take off his knees or his elbows. Once I told him to take off his thoughts.

"You don't want to get them wet," I said.

"Where are my thoughts?" Hank asked.

"Did you lose them?"

"No." He giggled.

"Then take them off."

"I can't," he said. "I don't know where they are."

"Hank, you really have to be more careful with your things. Mommy and Daddy won't keep buying you thoughts if you can't keep track of them."

"I know where they are," Hank said.

"Where?"

"Not here." And off he ran, naked.

Rex and I had a similar conversation when he was ten.

"I wonder where my mind is," he said.

"Where do you think?"

"It might be in my butt," he said.

"Do you have trouble thinking when your butt gets hurt?"

"Yeah," he said, "'cause I'm thinking about my butt."

We have more serious conversations about consciousness too. Lately we've been talking about how widespread it might be. We've wondered whether robots or computers might be conscious. We've wondered at the fact that anything is. At one point, I read Rex the passage from Huxley, where he marvels at the fact "that anything so remarkable as a state of consciousness comes about as the result of irritating nervous tissue."

We talked about it for a few minutes. Then Rex brought the conversation to a close.

"Can we take a break from consciousness?" he asked.

"Sure," I said.

"Good. You're irritating my nervous tissue."

11

INFINITY

What did you learn in school today?"

"Nothing."

"Really? Not a single thing? Not the whole day?"

"Nope," Rex said, exasperated that I'd asked. Then he added, "But I did figure something out."

"What's that?"

"The universe is infinite."

"Actually, scientists aren't sure," I said. "Some think it's infinite. But others think it's really, really, big—but finite."

"No, the universe *has* to be infinite," Rex said with surprising conviction for a seven-year-old whose entire physics education consisted of a handful of episodes of *How the Universe Works*.

"Why do you say that?"

"Well, imagine that you took a spaceship all the way to the edge of the universe. And then you punch right at the edge."

He punched the air in front of him.

"Your hand has to go somewhere, right?"

"What if it just stopped?"

"Well, then there'd be something stopping it," Rex said. "So you wouldn't be at the edge yet!"

. ⌒⌒ .

REX ISN'T THE FIRST PERSON to make that argument. It's commonly credited to an ancient Greek philosopher named Archytas. But that's just a matter of record keeping. Some seven-year-old probably thought of it first.

Archytas was Plato's friend. Once, Plato got in trouble with some toughs in Sicily, and Archytas (who also happened to be a politician—and mathematician) sent a ship to rescue him.

Here's how Archytas put Rex's argument:

> If I arrived at the outermost edge of the heaven . . . could I
> extend my hand or staff into what is outside or not? It would
> be paradoxical not to be able to extend it. But if I extend it,
> what is outside will either be body or place.

Hold up—that went fast. And it sounded weird. What would be paradoxical about not being able to extend your hand at the edge of the universe?

Rex had an answer, and so did Archytas. As Rex said, if you can't go further, there must be something stopping you. Let's say it's a wall made of Legos. If the bricks go on forever, the universe is infinite—and mostly made of Legos.* If the wall isn't infinite, and you can find a way to bust through, you should be able to keep going. At least, until something else gets in your way. But if you hit another obstacle, all you have to do is

---

*The speed at which we accumulate Legos suggests that they are, indeed, the main form of matter in the universe.

repeat Rex's argument. The conclusion seems inescapable: the universe is infinite.

But you don't have to take Rex's word for it. Or even Archytas's. The Roman poet and philosopher Lucretius made the same argument a few hundred years later. He imagined hurling a javelin toward the edge of the universe. Either the javelin sails through, in which case there wasn't an edge where you thought there was. Or something stops the javelin, in which case there's something beyond what looks to be the edge. As before, you can repeat the argument endlessly. Space simply won't quit.

Or so says Lucretius. But you'd probably like to hear from a scientist. Is Isaac Newton good enough for you? It turns out, he's with Rex: "Space extends infinitely in all directions," he said. "For we cannot imagine any limit anywhere without at the same time imagining that there is space beyond it."

Is Newton right? Whenever you imagine a bounded space, do you also imagine space outside it? Take a minute and see if you can see possibilities Newton didn't.

———

WHILE YOU WORK ON THAT, a few words about school. I have no idea what Rex was supposed to learn that day. I nearly never do, since Rex will never say. Mostly he reports how bored he was. But boredom has its benefits. In this case, a boy who hadn't mastered his times tables matched wits with Isaac Newton and came to the same view of space.

Rex feels some of the same frustrations about school that I did as a kid. It's too rigid, and it almost has to be. Teachers have lots of kids to wrangle, and a curriculum to march through too. That makes it hard to tailor the experience to particular kids. It's easier in some subjects than others. When it comes to reading, for instance, any half-decent librarian can help a kid find a book that matches his interests and abilities. But with math, it's more challenging to tailor the curriculum. You can move kids forward a bit or hold them back, but there's a standard progression everyone's expected to go through. There's little time for teachers to pursue the interests of individual kids.

I try to fill the gaps by asking the boys what they're curious about. And actually, that leads to better conversations than asking them what they learned at school. One day, Hank told me he was interested in infinity. Lots of kids are. Once you start learning math, it's natural to ask: What's the highest number?

Hank was sure it was infinity. But not because it came up in class. He heard it from a friend in first grade.

But his friend was wrong. Infinity is not the highest number. There is no highest number. And Hank *loved* learning that.

"Pick a super big number," I said.

"One million," Hank said.

"Okay. What number's next?"

"One million and one."

"I guess you're going to need a bigger number."

"One trillion," Hank said.

"Okay. What's next?"

"One trillion and one."

We went a couple more rounds, learning the words *quadrillion* and *quintillion* on the way. Then I asked, "How about a googol? Do you know what that is?"

"No."

"It's a crazy big number. It's a one with one hundred zeros after it. It's the biggest number I can name."

"Is that the biggest number?" Hank asked.

"Nope. What number do you think comes next?"

"A googol and one!" he said with glee.

"And after that?"

"A googol and two!"

"Wow! You just helped me learn new numbers."

Hank was proud of himself.

Then I asked: "Do you think we're ever going to run out of numbers? Or can we always add another one?"

"We can always add another one," he said.

"So is there a biggest number?"

"No."

"That's right," I said. "*Infinity* is the word we use to talk about the fact that numbers go on forever. They never stop, no matter how long you count."

FOR A LONG TIME, when I asked Rex what he was curious about, the answer was: space.

So let's get back to it!

Did you see any possibilities Newton didn't? When you picture a bounded space, do you have to imagine space outside it?

The answer is no. Newton was wrong. And so was Rex. For all we know, the universe might be infinite. But the argument that Rex offered doesn't work.

To see why, it helps to have a balloon. So I grabbed one when Rex had finished his argument.

"Let's look at the surface of this balloon," I said. "Is it finite? Or is it infinite?"

"I think it's finite," Rex said, hesitantly.

"What if we sliced it open and spread it out on a table? Would it go on forever?"

"No," Rex said, more confident this time. "It's finite."

"Good. Now imagine that there's an ant walking on the surface of this balloon. He sets out in one direction and just keeps going. Is he ever going to get stuck or hit an edge?"

"No," Rex said, as I traced the ant's path with my finger.

"What happens if he just keeps going?"

"He gets back to where he started," Rex said, as his finger traced the balloon too.

"That's right! He gets back where he started because the balloon folds back on itself."

We traced a few more paths to hammer the point home.

Then I explained: "The surface of this balloon is finite. But an ant can walk forever without hitting an edge. Because there are no edges!"

"Can the ant jump off?" Rex asked.

"Good question!" I said. "Let's say he can't. Imagine that the ant's completely flat. Because the surface of the balloon is the entire universe. There's no space above it, below it, or even inside it. So there's nowhere else he can go except on the surface of the balloon."

"Okay," Rex said, still studying the balloon.

"Space has three dimensions," I said, "not two like the surface of a balloon. But some scientists think it works the same way. It's finite, but it doesn't have any edges." Then I asked: "If the universe works like that, what do you think would happen if we set out in a spaceship and just kept going?"

"We'd get back where we started!" Rex said.

"Yeah!"

"Neat!"

"Just remember. We don't know if that's true. The universe might be infinite. But it could be finite and fold back on itself."

⁓

REX'S ARGUMENT ABOUT INFINITY reminded me that I also duplicated an ancient argument when bored at school. I was a tad older than Rex, though. I was in tenth grade.

I saw my friend Eugene in Mr. Jones's class, and I decided to share what I'd been thinking about all day.

"Hey, G! Can I punch you?" I asked.

Eugene was the biggest kid in school—by a long shot. When he was a freshman, the football team had to ask the Atlanta Falcons for help in getting a helmet, because they couldn't find one that fit his head. Later he went to college on a shotput scholarship.*

"Why?" he asked.

"I got something to prove," I said.

Now he did too. "Okay. It's not like it's gonna hurt."

I pulled my fist back. Then I stopped.

"I can't punch you," I said.

"It's cool, just do it."

"No, I mean, I *can't* punch you. It's not possible."

Then I showed him what I meant.

"To punch you, I've got to move my fist halfway to you."

I moved my fist halfway.

"Then I have to move halfway from here."

I moved my fist again.

"And again. And again. And again."

I moved my fist a little more each time.

"That means I can't get all the way to you. No matter how many times I go halfway, I'll always have further to go."

By this point, my fist was pressed against Eugene's chest. Happily for me, he was a gentle giant—and a math geek too.

"I know it feels like I'm touching you, G. But it's not possible."

Mr. Jones had been standing nearby the whole time. He finally chimed in: "Who taught you Zeno's paradox?"

"Who's Zeno?" I asked.

"Look him up," he said.†

---

*Also: Eugene set the record at our local wings place, eating 176 in one sitting. He stopped only because he took a break to call home—and his mom said she had dinner ready.

†A brief word about Billy Jones. He was a genius at keeping his students engaged. He taught Latin, German, and chemistry, but he could have taught a dozen other sub-

ZENO OF ELEA LIVED just before Archytas and Plato, around the same time as Socrates (in the fifth century BCE). He was friends with Parmenides, who had one of the most awesome ideas in all of philosophy: there is only one thing and it does not change; all appearances to the contrary are illusions. Philosophers call that *monism*.

Zeno developed many paradoxes, which lend support to that sort of monism. His most famous ones are about motion. My demonstration in Mr. Jones's class tracks the first of them. It's called *the dichotomy*, and it goes like this. If you're trying to move from one place to another, you have to go halfway first. Then you have to go half the remaining way. And then half the remaining way. And then half the remaining way. . . . And that goes on *forever*. Which seems like a problem.

Here's another way to think about it: At the start, Eugene is a fixed distance from my fist. To punch him, I need to travel 1/2 that distance, then 1/4 that distance, then 1/8, then 1/16, then 1/32, and so on *endlessly*. And again, that seems like a problem. The distances get smaller. But there are an infinite number of them, so it's not clear how I could ever cover them all.

And actually, we can make the paradox even more perplexing by flipping it around. At the start, I've got to go halfway. But to go halfway, I've first got to get halfway there (that is, a quarter of the way). And to go a

---

jects too. To an outsider, his classes would have looked like chaos, since every kid was working on something different. Kids moved at their own speed. If you finished work early, he gave you a new challenge. Many were puzzles he invented himself. He'd write your chemistry homework in a language you didn't speak, just to make it more difficult. Or he'd give you a brain teaser and require you to reply with a list of elements whose chemical symbols spelled the answer. (For instance, Archytas is **A**rgon, **C**arbon, **H**ydrogen, **Y**ttrium, **Ta**ntalum, **S**ulfur.) He also took an interest in your interests, helping you to build projects around them. No one was ever bored in Mr. Jones's class. We loved him for that, and we learned more from him than anyone else. I never met a better teacher, and I don't think I know a better person either.

quarter of the way, I've first got to get an eighth of the way. And to go an eighth of the way, I've first got to get a sixteenth of the way. And so on, *endlessly*.

That's true no matter how short the distance I want to travel is. So it seems I can't move at all—not even a little bit. To move just a short distance, I'd have to cover an infinite number of distances. But I don't have infinite time. So I'm stuck. Motion is just an illusion.

Or so said Zeno. He didn't persuade many people. On hearing the argument, Diogenes is said simply to have stood up and walked, refuting the claim with his feet. Which is cute. But it's not much of a refutation, as Zeno's whole point is that things may not be as they seem. To show that motion is possible, you have to find a flaw in Zeno's reasoning.

For a long time, I thought I had. A few days later, I was back in Mr. Jones's class, telling Eugene that I'd figured it out. To punch him, my fist has to travel through infinitely many finite distances. And it seems like there's no time to do it. But time can be cut up in the same way that space can. For every point in space I had to pass through, there was a point in time when I could be there.

A picture might help.

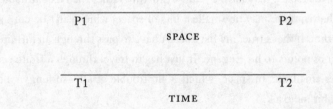

As I move from P1 to P2, I have to pass through infinitely many points in space. But there are infinitely many points in time between T1 and T2. So I've got all the time I need. Indeed, I've got exactly one point in time for every point in space I need to pass through.

That story satisfied me, so I stopped thinking about Zeno. It was only years later that I learned Aristotle had also suggested my solution.

But it doesn't completely solve the mystery (and Aristotle appreciated that). The problem is that it's not clear how time works on this picture. For a single second to go by, a half second has to go by first. For a half-second to go by, a quarter second has to go by first. And . . . well, you get the idea. That goes on forever, so it seems like even a single second must be infinitely long. And that doesn't make any sense.

<hr />

IT TOOK MODERN MATH to unravel the mystery—in particular the invention of calculus (by Newton and Gottfried Leibniz). There's still some disagreement on the details. But the key insight is that the sum of an infinite set of finite distances is not always infinite. Indeed, the sum of the series that interests us (1/2, 1/4, 1/8, 1/16 . . .) is just 1. So all those little distances don't pile up into a distance that's too far to travel in a finite period of time.

That said, there are some who think the solution doesn't actually lie in math—that it comes instead from physics. Zeno supposes that space is infinitely divisible—that we can chop it up into ever smaller bits. But that may not be true. Recent advances in quantum mechanics suggest that space may have a grainy structure rather than a continuous one. That is, there may be smallest bits of space, which can't be cut up any further. If that's true, my fist doesn't have to pass through an infinite number of points to hit Eugene. It just has to travel through a finite set of super small bits of space, which is no trouble at all—so long as he doesn't hit me back.

<hr />

I JUST SUGGESTED THAT the solution to Zeno's paradox lies in math or physics—not philosophy. And the answer to the question we started with—Is the universe infinite?—surely lies in science. So what are these questions doing in a book about philosophy?

They're here partly so that we can think about the relationship between philosophy and other fields. It's no accident that Archytas was a philosopher *and* mathematician. The list of thinkers who worked in both fields is long, and it includes bold-faced names like Descartes and Leibniz. That shouldn't come as a surprise, since philosophers and mathematicians employ more or less the same method—they think carefully about puzzles and problems. Aptitude for one is no guarantee of aptitude for the other, since the puzzles and problems aren't the same. But some people excel at both.

Philosophers have often been at the cutting edge of science too, not least Aristotle. Indeed, it wasn't until relatively recently that science was seen as something other than philosophy. For most of its history, science was simply called *natural philosophy*, to mark it off from other branches of philosophy, like *moral philosophy* or *aesthetics*. We see it as a separate endeavor mostly because it employs different methods. Scientists think carefully, of course. But they also investigate the world through observation and experimentation.

Philosophers have those tools in their kit too, but they use them less frequently. Many of the questions that interest philosophers most will not yield to an experiment. No experiment will tell you what justice is.* Or love. Or beauty. No experiment will tell you when punishment is justified. Or whether revenge is. Or what rights we have. No experiment will tell you what knowledge is. Or whether we have any hope of acquiring it.

The main tool we have for answering those sorts of questions is care-

---

*At least, no experiment of the sort that scientists conduct. Some philosophers, like the American pragmatist John Dewey, argue that we experiment with ethical ideas by trying them out—living with them and seeing how things go. I think there's a lot of truth in that. And it means that ethical knowledge, at least of a certain sort, is likely to be generated outside the academy, not within it. That said, there's still a role for professional philosophers to play—in refining ideas, generating new ones, working through their implications, and so on.

ful thought and conversation. And that leads some scientists to doubt that philosophy is a source of knowledge. It's just talk, they think. But it's important to say: if philosophy isn't a source of knowledge, science isn't either. At the end of the day, every experiment rests on an argument—that *this* is a way of finding out about the world. And every result requires interpretation. As I said before, scientists have to think carefully, just like philosophers. If their arguments aren't any good, the fact that they conduct experiments will not save their work. Science bottoms out in careful thought and conversation, just like philosophy.

Indeed, in the deepest sense, they are the same endeavor. We're all trying to make sense of the world, using whatever tools are appropriate to the task. What we see as separate fields—math, science, and philosophy—are all branches of the same tree. Philosophers pass problems along when other disciplines are better suited to solve them. That's what happened to Archytas's question about the size of the universe. Science helps us look deep into space—and deep into the past—to learn about the limits of the cosmos. It's also what's happened to Zeno's paradoxes of motion. Math helped us get a better grip on infinity. And science is laying bare the structure of space.

But as we're about to see, there are puzzles about infinity that are (for now) purely the province of philosophy.

——◦——

HERE'S ONE. Suppose the universe *is* infinite. What does that mean for us? Does it affect how we should act? It might seem like the answer is no. Even if the universe is not infinite, it's incredibly big. By some estimates, the observable bit is 93 billion light-years across. We'll never see most of it, of course. Few of us will ever escape this pale blue dot. At the moment, Mars is the furthest anyone has any plans to go. So we might wonder: What could it matter to us if the universe is infinitely big?

Nick Bostrom, who introduced us to the simulation hypothesis, thinks that it might matter a lot. At least, if you're attracted to a certain ethical outlook. A popular version of *utilitarianism* tells us that we ought to try to maximize the balance of pleasure over pain in the universe. It's an appealing idea. Our actions have consequences. We should want them to be good. And arguably, the most important measure of whether they are good is the impact they have on the pleasure and pain that people feel. And not just people. If pleasure and pain are what count, then presumably they count no matter who—or what—feels them. Hence the formula: act so as to maximize the balance of pleasure over pain in the universe.

Bostrom says that formula is fine, so long as the universe is finite. But it won't work if the universe turns out to be infinite. Why? Suppose the part of the universe we can't see is just like the part we can—full of galaxies, with stars and planets. It seems a safe bet that there are people on some of them. They might be just like us. Or perhaps they are differently constituted, yet still the sorts of characters who feel pleasure and pain. If so, their pleasures and pain contribute to the balance of pleasure over pain in the universe.

How many of those people are there? If the universe is infinite (and the rest is just like the bit we see), Bostrom says that we should expect that it has infinitely many people in it. Only a small portion of planets may have people. But if the universe goes on forever, there should be an infinite number of those planets. And that's a problem. If there are an infinite number of people in the universe, then there is infinite pleasure in the universe. And infinite pain too. And there's nothing we could ever do that would affect the balance between them.

IF YOU'RE A MATH GEEK, you might already see why. But no worries if not. We just need to learn a bit more about infinity. And we can do it with a puzzle I've presented the boys.

Imagine you're the night clerk at a place called Hilbert's Hotel.* The hotel has just one corridor. But it's long. Indeed, it's infinitely long, with infinitely many rooms off it, numbered consecutively.

Tonight every one of those rooms is filled. You have an infinite number of guests in your infinite hotel. So business is booming! And you're ready to relax. But as soon as you settle in, a tired traveler turns up. She asks whether you have room for her.

"Sorry," you say. "We're fully booked."

"Are you sure you can't squeeze me in?" she asks. "The weather out there is terrible."

You'd really like to help. But you just don't see how you could. True, you have an infinite number of rooms. But they're all occupied at the moment. No matter how far she treks down the corridor, she'll never find a free one.

She's just about to leave, and then it hits you. You *can* squeeze her in. You'll just have to inconvenience the other guests a bit.

Do you see how?

The boys didn't when I first asked them. But now that they know the answer, they like to pose the puzzle to other kids—and grown-ups too.

The solution is simple. To start, you get on the intercom, page every room, and ask every guest to pack up their stuff and move down to the next room. The guest in Room 1 will go to Room 2. The guest in Room 2 will go to Room 3. And so on, endlessly, all down the line.

Once they've done that, every guest in the hotel will have a new place to sleep. Except the first room will be empty. So you'll have just the space you need to squeeze in the tired traveler.

And there's a lesson here: infinity plus one is . . . infinity.

Even better, that trick works for any finite number of people that show up. If you've got two tired travelers, just ask everyone to move

---

*It's named after the great nineteenth- and twentieth-century mathematician David Hilbert.

down two rooms. If you've got three, three rooms. And so on. (Not endlessly—you can't ask people to move down an infinite number of rooms.)*

And there's a lesson there too: infinity plus any finite number is just . . . infinity.

⸙

BACK TO BOSTROM, THEN. If there's infinite pain in the universe, there's nothing I can do to increase the amount. To be sure, I can cause people pain. But despite what my exes might maintain, I can only cause finite pain.† And when you add finite pain to infinite pain, you just have . . . infinite pain.

The same is true of pleasure.

And here's the upshot: in an infinite universe, utilitarianism is completely indifferent to what we do. It doesn't matter whether we hurt people or help them. The balance of pleasure over pain will stay the

---

*But you can accommodate an infinite number of new guests! Just ask everyone to double their room number, and have the new guests take all the odd-numbered rooms. There are two lessons here. First, infinity plus infinity is infinity. And second, there are as many even numbers as there are even and odd numbers added together. Which just might be my favorite math fact.

And there's lots more you can do in Hilbert's Hotel! You can accommodate an infinite number of buses, each containing an infinite number of guests. You can accommodate one guest for every rational number (those that can be expressed as fractions). But there are some groups that are so large you cannot accommodate them—for instance, you can't accommodate a guest for every real number. Why not, if your hotel has infinitely many rooms? Because it turns out that there are different sizes of infinity. The set of real numbers (which includes irrational numbers, like π, that cannot be expressed as a fraction) is uncountably large—there are more of them than there are whole numbers, even though each set (the wholes and the reals) goes on forever. It turns out that math is *way* more fun than it seemed in school.

†I'm kidding. I married my high school sweetheart, so I don't have an ex—anywhere in the universe. Sometimes you see people say that in an infinite universe, everything that can exist does. That's false. Search the cosmos as long as you like, and you'll never find an ex of mine, even though Julie likes to point out that I could quickly have one.

same. We can't affect it at all. So we're free, I suppose, to do whatever we like, no matter how dreadful.

Unless utilitarianism is wrong. Which is too big a topic to take on here. But I want to say: I think it is. And Bostrom's argument is one indication of that. To my thinking, people matter, individually, not just as vessels for pleasure and pain.

Utilitarianism treats people like rooms to be filled. If an infinite number of us are already topped up with pleasures and pains, adding another doesn't make a difference.

I'd rather treat people like the traveler at the desk. It matters whether *she* has a place to stay, even though we can't increase the number of people who do by giving her one.

• ———— •

BUT WAIT A MINUTE. Does *she* really matter? Or, more important, since I made her up: Do *we* really matter?

There's a picture book I like to read with the boys. It's called *A Hundred Billion Trillion Stars*. It's filled with big numbers. It says that there are 7.5 billion people in the world. And 10 quadrillion ants. But the biggest number in the book is the title's hundred billion trillion. That's twenty-three zeros after a one. And it might be off by an order of magnitude. By some estimates, there are a thousand billion trillion stars in the observable universe. Or, more simply, a septillion. And, of course, infinitely more if the universe is infinite. But let's stick to a septillion. That's more than enough to make us think.

I like to read the book with the boys because I want them to ponder their smallness. Or, rather, *our* smallness. The universe is unimaginably big, even if it's not infinite. We occupy a small patch, and there's not much special about it. Worse yet, it won't even be ours for long. We'll get eighty years, give or take, if we're lucky. The universe has been around for more than thirteen billion already, and it has billions or trillions to go.

At best, we're a blip. And that makes us seem awfully insignificant.

⌣

"Do you think we matter?" I asked Rex one day as we were talking about the scale of the universe. He was ten.

"No, I don't think so," he said.

"Why not?"

"There's just so much out there," Rex said. "I don't see why we'd matter."

We kept walking and talking. After a while, I asked: "Can I punch you in the face?"

"No," he said, surprised.

"Why not?" I asked. "It doesn't matter."

"It matters to me," he said with a smile.

In a ten-minute span, Rex expressed two thoughts that are hard to hold in your head together.

If you take a step back and consider yourself from the perspective of the universe, you're small to the point of insignificant. The world wouldn't be that different if you'd never been born. And it won't be that different after you die.

The same is true for our entire species. The universe wouldn't be that different if we never came along. And it won't be that different after we're all gone.

From the outside, everything we do looks futile. Even if we succeed, it just gets washed away.

But from the inside, even the smallest things can seem significant.

We don't matter. But things matter to us.

⌣

Do you remember Tom Nagel? We met him in the last chapter. He's the guy who wants to know what it's like to be a bat. But he's also interested in the juxtaposition of those two thoughts: We don't matter. But things matter to us.

According to Nagel, holding those two thoughts in your head lends life an air of absurdity. And he means something specific by that. Nagel says that something's absurd when there's a mismatch between its seriousness and its significance. As a law student, I sat through a training on how to format citations for law journals. It included an endless, enthusiastic conversation about whether certain periods should be italicized. There was nothing at stake. It's really hard to tell whether a period is italicized. And no one cares. It was truly absurd.

Nagel thinks our entire lives are a little like that conversation. We take them seriously. We worry about our looks, our clothes, our careers, our projects, our plans—and all to what end? None, in the end. Because this will all come to an end, and it won't matter what happened to us.

We are insignificant. And we know that. And yet, we carry on as if it all matters.

Absurd.

SOME PEOPLE FIGHT THAT FEELING. They attempt to give up their attachments—to treat everything worldly as insignificant. If they can pull it off, they'll be less absurd. But hardly anybody can. (Indeed, the attempt is often absurd.)

Others insist that the universe was, in fact, made for them. They matter, they say, because they matter to the god who set it all in motion.

I'm skeptical about God, for reasons I'll explain later. But even if he exists, I think it presumptuous to think he cares about us. For all we know, in divine contemplation, we don't count for much more than ten quadrillion ants. For God, the drama might be elsewhere. We're not at the center of the universe; we're not even at the center of our solar system. Why would God put the creatures he cares about in some far-flung province? Or bother with the rest of creation? If we're what matters, what's the rest of it for?

I know, I know. You think God has a plan, mysterious as it may look to us. And he cares about all his creatures, wherever they are in the cosmos. Maybe so.

But I take a different lesson from this sort of appeal to God. The trick that some think he can play—making things matter simply by caring about them—we can do that too.

We can't make things matter in a cosmic sense, of course. But we can make them matter *to us*. All we have to do is care about them.

And I think that's something of a superpower. It's no exaggeration to say: we make our own meaning in the world. Not many creatures can do that.

⋅⁓⋅

SO WE SHOULD CARE about things, even if it's absurd to do so. We should care about our family, our friends, our fellow human beings, our projects, our plans. They make our lives meaningful.

Should we care about ourselves? I want to say yes. But I just read a paper by my friend Sarah Buss, which makes me wonder.

Buss is my colleague in the Michigan philosophy department. My boys love her, mainly because she brings them Christmas cookies each year. She's also one of the most astute moral philosophers I know.

Lately she's been thinking about moral courage—what it is and whether it can be cultivated. She wants to know why some people are willing to put their lives on the line, to make sacrifices, to oppose oppression, to help others at great cost to themselves.

Buss isn't sure; there could be many reasons. But she suspects that some people's courage stems from the fact that they attach little importance to themselves—and great importance to others. They see themselves as the cosmos might—small to the point of insignificant. But they let others loom large.

That's a hard trick to pull off, emotionally and intellectually. The main barriers are the love and sympathy we feel for ourselves—and the fear that comes with that. To gain courage of the right sort, you have to see yourself as insignificant. But it's not enough to recognize, intellectually, that what happens to you doesn't matter much. You have to *feel* it, in the same way that you presently feel your fear and self-love. Otherwise the fear is apt to win out when there's a conflict.

It's important to distinguish the attitude Buss is describing from low self-esteem. She doesn't want you to think that your life isn't worth living, or that you aren't a creature worthy of love and respect. For sure, she thinks you should look both ways before you cross the street. And you should expect others to treat you well. It's just that when the moment for courage comes, you want to feel your insignificance as surely as you feel your fear.

There's an intellectual challenge on top of that emotional one. If you see yourself as insignificant, it seems you should see others that way too. But that's dangerous. You don't want to be the sort of person who runs roughshod over others. And that will be tempting if you don't think they matter. So you have to hold on to your sense that others are important, even as you let go of your sense that you are.

That may not be a coherent way to see the world. But it's a beautiful way. A selfless way. A loving way.

And love isn't always coherent.

<hr />

I WANT MY KIDS to have moral courage. But that's a big ask. I'm not sure I have it myself. It's hard to know until you need to know.

At the least, I want them to grasp that there's a point of view from which they don't matter. I'd like them to practice seeing the world that way. I'd like them to be capable of putting things into perspective, by shifting to a perspective that sees them—and their present concerns—as insignificant.

That's why I talk to them about the size of the universe. And it's why I pulled *A Hundred Billion Trillion Stars* from the shelf one night. Hank was seven, and bedtime wasn't going so well. Julie had just exploded over the time it takes him to get ready for bed. (Infinite, it seems.) So he was sad as I settled in to read the book.

When we got to the end, I asked him the same question I'd asked Rex. "With all that's out there, do you think we matter?"

"No," he said. Then, all on his own, he added, "Well, we matter to us."

"For sure," I said. "You matter a lot to me."

Then I asked: "How do you feel when you think about all the galaxies, all the stars, and all the planets out there?"

"It doesn't help with my sadness," he said, in a way that signaled he saw through me.

So I sang him a lullaby and called it a night.

I'll keep trying, though.

I want my kids to care about things, passionately. That's how you make life meaningful.

But caring comes easy. It's hard to learn that the things you care about don't actually matter that much, even when they seem serious, even when they involve life and death.

If my kids come to see that, and they keep caring anyway, they'll be a bit absurd. But they already are. And they have good company. The rest of us are too.*

---

*It just doesn't matter much.

12

GOD

"Zack has God boots."

"What?" I said, turning my attention to Rex. I was in the kitchen, making dinner. Rex (then four) was at the table, eating the last of his pre-dinner snacks. The snacks serve a dual purpose in our house: they make it possible for us to cook dinner *and* make sure that our kids won't eat what we cook.

"Zack has God boots," Rex repeated, as if it were a revelation.

"ZACK HAS GOD BOOTS?!" I said, as if it really was a revelation. (Over-the-top enthusiasm is one of my go-to parenting moves. Good things happen when you get a kid excited about a conversation.)

"Yes! Zack has God boots," Rex said with increasing excitement.

"*Which* Zack? Big Zack? Little Zack? Grown-up Zack?" There were an absurd number of Zacks in the Giraffe Room.

"Little Zack!" said Rex, triumphantly.

"No way! Little Zack has God boots?!"

"Yeah!"

"Cool! But . . . what are God boots?"

"You know," Rex said, as if it was obvious.

"No, I don't, buddy. What are God boots?"

"They are boots with God on them."

"God is on Zack's boots!" I shouted, treating this as the shocking news it was. "Is God heavy? Can Zack walk in his boots? Is he stuck at school? SHOULD WE GO HELP HIM?"

"Not God, Daddy! Pictures of God."

"Oh, wow." I softened my voice. "What does God look like?"

"*You know*," said Rex, in a conspiratorial tone.

"No, I don't," I whispered. "What does God look like?"

"The man in the cowboy hat."

"Which man in the cowboy hat?"

"The one in the movie."

Now we were getting somewhere. Rex had only seen three movies. The first was *Curious George*. "Do you mean the man with the yellow hat?"

"No," he said, with a giggle.

The second was *Cars*. "Do you mean Mater?"

"No! Mater doesn't wear a cowboy hat," he said, in a way that suggested *he* was the one talking to a small child.

That left *Toy Story*. "Woody?"

"Yes! GOD!"

———

WHEN I WAS LITTLE, I was sure that God looked like Superman. Unless he looked like George Washington. He did have superpowers, which suggested the Son of Krypton. But he was also super good and super old, and George Washington was my main model for that.

I have no idea how Rex arrived at his view, but if you want to creep yourself out, imagine that Woody *is* God. Wherever you go, whatever you do, Woody's painted eyes are watching you. That is some scary shit.

But come to think of it, so is the standard story. Omniscience is omni-creepy.

· ~~~~ ·

So what does God look like? Washington? Woody? Superman? None of the above, say the major monotheistic religions. In fact, three out of four theologians say that God does not exist in space and time.* He created space and time, so he stands outside it. Except he doesn't really, because standing takes space, and outside is a place. And the point is that God is not a spatio-temporal being.† That means that God does not look like anything.

But wait! Weren't we created in God's image? And doesn't God sometimes appear in the Bible? Most theologians interpret "made in the image of God" metaphorically. The idea is not that we literally look like God—that God has two arms, two legs, and a creeping waistline. Rather, the idea is that we have some of God's attributes, like the ability to reason. And though God makes appearances in the Bible—think Moses and the burning bush—the people in those stories are not actually seeing God but, rather, something akin to an avatar.

Jesus is a more complicated case. And this Jew won't attempt to explain the Trinity. But I will say: Even according to Christianity, God is not completely spatio-temporal. Jesus surely looked like something (though surely

---

*The fourth recommends Crest. (No, I'm kidding. Everyone knows that Tom's is the best toothpaste.) But the statistic is not, in fact, a fact: I made it up to signal that there is some dispute about God's relationship to space and time. There are robust debates about, among other things, whether God is atemporal (i.e., does not exist within time) or eternal (i.e., exists at all points in time). The finer details of the theology won't matter for our purposes.

†So, no, he's not looking *down* on you—sorry about that!

not like Washington, Woody, or Superman). But God's other aspects—the ones that are said to still exist—don't have a location in space or time. Which means that we can't see them.

And that is awfully convenient.

⁙ ⸺ ⸺ ⁙

ANTONY FLEW WAS AN atheist philosopher* who taught at several universities in England in the second half of the twentieth century. He told a story that he adapted from a Cambridge philosopher, the improbably but impeccably named John Wisdom. Two guys are walking through the woods. They come to a clearing, where they find lots of flowers but also many weeds. The first guy says to the second, "A gardener must tend this plot."

The second guy says, "There is no gardener."

These are men of few words. Let's call them There Is and There Isn't.

The two decide to pitch their tents in the clearing and wait awhile. They never see a gardener. But There Is isn't dissuaded: "The gardener must be invisible," he says. So they build a barbed-wire fence. And because they want to make sure they catch the gardener if he comes, they electrify the fence. They also patrol the area with bloodhounds. But still, no gardener. The fence never shakes. They never hear a shriek from a shock. And the hounds never sound an alert. But There Is still isn't dissuaded. "There is a gardener," he insists, one that's "invisible, intangible, insensible to electric shocks, a gardener who has no scent and makes no sound, a gardener who comes secretly to look after the garden which he loves."

Finally fed up, There Isn't snaps: "How does an invisible, intangible, eternally elusive gardener differ from an imaginary gardener or from no gardener at all?"

---

*At least until a late-in-life conversion that some attributed to dementia.

FLEW THOUGHT THAT TALK about God was empty—meaningless. There Is said there was a gardener, so they set about looking for one. When they didn't see him, There Is qualified his claim. And he kept cutting it back until the claim was completely empty, since nothing could count against it.

Suppose you and I disagree about whether there is chicken in the fridge. I say there is; you say there isn't. How could we settle the dispute? Well, we could look. Suppose we do, and we don't see any chicken. You claim victory, but I stand fast. I never said the chicken could be seen. It's invisible chicken. So we start to feel about, and neither one of us feels a bird. You claim victory again, but I stand fast. I never said the chicken could be touched. It's intangible chicken.

At some point, you will decide that I'm deranged. Or endlessly obstinate. But either way, there would be no point in continuing to argue over whether there is chicken in the fridge, since I will not accept any evidence to the contrary.

Back in the day, people used to posit a role for God in the world. He tended the garden. They'd pray for rain. Or for the rains to end. Lots of people still do pray, of course. And some even pray for rain. But few of us think that every drizzle reflects a divine decision. We can explain why the rains come, so we don't need to posit a role for God. But as God has receded from the roles we assigned him, we have recast him as an invisible, intangible character whose traces in the world (if indeed there are any) are impossible to identify. That raises the worry that God is no more real than the invisible, intangible chicken that is not, in fact, in my fridge.

OR DOES IT? Chicken wouldn't be chicken unless you could see it, smell it, taste it, and touch it. Every chicken has a place in space and time. But why think that God has to exist in just the way that chicken does? There are other modes of existence.

⁓

I TAKE BEING AN UNCLE nearly as seriously as I take being a father. Which is to say, not so seriously. Once I persuaded my nephew that the number six did not exist.

"Hey, Ben, can you count to ten?" I asked when he was five.

"One, two, three, four, five, six, seven . . ." he started.

"WAIT! STOP! What did you just say?"

"Seven."

"No, before that."

"Six."

"What's six?"

"A number."

"No, it's not."

"Yes, it is!"

"No, Ben. It's not. When you count to ten, it goes like this: one, two, three, four, five, seven, eight, nine, ten."

He wasn't convinced at first, but I am persistent and persuasive. Eventually, he padded off to his mother.

"Uncle Scott says there's no such thing as the number six."

"Well, Uncle Scott is very good at math," his mother said. And with that, let us pause to observe that the woman my kids call Aunt Nicole is all kinds of awesome, not least because she let me gaslight her kid.

I toyed with him until he was fully convinced that the number six was a creation of the kindergarten-industrial complex. But as soon as he signed on to the conspiracy theory, I dropped it and told him the truth: the number six does, in fact, exist.

But it is not a spatio-temporal thing. The questions "Where is the number six?" or "When is the number six?" do not make sense, since the number six doesn't have a location in space or time. There is no point in asking what it looks like either, since six is not the sort of thing that can bounce photons into your face.

Wait! you might be thinking, *I know what six looks like. It looks like this:*

6

But *6* is just a symbol for the number, in the same way that the three-letter word *God* is just a symbol for the almighty deity we call by that name. The number itself can also be symbolized this way:

VI

Or this way:

Six

Or any other way you want, so long as you tell people what your symbol means. But the symbol is a separate thing from the number.

WHAT IS THE NUMBER SIX? Why does it exist? Philosophers of math argue about that. At a minimum, we might say something like this: Six exists because of the role it plays in a system. It's the successor of five and predecessor of seven. And it bears countless other relations to entities whose existence is mutually defined by their relations to one another. That's why I had to let my nephew off the hook. Without six, the rest of math would go wacky.

But saying that six exists because of the role it plays in a system puts off the hard questions: Did people *create* that system, or did we *discover* it? Would numbers exist if we did not? I am inclined to think that they would, though I am not in a position to defend that view, and you would abandon this book if I tried. It would get super hard and super boring, super fast.

But the point I want to make is just this: Not everything that exists exists in the same way. Chicken exists in space and time. So do gardeners. But the number six does not. And if six can exist without having a place in space or time, why not God?

<hr />

"Is God real?" Rex asked a lot when he was little. We send him to religious school, so he's learned a lot about God, or at least the stories that Jews tell about God. We send him, in large part, so that he will know those stories. We want him to feel at home in his community and culture.

But as he learned the stories, he'd ask, insistently, "Is God real?" From all I've said so far, you might think that I tell him no. But I don't, for two reasons. First, I am not sure; I'll say more about why in a moment. Second, and more important, when a kid asks a Big Question, I think it important to start a conversation, not cut one off.

So I never say yes or no. Instead, I share a range of views: "Some people think that God is real and that the stories we read in the Bible happened, just the way they are told. Other people think that those stories are just stories, which people made up to explain things they didn't understand." Then, I ask: "What do you think?" And I take Rex's response seriously, not as a conversation stopper but as a conversation starter. If Rex says that God is real, then I'll want to know what makes him think so, whether he's noticed that the stories in the Bible don't quite add up (there are two creation stories, for instance), and why so many bad things happen in the world if God is real and could stop them. If he takes the other path, if he says that the stories are just stories, then I'll ask him why so many people take them so seriously, how he would explain the existence of the world, and so on.

The conversation has to be pitched to a kid's capabilities. And you shouldn't think that Rex and I spend hours sitting by the fire, sipping brandy, and sifting life's mysteries. Most of these conversations are short—often just a minute or two. But they add up over time. Sometimes in surprising ways.

⁘ ⌇ ⁘

"Is God real?" Rex asked. He was four. We weren't far past the Woody revelation.

We'd had this conversation a lot, so I skipped straight to the question: "What do you think?"

"I think that, for real, God is pretend, and for pretend, God is real," Rex announced.

I was stunned. That's a profound thought for a four-year-old. It's a profound thought for a forty-year-old too. I asked Rex to explain what he meant.

"God isn't real," he said. "But when we pretend, he is."

⁘ ⌇ ⁘

Philosophers have a name for this sort of view. They call it *fictionalism*. When I say, "I teach at the University of Michigan," I am saying something that is true—here, now, in this world. But suppose I say, "Dumbledore teaches at Hogwarts." If that was a claim about this world, it would be false. Hogwarts doesn't exist in this world, and neither does Dumbledore, so he can hardly teach there. But they do exist in a different world—the fictional world that Harry Potter lives in. The sentence "Dumbledore teaches at Hogwarts" is true *in that fiction*. And when I say that sentence, you immediately understand that I am talking about that fiction, so you hear what I say as true, even though it's not true in this world.

To be a fictionalist about Dumbledore is just to accept that he exists in a fiction rather than in our world. Nobody, of course, denies that. Dumbledore is obviously fictional. But some philosophers think we should be fictionalists about things that are not obviously fictional. For instance, some philosophers think that morality is fictional. According to these philosophers, rights are make-believe, just like Dumbledore.

That is a sad thought. People care about rights. They fight for rights. For real. So it would suck if rights weren't really real.

"But don't despair!" say the philosophers who think morality is make-believe. "The stories we tell about rights are good stories, with good consequences, so we should go right on telling them. We should fight for our fictional rights!"

I AM NOT ONE of those philosophers. I think that rights are every bit as real as the visible, tangible chicken in my fridge. Or the number six. But some philosophers would say I am wrong about that too. They think that numbers are make-believe. There is no six or seven or seventy-two, except in stories that we tell.

That is another sad thought. Think of the hours lost to long division!

"But those hours weren't wasted!" these philosophers will say. "The stories we tell about numbers are super-duper awesome. We could not live without them. So whatever you do, don't stop talking about numbers, even though we totally, totally made them up!"

I'M NOT ONE of those philosophers either. We could not make sense of the world without math. The laws of physics (like $E = mc^2$ or $F = ma$) are expressed in mathematical terms. And certain numbers seem to be written into the fabric of the universe, like c, which denotes the speed of light in a vacuum (roughly 186,000 miles per second). That's the fastest anything around here—or anywhere else—can travel. It would be weird if physics rested on something fictional—if made-up math was the key to explaining the world as we find it. So I'm not a fictionalist about math any more than I'm a fictionalist about morality.

BUT I MUST CONFESS: I think Rex is right. For real, God is pretend, and for pretend, God is real. I am a fictionalist about God.

We recently switched synagogues. At the old one, the service was mostly in Hebrew, and I don't speak much Hebrew. I know how to say all the prayers; I just don't know what most of them mean. So at synagogue, I would sing along and let the words wash over me. I liked that.

At the new synagogue, we sing a lot of the same songs and say a lot of the same prayers. But we say many more of them in English. And I find that almost intolerable. It turns out, I like my religion inscrutable.

I just don't believe the stories that we tell. And hearing them in English forces me to confront that, over and over again.

THERE'S AN OLD JOKE that Jews pass around.

A kid comes home from Sunday school, and his father asks what he learned.

"Today we learned how Moses freed the Jews from bondage in Egypt."

"How did he do it?" his dad asked.

"They left fast, so fast they couldn't bake bread. And when they got to the Red Sea, the Egyptians were hot on their tail. So they had to work quick. They built a bridge, rushed across, and when they reached the other side, they blew the bridge up."

"Really?" his dad asked. "That's what they taught you?"

"No," said the kid. "But if I told you what they told me, you wouldn't believe it either."

I AM THE KID in that joke.

I don't believe, and I never did, not from the first time I heard the stories.

But here's the thing: I pretend. And I don't plan to stop. Because pretending makes the world a better place.

At our house, we light Shabbat candles on Friday night, and when we do, we pray to God. It's a peaceful moment in a busy week, and it gives us a reason to gather together and give thanks for all that we have.

Throughout the year, we celebrate holidays, joyous and solemn. When we do, we come together with family and friends. We sing songs and say prayers that our people have said for generations.

We mark the major events in our lives with religious rituals: the bris or baby naming for a newborn, the bar or bat mitzvah at the end of childhood, the wedding at the start of a new family, and the laying to rest at the end of life.

There are ways to make these events meaningful without God. But many nonbelievers miss out because they fail to fashion alternative traditions.

The solution is not to believe. It is to pretend.

⁘

AT LEAST, that is my solution. I do not begrudge anyone their faith. But what is faith, exactly? And why don't I have it? Ludwig Wittgenstein was one of the most influential (and enigmatic) philosophers of the twentieth century. He told super short stories. Here's one:

> Suppose someone were a believer and said: "I believe in a Last Judgment," and I said: "Well, I'm not so sure. Possibly." You would say that there is an enormous gulf between us. If he said "There is a German aeroplane overhead," and I said "Possibly. I'm not so sure," you'd say we were fairly near.

Why are we close in one case and far apart in the other? When we're discussing whether there's an airplane overhead, we share an orientation toward the world. We are trying to figure out the facts. All we disagree about is how to assess the evidence. And our disagreement isn't very deep. I think you might be right about the airplane; I'm just not sure.

In the first exchange—about the Last Judgment—something altogether different is happening. Even though you say that you "believe" in the Last Judgment, you're not really telling me that you've assessed the evidence and concluded that, in fact, there will be a Last Judgment. Because, let's be honest: the evidence isn't so good. Rather, you're professing your faith. And as Berkeley philosopher Lara Buchak has pointed out, faith has more to do with action than belief.

To see what she means, let's try another story. Suppose you are concerned that our friend is lying about something significant. I hear you out, then say, "I see why you're worried, but I have faith in her." When I say that, I'm not arguing with you. I'm not even telling you that I assess the evidence differently. Rather, I'm telling you that I plan to act as if our friend is telling the truth—that I'm taking a chance on her—even in the face of evidence to the contrary. And if I really have faith, then I'm telling you that I'm willing to rest on the evidence that we've got. (If I asked you to check up on her, that would be a sure sign that I *lacked* faith.)

A person who has faith in God is similarly willing to take a chance. She chooses to act as if God exists, without waiting for confirmation or seeking further evidence. She might allow that there are grounds for doubt—maybe even that the evidence isn't so good. But she's willing to orient her life around God despite the doubt.* Likewise, when you tell me that you believe in the Last Judgment, you are telling me that you

---

*Interestingly, if she's certain that God exists, she doesn't have faith. Faith makes sense only when there's a risk that you're wrong. I wouldn't say, for instance, that I have faith that Tiger Woods is a golfer. I'm certain that he is; no faith needed. But notice that I can have faith that Woods will win the Masters; similarly, someone who is certain that God exists can have faith that God is watching over her, or some such, so long as it is in doubt. As the New Testament explains, "Faith is confidence in what we hope for and assurance about what we do not see" (Hebrews 11:1, NIV).

are committed to seeing the world a certain way and acting accordingly. If I respond, "Well, I'm not so sure. Possibly," I'm telling you that I lack the commitment you've made. There's a gulf between us, and it *is* enormous. You've made a leap of faith. I'm still standing on the other side.

*

SHOULD I TAKE THE LEAP TOO? I don't think that's the right question, as I doubt you can reason your way to faith in God. But some philosophers disagree.

Blaise Pascal, the famous seventeenth-century French mathematician, also dabbled in philosophy. He thought you could reason your way to faith. His argument went like this: Suppose there is a God. If you bet on him—by believing in him—he'll be pleased, and you'll reap the benefits for all eternity. But if you wager the other way, he'll be upset. And, well, you can guess how that would go. Now suppose that there is no God. Believing won't cost you very much. Sure, you waste some time in church or, um, doing good deeds. But good deeds have value even absent God. And if you hadn't gone to church, you'd probably just waste the time on *Candy Crush*. Or, as Pascal put it before *Candy Crush* came along: "If you gain, you gain all; if you lose, you lose nothing. Wager, then, without hesitation that He is."

That argument is called Pascal's Wager. But you could also call it Hank's Wager. When he was seven, I asked him whether God was real. We talked about it for a few minutes, then he begged off.

"I don't like to talk about this," he said.

"Why?"

"Because God would find it insulting—if he's real."

I laughed and taught him a bit about Pascal. "You're thinking the same thing he was—that you should believe in God so that you don't upset him—if he's real."

"I've always thought that," said Hank. "That's why I never want to talk about it."

Philosophers bicker about whether Pascal's Wager works. We don't need to pass judgment. But I will say: if you commit to God for self-interested reasons, I doubt you're getting full credit in the afterlife. So I suspect that Hank and Pascal are off, perhaps wildly, in calculating the wages of their wagers.

·⁓·

THOUGH I DON'T THINK you can reason your way to faith, I can explain why I lack it—and why I'm not tempted to take the leap. As I just said, a person who has faith orients her life around God. In a way, that's the opposite of the orientation I've adopted. I am a person who questions, a person who doubts, a person who wants to understand the world and our place within it. I would rather steep in a mystery than assume a solution. So faith calls for a commitment I can't make, at least not without remaking myself.

For many, it works the other way round, and as I said, I do not begrudge anyone their faith. Indeed, I admire many believers for the good works their faith inspires. The world is a richer place for religious art and activism. And that is not an accident. Faith is, for many, a source of purpose, direction, and deep motivation. For Jews, the aim is *tikkun olam*—repairing the world. But many faiths—and many people of faith—share similar ambitions. And the world is no doubt better for all that they do.

But belief breeds hate too. And that is not an accident. No one who holds fast to the first bit of Rex's formula—for real, God is pretend—is apt to hate in the name of God.* I can tell my stories, and you can

---

*Such a person might, of course, hate for other reasons. The claim I am making here is not comparative. I mean simply to say that religion is *a* source of hatred. We are all familiar with others: nationalism, racism, sexism, and on . . . and on . . . and on. All these belief systems share something in common with religion: they license a sense of superiority for those who see themselves as part of the in crowd. And that, I suspect, is the cornerstone of much of the hatred that they generate.

tell yours. It is only when we believe them that they become incompatible.

It is possible, of course, to believe without hate, and many people do. But religious hatred is the source of so much conflict in the world that I wish that Rex's view was more widespread. If I got to choose, we'd be fictionalists about God and put our faith elsewhere—in each other and in our collective capacity to repair the world.

If we did that—if we worked together to repair the world—I suspect God would be pleased. If God exists. You can call that Scott's Wager. It's a better bet than Pascal's.

<hr>

ONE NIGHT, I told Rex (then nine) that I was writing about our conversations about God. He looked at me anxiously. "That could be offensing to some people," he said.

I smiled. I miss his mispronunciations. And I didn't dare correct that one. I want to hold on to my little boy as long as I can.

Rex is right. Lots of people won't like the idea that the Almighty is make-believe. But as I explained to Rex, a philosopher has to say what he thinks, even if he doesn't think others will like what he says. That's the job.

But I owe you my doubts as well as my thoughts.

There is so much about the world that we do not understand. We do not know what consciousness is, why it exists, or how widespread it is. And, more fundamentally, we do not know why the world exists, why the laws of physics are what they are, or even why there are laws of physics in the first place.

God is the answer that many people give. Most religions start with a creation story. None of them are true. But even if they were, they wouldn't solve the mystery. They would just push it to a different place. If there is a God—and if God created the world we know—we'd still have to wonder: Why does God exist?

MAYBE GOD MUST EXIST. Some philosophers have thought so. In the eleventh century, Saint Anselm said that he had an argument that proved that God existed. It started with an odd thought: we can conceive, Anselm said, of a being greater than any other being that could be conceived. Which is just a fancy way of saying we can think of something more awesome than anything else we could possibly think up.

Actually, let's run that experiment. Think of the most awesome thing you can possibly think of. I'll do it too.

I got tacos. What did you get? Tacos? I thought so.

Well, Anselm got God. (To be fair, he'd never had tacos.) Moreover, Anselm said God must exist, since actually existing makes a great guy even greater. God just *is* the greatest guy possible, Anselm said, so he's got to be real. Booyah! (Or, as logicians like to say: QED.)*

If you feel like Anselm is trying to slip something past you, you aren't alone. His argument was mocked by a monk named Gaunilo almost as soon as the ink was dry. Gaunilo said he could conceive of an island greater than any other island that could be conceived. Actually existing makes a great island even greater. So by Anselm's logic, that perfect honeymoon hotspot must exist!

Philosophers gave Anselm's argument a fancy name—they call it the Ontological Argument. Rex, for the record, says the argument is ridiculous: "Just 'cause I can think of something doesn't make it real." Which is more or less the diagnosis most philosophers would give. There have been attempts to improve the argument over the years. But I don't know anyone who believes in God simply on the basis of Anselm's argument.

(If you do, I've got an island I'd like to sell you. Gaunilo says it's *awesome*.)

---

*QED is short for *quod erat demonstrandum*. Roughly, it means "that which was to be demonstrated." And it is used to signal the successful conclusion of a proof.

ULTIMATELY, I DON'T THINK God can help us explain the existence of the world. As I said, God just moves the mystery.

So how else can we explain the world, if not through God? Maybe there is something else that must exist that explains why the world exists. Albert Einstein once said that he wanted to figure out "whether God had any choice in the creation of the world." But Einstein meant *God* metaphorically. He wasn't asking a theological question. He was wondering whether the laws of physics have to be what they are. Discovering that the laws of physics could only be one way is, I suspect, the only hope we have of finding a satisfying explanation for why the world is the way it is. But even that may not tell us why the world exists.

Why are there laws of physics in the first place? Why not nothingness? That is, perhaps, the biggest question of all.

Maybe there is no explanation for the existence of the world. Maybe it just is. Maybe we cannot know. Or maybe I am wrong and God is the key to the mystery.

I do not insist that God does not exist because that is a stronger commitment than I am prepared to make.

I doubt. And I doubt my doubts. That is the best disposition for a philosopher. And it's the one I work to cultivate in my kids.

"DO YOU THINK THAT GOD IS REAL?" I asked Rex, as I was wrapping up this book. He was eleven.

"No," he said, without hesitation.

"Why not?"

"If God was real, he wouldn't let all those people die." The pandemic was on. By that point, more than 2.5 million people had died from COVID-19.

"Why do you say that?"

"God is supposed to care about us," he said. "That doesn't seem like something you'd let happen if you cared—and could stop it."

This is the Problem of Evil—well-known, I suspect, to everyone who ponders God, even if not by that name. The problem was best explained by J. L. Mackie, an inveterate skeptic, about both morality and God. "In its simplest form," Mackie said, "the problem is this: God is omnipotent; God is wholly good; and yet evil exists." Mackie thought that the presence of evil in the world made it irrational to believe in an omnipotent and wholly good God.*

You can solve the problem by dropping the idea that God is both omnipotent and wholly good. Take either one away, and it's easy to explain the existence of evil. God can't stop it, or can't be bothered. But matters are more tricky if you insist—as many believers do—that God *is* omnipotent and wholly good. Then the presence of evil poses a puzzle— roughly, Rex's. Why would a wholly good God allow people to suffer when he could stop it?

People have proposed many answers to that question, but most are poorly reasoned. For instance, some say that good requires evil—that it can't exist without it. It's not clear why that would be true. But it doesn't matter, because if you take that view, you're calling into question God's omnipotence. It turns out there's something he can't do: create good without evil. But also: if good requires evil, maybe just a bit would do. Is absolutely every evil in the world essential? Why can't we have a world that's just like this one—except without that twinge of pain I felt last Tuesday? What kind of God can't give me a little less sciatica? My physical therapist, Tony, makes my back feel better, and he doesn't even claim to be a deity.

He is a hero, though. And some say that's why God allows evil in the

---

*To show that it's irrational, Mackie noted, you have to make a few additions to his statement of the problem: "These additional principles are that good is opposed to evil, in such a way that a good thing always eliminates evil as far as it can, and that there are no limits to what an omnipotent thing can do."

world. He doesn't care about pleasure and pain. He cares what they make possible: compassion, charity, and heroic acts, like Tony tweaking my back. Of course, pleasure and pain also make spite, malice, and callousness possible. And it's not clear which side is winning. Some days, it seems like the bad guys are getting the best of us.

"But that's not God's fault!" say his supporters. God wants us to have free will. That's the good he's after. And to get it, he's got to give up control. If we choose poorly, that's on us, not him. This is, historically, the most influential answer to Rex's question. But I don't buy it, for reasons well put by Mackie: "If God has made men such that in their free choices they sometimes prefer what is good and sometimes what is evil, why could he have not made men such that they always freely choose the good?" It's no answer to say that we wouldn't be free if God ensured that we always chose the good. Mackie's not imagining that God controls our choices. He's just observing that God can foresee what we will choose. So he could, if he wished, create only people who would choose well each and every time.

Some say that's not possible, even for God. Remember way back in the Introduction, when Hank complained that Julie had predicted him by preparing a hamburger before he'd decided what he wanted for lunch? Some doubt that foreknowledge of what another will do is compatible with free will. I don't. Hank chose, even though we knew what he'd do. And God should be even better at that game. He should be able to predict what Hank would do in any circumstance. And not just Hank. He should be able to predict what any of us would do in any situation, since omnipotence implies omniscience. Or so it would seem. But if you still want to say My Most Holy Dude can't do that, notice that he's sounding more impotent than omnipotent.

I think the Problem of Evil poses a serious barrier to belief, and I've got little patience for those who brush it off with bromides. Leibniz insisted that we live in the best of all possible worlds. If there could have been a better one, God would have created it instead. So we can rest assured that this is as good as it gets, sciatica (and, um, slavery) aside. I think that's silly. (So did Voltaire.) It lets God off the hook for an awful lot of suffering, simply on the supposition that he'd have done better if he could. I think the Problem of Evil calls for a more persuasive—and perspicuous—solution.

So did Marilyn McCord Adams. She was a philosopher—and an Episcopal priest. She was the first woman to serve as the Regius Professor of Divinity at Oxford. And in 1978, she helped start the Society of Christian Philosophers, which she later led. (If I've left you with the impression that there's any conflict between philosophy and faith, Adams is clear testament to the contrary. Historically, many philosophers were deeply devout, and that remains true down to the present day.)

Adams didn't think that we could solve the Problem of Evil by considering the world as a whole. She thought that God had to answer for the presence of horrendous evils in the lives of particular people, not all at once, but one by one. She listed the sort of evils that concerned her: torture, rape, starvation, child abuse, genocide, and other horrors so horrific I won't mention them here. Perhaps, she said, such evils could exist in a maximally good world—for reasons we'd struggle to understand. But she didn't like the idea of a God that would let people suffer horrors as a "means to His end of global perfection." She wondered: "Could the truck driver who accidentally runs over his beloved child find consolation in the idea that this . . . was part of the price God accepted for a world with the best balance of moral good over moral evil He could get?" Adams didn't think so. In her eyes, God couldn't count as "good or loving" if he allowed anyone's life to be swallowed up by evil.

And yet many lives seem to be. So how are we to solve this problem? Adams didn't think there was a secular solution. Any adequate answer to the Problem of Evil, she suggested, would have to draw on religious ideas—the sort you could access only if you'd taken a leap of faith. She argued that intimacy with God could *engulf* a person's life, making it worth living, no matter what she'd suffered. It would all pale in comparison to God's love. But more than that, she argued, God might *defeat* the evil in our lives by incorporating it into an organic whole, which was itself valuable in part in virtue of the suffering. (To illustrate the idea, Adams observed that a small patch of a painting might be ugly on its own, yet contribute to the aesthetic value of the entire work.) How could horrendous evils contribute to something of value? Adams speculated that "human experience of horrors" might be "a means of *identifying* with Christ," since he "participated in horrendous evil through His passion and death." Alternatively, she suggested, God might express gratitude for one's suffering, and thereby shift its significance.

Adams wasn't sure what the answer was, but she wasn't worried about that either. We should accept, she said, that "there are reasons we are cognitively, emotionally, and/or spiritually too immature to fathom." A two-year-old child, she explained, might not understand why his mother would permit him to have painful surgery. Nevertheless, he could be convinced of his "mother's love, not by her cognitively inaccessible reasons, but by her intimate care and presence" through the painful experience.

For those that feel the presence of God, or have faith that they will feel it later, I think Adams is onto an answer. And I think it fair to repair to religious ideas to defend religious doctrine. But if I'm honest, it sounds too optimistic to me—a just-so story that aims to justify the unjustifiable. That might be because I grew up in a tradition that doesn't take God's goodness for granted. Indeed, Abraham, the very first Jew, argued with God about his plan to destroy Sodom and Gomorrah.

"Will you destroy the righteous with the wicked?" Abraham asked. "Suppose you can find fifty people that are righteous."

God said he'd spare the cities if he found fifty righteous people.

"What about forty-five?" Abraham asked. "Would you destroy them for a lack of five?"

"No," God answered. "Forty-five would be fine."

"Forty?"

"Sure."

"Thirty?"

"Yeah."

Abraham talked God down to ten. But God might have been humoring him. As it happens, he didn't find even ten righteous souls, so he destroyed the cities—and all within them.* He must have known that's how it would go, if indeed he's omniscient.

But notice that Abraham didn't assume that God's plan was good. He fought for a better one, and God gave in.

I don't expect to meet God when I die. But if I do, I plan to follow Abraham's lead and argue. There's lots of suffering in the world. Indeed, there's lots of suffering in every human life.

If God exists, I want answers. I think we're owed them.

—•———•—

AFTER REX INSISTED THAT GOD didn't exist, I asked if he remembered what he thought when he was little.

He didn't, so I told him what he'd said: "For real, God is pretend, and for pretend, God is real."

"That sounds smart," he said.

"Yeah, I thought so too. Do you think that's right?"

"Maybe," he said.

And we talked about it for a while. I told him about fictionalism and how, at four, he'd hit on a sophisticated philosophical idea. Then I asked again. "What do you think? Were you right back then?"

---

*I wonder what Adams would make of the people God killed. Were they too engulfed by God's goodness? Christians of a certain sort would say they deserved it, and settle at that. But if any of us might be damned, Adams thought, human life would be a bad bet—and inconsistent with the idea of a loving God. She cared about evildoers, as well as those who suffered at their hands.

"I'm not sure," he said. "It's complicated. I don't know what to think."

"That sounds smart too," I said.

Childhood is ephemeral. And so are some of the thoughts that come with it. I think Rex was right when he was little. But I also appreciate the reticence he has now.

He's thinking it through. I hope he never stops.

HOW TO RAISE A PHILOSOPHER

Rex and his friend James were packing up to head home from school.

"What makes that locker that locker?" Rex asked.

"What do you mean?" James said.

"I mean, if you took the door off and put on a new one, would it be the same locker?"

"Yeah," James said. "It would just have a new door."

"Then what if you changed the box that the door is on. Would it be the same locker then?"

"I don't know," said James. "That's a weird question."

"It would still be in the same spot," Rex said. "But it wouldn't be made of the same metal."

"I think it would be a different locker," James said.

"I'm not sure," Rex said. "It would still be my locker."

REX TOLD ME about that conversation when he got home from school.

"I asked James about Theseus's ship!" he said. "Well, I didn't ask about the ship—I asked about my locker—and whether it would still be the same locker if we changed the door."

Theseus's ship is an ancient puzzle about identity. Rex read about it in the Percy Jackson series. He was excited to share it with me—and surprised that I'd already heard about it. But it's one of the most famous puzzles in philosophy.

The classic version runs like this. The ship that Theseus sailed home from Crete was preserved in the port of Athens. But over time, the wooden planks started to rot. As each plank rotted, it was replaced with a new plank, until all the original planks were gone. According to Plutarch, philosophers were divided over whether the ship in the harbor was Theseus's ship, or an entirely new one.

If you're inclined to say it was a different ship, ask yourself: At what point did it cease to be Theseus's ship? When the first plank was replaced? That doesn't sound right. You can't get a new car just by replacing a panel on your old one. Or a new house by replacing the roof. Objects, it seems, can survive some change.

But how much change? Was it Theseus's ship up until the day the last plank was replaced? Or was there some tipping point in the middle— say, when half the planks had been swapped out? That sounds off too, since it suggests that a single plank made the difference—the plank that pushed things over 50 percent. But how could the identity of the ship depend on one plank out of hundreds or thousands?

If no single plank can make a difference, maybe none of them do. Perhaps it's the arrangement of the planks that matters, not whether they were original to the boat. In that case, the ship in the harbor *is* still the ship of Theseus.

But don't get too comfortable with that conclusion either. Our old friend Thomas Hobbes tacked a new puzzle onto the old one. He supposed that, as each plank was pulled off Theseus's ship, it was secreted away and preserved. (Perhaps the planks weren't rotten—maybe they just got grimy.) Once all the planks had been replaced, an enterprising ship builder reassembled the originals.

Surely *that's* Theseus's ship! It's got all the same parts arranged in just the same way. (If you take apart your car and reassemble it on the other side of your garage, it's still the same car, right?) But if the reassembled ship is Theseus's ship, what's the ship in the harbor? They can't both be Theseus's ship. They aren't the same ship.

Is there a solution to this puzzle? Actually, I think there are *many* solutions. Answers to questions about identity, I tend to think, depend on the reasons we're interested in them. If you're hoping to touch a thing that Theseus touched, then no, the ship in the harbor is not, in the relevant sense, his ship. If you're hoping to gawk at the object that has been venerated for generations, then yep, that's the right one. (Suppose you return home from your trip to Athens and a friend asks: "Did you see Theseus's ship?" "Yes, but I realized it wasn't actually Theseus's ship" is a coherent answer, reflecting different ways of thinking about identity.) The original problem is puzzling, I think, because it's not clear why we care whether the ship is Theseus's. Absent a reason to care, we're at a loss to say whether it's his.

As with lots of puzzles we've seen, the paradox of Theseus's ship might seem silly. But an awful lot can turn on questions of identity. For instance, a painting by Leonardo da Vinci is a very valuable thing. But suppose that restorers removed or covered some of Leonardo's paint. Would the painting still be a Leonardo? If you say no, then even the Mona Lisa wouldn't count any longer, since it's been messed with many times. A Leonardo, it seems, doesn't have to be just what he painted. But how much can we mess with a painting before it's no longer his? Millions of dollars might depend on the answer.

And we can make these sorts of questions more personal. What makes you the same person you were last week? Or last year? Or the person in your pictures from prom? Your planks have been slowly replaced. Does that make you a different person? Or are you the same person in a different body? Or the same person in the same body, even though it's neither made of the same stuff nor arranged in the same way? Again, I think the answer depends on why we're asking. There are senses in which I'm the same person as the kid you met in the Introduction—the one worried about what red looked like to his mother. And there are senses in which I'm not even the person who wrote the Introduction. So much has happened since then. (Hi, COVID!)

We won't take these puzzles any further. I'll leave you to work them through on your own. Or with your own, personal James. Every philosopher needs an interlocutor, ideally more than one.

⁘ ⸺ ⸻ ⸺ ⁘

THE BOYS HAVE LONG been mine. But I thought it was super cool when Rex started talking philosophy with his friends. The toddler who loved his time-out had become the Socrates of Second Grade. I just hope it ends better for him than Socrates. (Socrates was executed for corrupting the youth of Athens by . . . asking annoying questions.)

For a long time, it's been clear that we're raising a philosopher—two, in fact. Should you try to do it too? I don't think that's the right question. If you've got a young kid, you *are* raising a philosopher, whether you know it or not. The only question is whether you will support it, ignore it, or attempt to extinguish it. And it won't come as a surprise that I think you ought to support it.

Why? Remember what Rex taught us about philosophy right at the start: *It's the art of thinking.* And that's an art you want your kid to master. The aim is *not* to raise a professional philosopher. It's to raise a person who thinks clearly and carefully. It's to raise a person who thinks for themself. It's to raise a person who cares what others think—and thinks with them. In short, the aim is to raise a person who thinks.

How DO YOU RAISE a philosopher? The simplest way is to talk to your kids. Ask them questions and question their answers. The questions don't have to be complicated, and you don't need to know any philosophy to ask them. In fact, a set of stock questions will get you through most situations.

- What do you think?

- Why do you think so?

- Can you think of reasons you might be wrong?

- What do you mean by . . . ?

- What is . . . ?

The aim is to make the kid make an argument—and get them to see the other side. So let the kid do most of the talking. But don't hesitate to help when they're stuck. And above all else: approach it as a conversation between equals. Take what your kid says seriously, even if you disagree—even if it strikes you as silly. Reason with your child—and resist telling them what to think.

How DO YOU GET a philosophical conversation going? You can set them up, and in the Appendix I'll point you to resources that will get you started: books, podcasts, and websites. Just about every picture book raises some question in philosophy; you've just passed them by. And that's okay. I let most pass by too. Some nights, you just want to enjoy the story. Or get to the end of the book. But it's fun to have a conversation when you can.

That said, you don't need books, or anything else, to get a conversation started. If you simply listen to your kids—their complaints and curiosities—philosophical questions will crop up often. When a kid says something's not fair, ask what fairness is. Or whether it's your job to make things fair. Or whether she ever benefits from unfairness. You don't have to have answers in mind to ask questions. Just see where the conversation goes.

It's hard to have a deep conversation with a kid that's distraught. But in my experience, philosophy can help calm a kid down. Remember Hank sobbing at the thought that he didn't have a right to Rex? I talked to him softly and took him seriously. And he got a grip on himself sufficient to allow us to have a serious conversation. It doesn't always work. Sometimes a kid just needs a hug. Or some time to herself. But it can be soothing to be taken seriously.

Curiosities work just as well as complaints. Don't waste wonder. And don't worry whether you know the answer. Talk for a while. Then do research together. Do this for science for sure. But do it with questions about *everything*. When I was a little kid, I was constantly curious to know what the best of something was. My father would always answer.

"What's the best music?"

"*Rhapsody in Blue*," he said.

"What's the best TV show?"

"*The Lone Ranger*."

The answers were idiosyncratic to him. But also: a missed opportunity.

"What's the best music?"

"That's a good question," I'd say. "What do you think makes music good?"

And with that, we'd be off and running on a conversation about aesthetics. And no, you don't need to know anything about aesthetics to have the conversation. I sure don't. Just see what the kid says and share your thoughts about it.

Above all, lean into the weird questions that kids ask. If your kid wonders whether he's dreaming his entire life, don't dismiss him. If she wants to know why the days keep coming, see what she thinks the answer is. And if a kid asks a question that leaves you completely stumped, stop and wonder at the world together.

·⁓·

REMEMBER THE NIGHT I tried to argue Hank out of his relativism? We had our man-to-man chat at bedtime, and I broke him by insisting that he was six when he was actually eight.

I didn't tell you what happened just before that.

As we were arguing about truth, Hank asked why I cared so much.

"I'm a philosopher," I said. "We want to understand everything. But especially truth."

"You're not a very good philosopher," Hank said.

"Why not?"

"Your arguments aren't persuasive."

I laughed—and decided then that his relativism wouldn't last the night. It was sort of like the time Rex gave me advice on how to play air hockey—just a few minutes into his first game ever.

You don't think I know what I'm doing, kid? Watch this.

So I broke Hank. But I regret it, a little. Because persuading people is not really the aim of philosophy. Or at least, it's not my aim in philosophy.

Robert Nozick—one of the great political philosophers of the twentieth century—described a style he called *coercive philosophy*. Its practitioners, he said, are searching for "arguments so powerful they set up reverberations in the brain: if a person refuses to accept the conclusion, he *dies*." No one, of course, achieves that. But the ambition—to subdue others through the force of one's intellect—is all too common in the field. Many think the measure of success is just what Hank suggested: How persuasive have you been? Did you win people over to your side?

My ambition is to understand things, in a deeper way than I did before. If I find answers, great. And if other people see promise in them, even better. But I see philosophy the way Bertrand Russell did: "Philosophy, if it cannot *answer* so many questions as we could wish, has at least the power of *asking* questions which increase the interest of the world, and show the strangeness and wonder lying just below the surface even in the commonest things of daily life."

Kids are alive to that strangeness and wonder. At least until we train them not to be. I hope you'll help the kids in your life hold on to it. And I hope, just as much, that you'll find it for yourself.

ACKNOWLEDGMENTS

"What are you working on next?" Rex asked, as I submitted the last draft of this book.

"I have to write acknowledgments," I said.

"Since you're telling stories about Hank and me, will we get one of those?"

Indeed you will, kid.

To start, a huge thank-you to Rex and Hank for letting me tell stories about them—and for letting me tell stories that are true, even when they don't love all the details. I also appreciate their willingness to share their ideas—and let me share them with you. The boys are, in important ways, authors of this book.

But I owe them thanks for a lot more than that. Rex and Hank make me smile. They make me laugh. They make me think. They inspire me—in philosophy and out. And I haven't done them justice, not even close; there's so much more to both boys than shows up on the page.

Rex is the sweetest, kindest person I know. He's not just smart; he's wise. And he's funny too. When I grow up, I'd like to be a little more like him.

Hank laughs easily, and his smile is the best I've ever seen. He's got a sharp mind and a good heart. He's always up to something, and it's (almost) always something good. I hope he never grows up—not completely. We should all have a little Hank in us.

I met Julie on a bus to camp. She was sixteen; I was seventeen. She was cute and kind. So I sought her out at dinner. It remains the best decision I ever made.

Julie's my best friend—and a better partner than I deserve. I love her more than I could possibly say. She's a supporting character in this book, but a star to everyone who knows her—and especially those of us lucky enough to live with her. I wouldn't have started this project without Julie's encouragement, or finished it without her support. And that's true of more or less everything that I do.

When the kids were little, Julie and I took turns with the nighttime routine. One night she did bath and I did bedtime; the next night we switched. That broke down when I was up for tenure. Julie did both jobs most nights as I rushed to complete my file. Rex was not happy when I returned to the rotation.

"Go upstairs and type, Daddy!" he demanded on my first night back at bath. He wanted his mother. And I get that. I like her more than me too.

Years later, he got his wish. I've spent a lot of time typing, often late into the night. As a result, I've been tired and grumpy on more occasions than I care to count. Not only did Julie and the boys put up with me; they've welcomed me back more readily than Rex did when he was little. I'm blessed to be part of this brood.

Aaron James was the first person to suggest that I write about my kids and philosophy. This book wouldn't exist if he hadn't planted the seed.

Years later, I told Scott Shapiro about the idea, and he liked it. Better yet, he told Alison MacKeen about it, and she liked it too. She also knew how to bring a book into the world. I could not ask for a better agent. Alison—and the rest of her team at Park & Fine—have been terrific advocates for both me and the book. Alison has also been a great friend. (And so has Scott, for several decades now.)

I met Ginny Smith Younce on a video chat. It was love at first Skype. She grokked the book immediately, and improved it in countless ways. So did Caroline Sydney. Together they asked all the right questions—and saved me from many mistakes. The entire team at Penguin Press has been terrific.

When I wasn't writing upstairs, I was often writing at Lake Michigan—in a house owned by David Uhlmann and Virginia Murphy. When Rex was little, he called it the "house beach" and the name stuck. I don't think I would have finished the book without the solitude the house beach provided—or support from David and Virginia, the best friends one could hope to have.

Angela Sun provided first-rate research assistance—and sound advice on so many issues. It would have taken twice the time to write this book without her—and it wouldn't have been nearly as good.

Writing a book that addressed so many questions in philosophy was a serious challenge. And I couldn't have pulled it off without the help of many friends and philosophers.

Don Herzog continued his streak of reading every word I write. His influence runs deep, even where we disagree. He's an all-star colleague and an even better friend.

Chris Essert also read the entire manuscript. He encouraged me where I needed encouraging, and reined me in where I didn't. I'm always grateful for his good judgment.

I'm also grateful to the long list of people who commented on large chunks of the manuscript, or talked me through important bits of it: Kate Andrias, Nick Bagley, Dave Baker, Gordon Belot, Sarah Buss, Murrey Cohen, Nico Cornell, Robin Dembroff, Daniel Fryer, Megan Furman, Fiona Furnari, Daniel Halberstam, Jerry Hershovitz, Julie Kaplan, Ellen Katz, Kyle Logue, Alison MacKeen, Gabe Mendlow, William Ian Miller, Sarah Moss, Virginia Murphy, Kristina Olson, Aaron Olver, Steve Schaus, Scott Shapiro, Nicos Stavropoulos, Eric Swanson, Laura Tavares, Will Thomas, Scott Weiner, and Ekow Yankah. The book is better for all their contributions—and for the contributions of someone I'm surely forgetting.

Special thanks to Aaron Olver and Scott Weiner, for soothing anxieties and offering sound advice, in addition to first-rate friendship.

I don't come from a family of philosophers. But I do come from a family that took me seriously. I didn't grow up in a seen-and-not-heard sort of house. We had real conversations. My parents let me argue a lot. And my brother treated me like a peer, even though I was years behind him. I think my family is puzzled by my interest in philosophy, but without doubt they helped me stay a philosopher. All kids should be so lucky.

APPENDIX

SUGGESTED RESOURCES

BOOKS FOR GROWN-UPS

ON KIDS AND PARENTING

Gopnik, Alison. *The Philosophical Baby: What Children's Minds Tell Us about Truth, Love, and the Meaning of Life.* New York: Farrar, Straus and Giroux, 2009.

Kazez, Jean. *The Philosophical Parent: Asking the Hard Questions about Having and Raising Children.* New York: Oxford University Press, 2017.

Lone, Jana Mohr. *The Philosophical Child.* London: Rowman & Littlefield, 2012.

———. *Seen and Not Heard: Why Children's Voices Matter.* London: Rowman & Littlefield, 2021.

Matthews, Gareth B. *Dialogues with Children.* Cambridge, MA: Harvard University Press, 1984.

———. *Philosophy & the Young Child.* Cambridge, MA: Harvard University Press, 1980.

———. *The Philosophy of Childhood.* Cambridge, MA: Harvard University Press, 1994.

Wartenberg, Thomas E. *A Sneetch Is a Sneetch and Other Philosophical Discoveries: Finding Wisdom in Children's Literature.* West Sussex, UK: Wiley-Blackwell, 2013.

———. *Big Ideas for Little Kids: Teaching Philosophy through Children's Literature.* Plymouth, UK: Rowman & Littlefield Education, 2009.

ON THE TROLLEY PROBLEM

Edmonds, David. *Would You Kill the Fat Man?: The Trolley Problem and What Your Answer Tells Us about Right and Wrong.* Princeton, NJ: Princeton University Press, 2014.

ON PUNISHMENT

Murphy, Jeffrie G., and Jean Hampton, *Forgiveness and Mercy.* New York: Cambridge University Press, 1988.

ON KNOWLEDGE

Nagel, Jennifer. *Knowledge: A Very Short Introduction.* Oxford: Oxford University Press, 2014.

ON CONSCIOUSNESS

Dennett, Daniel C. *Consciousness Explained.* Boston: Little, Brown, 1991.

Godfrey-Smith, Peter. *Other Minds: The Octopus, the Sea, and the Deep Origins of Consciousness.* New York: Farrar, Straus and Giroux, 2016.

Goff, Philip. *Galileo's Error: Foundations for a New Science of Consciousness.* New York: Pantheon Books, 2019.

Koch, Christof. *Consciousness: Confessions of a Romantic Reductionist.* Cambridge, MA: MIT Press, 2012.

ON THE HISTORY OF PHILOSOPHY

Warburton, Nigel. *A Little History of Philosophy.* New Haven, CT: Yale University Press, 2011.

FURTHER FUN PHILOSOPHY

Edmonds, David, and John Eidinow. *Wittgenstein's Poker: The Story of a Ten-Minute Argument Between Two Great Philosophers.* New York: Ecco, 2001.

Holt, Jim. *Why Does the World Exist?: An Existential Detective Story.* New York: W. W. Norton, 2012.

James, Aaron. *Assholes: A Theory.* New York: Anchor Books, 2012.

———. *Surfing with Sartre: An Aquatic Inquiry into a Life of Meaning.* New York: Doubleday, 2017.

Setiya, Kieran. *Midlife: A Philosophical Guide.* Princeton, NJ: Princeton University Press, 2017.

BOOKS FOR KIDS

BOARD BOOKS

Armitage, Duane, and Maureen McQuerry. Big Ideas for Little Philosophers series, including titles like *Truth with Socrates* and *Equality with Simone de Beauvoir.* New York: G. P. Putnam's Sons, 2020.

ON THE UNIVERSE

Fishman, Seth. *A Hundred Billion Trillion Stars.* New York: HarperCollins, 2017.

ON RULES AND WHEN IT'S OKAY TO BREAK THEM

Knudsen, Michelle. *Library Lion.* Somerville, MA: Candlewick Press, 2006.

ON INFINITY

Ekeland, Ivar. *The Cat in Numberland.* Chicago: Cricket Books, 2006.

A COMPENDIUM OF PHILOSOPHICAL PUZZLES (APPROPRIATE FOR A TEENAGER)

Martin, Robert M. *There Are Two Errors in the the Title of This Book: A Sourcebook of Philosophical Puzzles, Problems, and Paradoxes.* Peterborough, ON, Canada: Broadview Press, 2011.

THE MOST IMPORTANT BOOKS YOU CAN BUY A KID

Watterson, Bill. *The Complete Calvin and Hobbes.* Kansas City, MO: Andrews Mc-Meel, 2012. Calvin and Hobbes inspired my philosophical musings as a kid. Now they're doing the same for Rex. And, of course, they're entertaining him too. I'm not sure there's a better entry point into philosophy, for grown-ups or kids.

WEBSITES

Teaching Children Philosophy (www.prindleinstitute.org/teaching-children-philosophy): If you want to talk to kids about philosophy, this is the single best resource you'll find. It has teaching modules for picture books, many of which you might have already. It provides an overview of the philosophical questions each book raises, and it suggests questions you can ask as you read.

University of Washington Center for Philosophy for Children (www.philosophyforchildren.org): This is another terrific resource for talking to kids about philosophy. It has teaching modules for picture books, lesson plans for teachers, and advice for starting philosophy programs in schools. The center also runs workshops for teachers and parents.

Wi-Phi (www.wi-phi.com): This site has lots of short videos explaining topics in philosophy. Rex and I like to watch them together.

PODCASTS

Hi-Phi Nation (https://hiphination.org): A story-driven podcast about philosophy, aimed at grown-ups.

Philosophy Bites (https://philosophybites.com): Short interviews with top philosophers.

Pickle (www.wnycstudios.org/podcasts/pickle): A short-lived kids' podcast from WNYC about philosophy. Its Australian cousin, *Short & Curly* (www.abc.net.au/radio/programs/shortandcurly/), has many more episodes.

Smash Boom Best (www.smashboom.org): This podcast is all about making arguments. It's silly, and not exactly philosophy. But Hank likes it a lot.

NOTES

I have tried to make the notes that follow as useful as possible for a lay reader. When I had a choice, I cited sources that are freely available, rather than journal articles locked behind paywalls. Many notes also point toward online encyclopedias—the *Stanford Encyclopedia of Philosophy* and the *Internet Encyclopedia of Philosophy*—that are available to anyone.

The *Stanford Encyclopedia*, in particular, is an excellent resource. There are entries for just about every philosophical topic you might be interested in. And the bibliographies at the end of each entry will point you in the right direction if you want to dig into the academic literature.

INTRODUCTION: THE ART OF THINKING

5   *shifted color spectrum*: More commonly, this problem is presented through an inversion of the color spectrum—a 180-degree shift from red to green. For an overview of the problem and its implications for philosophy, see Alex Byrne, "Inverted Qualia," *Stanford Encyclopedia of Philosophy* (Fall 2020 edition), ed. Edward N. Zalta, https://plato.stanford.edu/archives/fall2020/entries/qualia -inverted.

6   **students recall pondering**: Daniel C. Dennett, *Consciousness Explained* (Boston: Little, Brown, 1991), 389.

6   **"Imputation of *Falshood*"**: Here's the rest of what Locke had to say (as you'll see,

it's more or less what I said to my mom): "For since this could never be known: because one Man's Mind could not pass into another Man's Body, to perceive, what Appearances were produced by those Organs; neither the Ideas hereby, nor the Names, would be at all confounded, or any Falshood be in either. For all Things, that had the Texture of a Violet, producing constantly the Idea, which he called Blue, and those which had the Texture of a Marigold, producing constantly the Idea, which he as constantly called Yellow, whatever those Appearances were in his Mind; he would be able as regularly to distinguish Things for his Use by those Appearances, and understand, and signify those distinctions, marked by the Names Blue and Yellow, as if the Appearances, or Ideas in his Mind, received from those two Flowers, were exactly the same, with the Ideas in other Men's Minds." John Locke, *An Essay Concerning Human Understanding*, ed. Peter H. Nidditch (New York: Oxford University Press, 1975), 389.

9 **Sarah (age four) asked:** Gareth B. Matthews relays the story in his book *The Philosophy of Childhood* (Cambridge, MA: Harvard University Press, 1994), 1.

10 **At the time, Matthews was teaching:** For an overview of the Cosmological Argument, see Bruce Reichenbach, "Cosmological Argument," *Stanford Encyclopedia of Philosophy* (Spring 2021 edition), ed. Edward N. Zalta, https://plato.stanford.edu/archives/spr2021/entries/cosmological-argument.

10 **"the First Flea":** Matthews, *Philosophy of Childhood*, 2.

10 **the *pre-operational stage*:** Matthews, *Philosophy of Childhood*, 2.

10 **Piaget simply fails:** Gareth B. Matthews, *Philosophy & the Young Child* (Cambridge, MA: Harvard University Press, 1980), 37–55.

11 **Matthews didn't stop:** Gareth B. Matthews collects many of his conversations with kids in *Dialogues with Children* (Cambridge, MA: Harvard University Press, 1984) and *Philosophy and the Young Child*.

11 **little boy named Ian:** Matthews, *Philosophy and the Young Child*, 28–30.

12 **"cultivate the naiveté":** Matthews, *Philosophy of Childhood*, 122.

12 **"spontaneous excursions into philosophy":** Matthews, *Philosophy of Childhood*, 5.

12 **By eight or nine:** Matthews, *Philosophy of Childhood*, 5.

12 **"a freshness and inventiveness":** Matthews, *Philosophy of Childhood*, 17.

12 **Michelle Chouinard listened:** Michele M. Chouinard, P. L. Harris, and Michael P. Maratsos, "Children's Questions: A Mechanism for Cognitive Development," *Monographs of the Society for Research in Child Development* 72, no. 1 (2007): 1–129. For a discussion of Chouinard's study, see Paul Harris, *Trusting What You're Told: How Children Learn from Others* (Cambridge, MA: Belknap Press, 2012), 26–29.

12 **In another study, researchers found:** Brandy N. Frazier, Susan A. Gelman, and Henry M. Wellman, "Preschoolers' Search for Explanatory Information within Adult-Child Conversation," *Child Development* 80, no. 6 (2009): 1592–1611.

13 **"What is time, anyway?":** Augustine, *Confessions* 11.14, cited in Matthews, *Philosophy of Childhood*, 13.

14 **"the ungainly attempt":** David Hills, Stanford University, Department of Philosophy, accessed October 13, 2021, https://philosophy.stanford.edu/people/david-hills.

14 **each brings something different**: See Matthews, *Philosophy of Childhood*, 12–18, and Matthews, *Dialogues with Children*, 3.

15 **Philosophy is partly play**: See Matthews, *Philosophy and the Young Child*, 11.

15 *days keep coming*: In her book *Seen and Not Heard*, Jana Mohr Lone also reports meeting a mother whose daughter asked this question. (Lone may well be Matthews's successor to the title of philosopher most engaged with children; her book shares what she's learned through countless conversations with kids about philosophy.) It's possible we both spoke with the same mother. If we didn't, kids are spookily concerned with this question. See Jana Mohr Lone, *Seen and Not Heard: Why Children's Voices Matter* (London: Rowman and Littlefield, 2021), 8.

16 **about continuous creation**: For an introduction to continuous creation, see David Vander Laan, "Creation and Conservation," *Stanford Encyclopedia of Philosophy* (Winter 2017 edition), ed. Edward N. Zalta, https://plato.stanford.edu/archives /win2017/entries/creation-conservation.

18 **doesn't teach them philosophy**: Jana Mohr Lone, "Philosophy with Children," *Aeon*, May 11, 2021, https://aeon.co/essays/how-to-do-philosophy-for-and-with -children.

19 **Indeed, he thought**: Thomas Hobbes, *Leviathan*, ed. A. R. Walker (Cambridge: Cambridge University Press, 1904), 137.

19 **"nasty, brutish, and short"**: Hobbes, *Leviathan*, 84.

CHAPTER 1: RIGHTS

28 **can, may, and should**: On the interchangeability of *can* and *may*, see "Usage Notes: 'Can' vs. 'May,'" *Merriam-Webster*, accessed July 5, 2021, www.merriam -webster.com/words-at-play/when-to-use-can-and-may#.

29 **theory of rights**: Judith Jarvis Thomson, *The Realm of Rights* (Cambridge, MA: Harvard University Press, 1990), 123.

30 **It's called *consequentialism***: For an overview of consequentialism, see Walter Sinnott-Armstrong, "Consequentialism," *Stanford Encyclopedia of Philosophy* (Summer 2019 edition), ed. Edward N. Zalta, https://plato.stanford.edu/archives /sum2019/entries/consequentialism.

31 **take rights seriously**: Ronald Dworkin, *Taking Rights Seriously* (Cambridge, MA: Harvard University Press, 1977).

31 **rights *trump* concerns about welfare**: Ronald Dworkin, "Rights as Trumps," in *Theories of Rights*, ed. Jeremy Waldron (Oxford: Oxford University Press, 1984), 153–67.

31 **commonly called Transplant**: See Judith Jarvis Thomson, "The Trolley Problem," *Yale Law Journal* 94, no. 6 (May 1985): 1396.

31 **the first Bystander at the Switch**: Thomson, "Trolley Problem," 1397.

33 **This one's called Fat Man**: Thomson, "Trolley Problem," 1409.

34 **Kant insisted that**: For an overview of Kant's moral philosophy, see Robert Johnson and Adam Cureton, "Kant's Moral Philosophy," *Stanford Encyclopedia of*

Philosophy (Spring 2021 edition), ed. Edward N. Zalta, https://plato.stanford.edu /archives/spr2021/entries/kant-moral.

35   **an unfortunate by-product:** Another proposed solution to the Trolley Problem also exploits the fact that the death of the single worker on the spur is foreseen but not intended. This is the famous *doctrine of double effect*, which figures prominently in Catholic teachings about abortion. According to the doctrine, it is sometimes permissible to cause harm in the pursuit of a worthwhile end, so long as the harm itself is not intended. As it happens, the very first appearance of trolleys in philosophy was in an article by Philippa Foot, titled "The Problem of Abortion and the Doctrine of the Double Effect," *Oxford Review* 5 (1967): 5–15. For an overview of the doctrine of double effect, and some doubts about it, see Alison McIntyre, "Doctrine of Double Effect," *Stanford Encyclopedia of Philosophy* (Spring 2019 edition), ed. Edward N. Zalta, https://plato.stanford.edu /archives/spr2019/entries/double-effect.

35   **she considered the solution:** Thomson, "Trolley Problem," 1401–3.

35   **This one's called Loop:** Thomson, "Trolley Problem," 1402.

36   **Some philosophers think:** For an exploration of the possibility that it does, see John Mikhail, *Elements of Moral Cognition* (Cambridge: Cambridge University Press, 2011), 101–21.

37   **Fat Man Trapped:** Mikhail calls this case Drop Man. See his *Elements of Moral Cognition*, 109.

37   **sometimes called Trolleyology:** For a fun tour through Trolleyology, see David Edmonds, *Would You Kill the Fat Man? The Trolley Problem and What Your Answer Tells Us about Right and Wrong* (Princeton, NJ: Princeton University Press, 2014).

37   **letter to the *Globe and Mail*:** Wilson's letter is reprinted in Thomas Hurka, "Trolleys and Permissible Harm," in F. M. Kamm, *The Trolley Problem Mysteries*, ed. Eric Rakowski (Oxford: Oxford University Press, 2015), 135.

37   **Thomson's last word:** On this topic, discussed in the footnote, see Judith Jarvis Thomson, "Turning the Trolley," *Philosophy & Public Affairs* 36, no. 4 (2008): 359–74.

40   **Trolleys were introduced:** Foot, "Problem of Abortion."

CHAPTER 2: REVENGE

48   **steal their stickers:** Nadia Chernyak, Kristin L. Leimgruber, Yarrow C. Dunham, Jingshi Hu, and Peter R. Blake, "Paying Back People Who Harmed Us but Not People Who Helped Us: Direct Negative Reciprocity Precedes Direct Positive Reciprocity in Early Development," *Psychological Science* 30, no. 9 (2019): 1273–86.

48   **seek to satisfy hunger:** See Susan Cosier, "Is Revenge Really Sweet?" *Science Friday*, July 1, 2013, www.sciencefriday.com/articles/is-revenge-really-sweet/; and Eddie Harmon-Jones and Jonathan Sigelman, "State Anger and Prefrontal Brain Activity: Evidence That Insult-Related Relative Left-Prefrontal Activa-

tion Is Associated with Experienced Anger and Aggression," *Journal of Personality and Social Psychology* 80, no. 5 (June 2001): 797–803.

48 **revenge is sweet**: Homer, *The Iliad*, trans. Peter Green (Oakland: University of California Press, 2015), 18.108–10. In this passage, Achilles says "resentment" is "sweeter than honey," but it's resentment in contemplation of revenge that he has in mind.

48 **"At a boozy dinner"**: The quote related in the footnote is from Simon Sebag Montefiore, *Young Stalin* (New York: Vintage Books, 2008), 295.

50 **the roles of debtor and creditor**: See William Ian Miller, *An Eye for an Eye* (New York: Cambridge University Press, 2006), 68–69.

50 **"Vengeance is mine"**: Rom. 12:19 (King James Version).

50 **Aristotle drew a distinction**: Aristotle, "Book V: Justice," *Nicomachean Ethics*, trans. C. D. C. Reeve (Indianapolis: Hackett, 2014), 77–97.

50 **a rather genius one**: Miller, *An Eye for an Eye*, especially chapter 4 ("The Proper Price of Property in an Eye").

52 *Saga of Gudmund the Worthy*: Discussed in William Ian Miller, *Bloodtaking and Peacemaking: Feud, Law, and Society in Saga Iceland* (Chicago: University of Chicago Press, 1997), 1–2.

53 **"willing to pay more"**: Miller, *Bloodtaking and Peacemaking*, 2.

54 **"Honor was what provided"**: Miller, *An Eye for an Eye*, 101.

55 **case about Kay Kenton**: *Kenton v. Hyatt Hotels Corp.*, 693 S.W.2d 83 (Mo. 1985).

56 **counted as reasonable compensation**: As Miller explains (*An Eye for an Eye*, 53–54), there were often customs about what counted as reasonable compensation for particular injuries—like the one that Gudmund flouted when he set the price for Skæring's hand.

56 **"odd to get even"**: Miller, *An Eye for an Eye*, 9.

57 **"cheap, nasty, and brutish"**: Miller, *An Eye for an Eye*, 55.

57 **little value on life and limb**: For this and the "less of our virtue" quote in the footnote, see Miller, *An Eye for an Eye*, 57.

57 **"every road fatality"**: Miller, *An Eye for an Eye*, 55.

57 **a debt slave**: Miller, *An Eye for an Eye*, 54.

59 *self-respect* **is at stake**: See Pamela Hieronymi, "Articulating an Uncompromising Forgiveness," *Philosophy and Phenomenological Research* 62, no. 3 (2001): 529–55.

59 **ought to feel anger and resentment**: Hieronymi, "Articulating an Uncompromising Forgiveness," 530.

60 **a matter of self-respect**: Jeffrie G. Murphy and Jean Hampton, *Forgiveness and Mercy* (New York: Cambridge University Press, 1988).

60 **If Hank resents Caden**: Hieronymi, "Articulating an Uncompromising Forgiveness," 546.

63 **correct the messages**: See Scott Hershovitz, "Treating Wrongs as Wrongs: An Expressive Argument for Tort Law," *Journal of Tort Law* 10, no. 2 (2017): 405–47.

63 **about Taylor Swift**: The argument in this section is adapted from my "Taylor

Swift, Philosopher of Forgiveness," *New York Times*, September 7, 2019, www
.nytimes.com/2019/09/07/opinion/sunday/taylor-swift-lover.html.

CHAPTER 3: PUNISHMENT

68   **Wrongdoers incur a debt**: For an overview of different ways of thinking about
retribution, see John Cottingham, "Varieties of Retribution," *Philosophical
Quarterly* 29, no. 116 (1979): 238–46. For skepticism about the leading forms of
the idea, see David Dolinko, "Some Thoughts about Retributivism," *Ethics* 101,
no. 3 (1991): 537–59.

70   **school for animal trainers**: Amy Sutherland, *What Shamu Taught Me about Life,
Love, and Marriage* (New York: Random House, 2009).

70   **"What Shamu taught me"**: Amy Sutherland, "What Shamu Taught Me about a
Happy Marriage," *New York Times*, June 25, 2006, www.nytimes.com/2019/10/11
/style/modern-love-what-shamu-taught-me-happy-marriage.html.

70   **"a sea lion"**: Sutherland, "What Shamu Taught Me about a Happy Marriage."

71   **It's called "Freedom and Resentment"**: P. F. Strawson, *Freedom and Resentment
and Other Essays* (London: Methuen, 1974), 1–25.

72   **"to be managed or handled"**: Strawson, *Freedom and Resentment*, 9.

72   **"closer to perfect"**: Sutherland, "What Shamu Taught Me about a Happy Marriage."

72   **we feel anger and resentment**: Strawson, *Freedom and Resentment*, 6–7.

74   **Feinberg saw a problem**: Joel Feinberg, "The Expressive Function of Punishment," *The Monist* 49, no. 3 (1965): 397–423.

75   **"hostility is self-righteous"**: Feinberg, "Expressive Function of Punishment," 403.

76   **"slave of the passions"**: David Hume, *A Treatise of Human Nature* (London:
Deighton and Sons, 1817), 106.

79   **"managed or handled"**: Strawson, *Freedom and Resentment*, 9.

81   **a fair bit of research**: Adam Grant collects some of the studies together in "Raising a Moral Child," *New York Times*, April 11, 2014, www.nytimes.com/2014/04/12
/opinion/sunday/raising-a-moral-child.html.

81   **you really are upset**: As Strawson put it, "Rehearsals insensibly modulate toward
true performances." Strawson, *Freedom and Resentment*, 19.

83   **Punishment signals that**: I develop this view of corrective and retributive justice
in "Treating Wrongs as Wrongs: An Expressive Argument for Tort Law," *Journal of Tort Law* 10, no. 2 (2017): 405–47.

83   **sentence handed down**: Chanel Miller recounts her experience of the assault and
its aftermath in *Know My Name: A Memoir* (New York: Viking, 2019).

83   **sentence sparked outrage**: See Liam Stack, "Light Sentence for Brock Turner in
Stanford Rape Case Draws Outrage," *New York Times*, June 6, 2016.

83   **for petty theft**: Cal. Penal Code §§ 487–88 (2020).

83   **more people per capita**: Roy Walmsley, "World Prison Population List," 12th ed.,
Institute for Criminal Policy Research, June 11, 2018, www.prisonstudies.org
/sites/default/files/resources/downloads/wppl_12.pdf.

85 **"In every good marriage"**: Ruth Bader Ginsburg, "Ruth Bader Ginsburg's Advice for Living," *New York Times*, October 1, 2016, www.nytimes.com/2016/10/02 /opinion/sunday/ruth-bader-ginsburgs-advice-for-living.html.

85 **"take his faults personally"**: Sutherland, "What Shamu Taught Me about a Happy Marriage."

85 **"too entrenched, too instinctive"**: Sutherland, "What Shamu Taught Me about a Happy Marriage."

85 **"strains of involvement"**: Strawson, *Freedom and Resentment*, 10.

CHAPTER 4: AUTHORITY

90 **distinction between power and authority**: See Joseph Raz, *The Authority of Law: Essays on Law and Morality*, 2nd ed. (Oxford: Oxford University Press, 2009), 19–20.

91 **power over a person's**: See, e.g., Joseph Raz, *Ethics in the Public Domain* (Oxford: Oxford University Press, 1994), 341 ("[T]o have authority is to have a right to rule those who are subject to it. And a right to rule entails an obligation to obey"); Robert Paul Wolff, *In Defense of Anarchism* (Berkeley: University of California Press, 1998), 4 ("Authority is the right to command, and correlatively, the right to be obeyed").

91 **with a stickup**: See Wolff, *In Defense of Anarchism*, 4.

92 **obligated to *take responsibility***: Wolff, *In Defense of Anarchism*, 12–15.

92 **aims to act *autonomously***: Wolff, *In Defense of Anarchism*, 13.

92 **she has responsibilities**: Wolff, *In Defense of Anarchism*, 13.

92 **autonomy and authority are incompatible**: Wolff, *In Defense of Anarchism*, 18–19.

93 **reason to defer**: Raz, *Authority of Law*, 13–15.

93 **only because *you* decided**: See Scott J. Shapiro, "Authority," in *The Oxford Handbook of Jurisprudence and Philosophy of Law*, ed. Jules L. Coleman, Kenneth Einar Himma, and Scott J. Shapiro (New York: Oxford University Press, 2002), 383–439; and Raz, *Authority of Law*, 3–36.

93 **responsibility in proportion**: Re the footnote, see Wolff, *In Defense of Anarchism*, 12–13.

95 **help you do a better job**: Raz calls this the *normal justification thesis*. See Joseph Raz, *Morality of Freedom* (Oxford: Clarendon, 1986), 53. For my sketch of the thesis—and concerns about it—see Scott Hershovitz, "Legitimacy, Democracy, and Razian Authority," *Legal Theory* 9, no. 3 (2003): 206–8.

95 *service conception of authority*: Raz, *Morality of Freedom*, 56.

95 **might know better**: Raz, *Morality of Freedom*, 74–76.

95 **call these situations *coordination problems***: Raz, *Morality of Freedom*, 49–50.

96 **a reason for the players**: Raz, *Morality of Freedom*, 47.

98 **set out to show**: My critique of Raz's view of authority is spread across three papers: Hershovitz, "Legitimacy, Democracy, and Razian Authority," 201–20; and Scott Hershovitz, "The Role of Authority," *Philosophers' Imprint* 11, no. 7

(2011): 1–19; and "The Authority of Law," in *The Routledge Companion to the Philosophy of Law*, ed. Andrei Marmor (New York: Routledge, 2012), 65–75.

100 **right to boss you around**: See Hershovitz, "Role of Authority"; Stephen Darwall, "Authority and Second-Personal Reasons for Acting," in *Reasons for Action*, ed. David Sobel and Steven Wall (Cambridge: Cambridge University Press, 2009), 150–51; and Ken Himma, "Just 'Cause You're Smarter Than Me Doesn't Give You a Right to Tell Me What to Do: Legitimate Authority and the Normal Justification Thesis," *Oxford Journal of Legal Studies* 27, no. 1 (2007): 121–50.

101 **rest of the role**: The view set out in this section is developed at length in my paper "Role of Authority."

102 **Peter Parker principle**: Massimo Pigliucci, "The Peter Parker Principle," *Medium*, August 3, 2020, https://medium.com/@MassimoPigliucci/the-peter-parker -principle-9f3f33799904.

102 **some role of authority**: On the idea that ownership is a role of authority, see Christopher Essert, "The Office of Ownership," *University of Toronto Law Journal* 63, no. 3 (2013): 418–61.

104 **political sign on your lawn**: Robert McGarvey, "You Can Be Fired for Your Political Beliefs," *The Street*, April 28, 2016, www.thestreet.com/personal-finance /you-can-be-fired-for-your-political-beliefs-13547984.

104 **wear your hair**: Roger S. Achille, "Policy Banning Extreme Hair Colors Upheld," Society for Human Resource Management, March 14, 2018, www.shrm .org/resourcesandtools/legal-and-compliance/employment-law/pages/court -report-policy-banning-extreme-hair-colors-upheld.aspx.

104 **most oppressive government**: Elizabeth Anderson, *Private Government: How Employers Rule Our Lives (and Why We Don't Talk about It)* (Princeton, NJ: Princeton University Press, 2017).

104 **search employees' belongings**: See *Frlekin v. Apple, Inc.*, 2015 U.S. Dist. LEXIS 151937, cited in Anderson, *Private Government*, xix.

104 **They schedule shifts**: Stephanie Wykstra, "The Movement to Make Workers' Schedules More Humane," *Vox*, November 5, 2019, www.vox.com/future-perfect /2019/10/15/20910297/fair-workweek-laws-unpredictable-scheduling-retail -restaurants.

104 **rules for hair and makeup**: Achille, "Policy Banning Extreme Hair Colors Upheld."

104 **Workers in warehouses**: Colin Lecher, "How Amazon Automatically Tracks and Fires Warehouse Workers for 'Productivity,'" *The Verge*, April 25, 2019, www .theverge.com/2019/4/25/18516004/amazon-warehouse-fulfillment-centers-pro ductivity-firing-terminations.

104 **even their trips**: See Oxfam America, *No Relief: Denial of Bathroom Breaks in the Poultry Industry* (Washington, DC, 2016), 2, https://s3.amazonaws.com/oxfam -us/www/static/media/files/No_Relief_Embargo.pdf, cited in Anderson, *Private Government*, xix.

106 "war of every man": Thomas Hobbes, *Leviathan*, ed. A. R. Walker (Cambridge: Cambridge University Press, 1904), 137.

106 "The weakest has strength": Hobbes, *Leviathan*, 81.

106 no machines, no buildings: Hobbes, *Leviathan*, 84.

106 In the state of nature, life: Hobbes, *Leviathan*, 84.

106 saw a way out: Hobbes, *Leviathan*, 84–89.

107 separation of powers: John Locke, *Two Treatises on Civil Government* (London: Routledge, 1884), 267–75.

107 popular representation in the legislature: Locke, *Two Treatises*, 306–7.

CHAPTER 5: LANGUAGE

111 "For a simple demonstration": Neil deGrasse Tyson, *Astrophysics for Young People in a Hurry* (New York: Norton Young Readers, 2019), 16.

113 "slam a door": Rebecca Roache, "Naughty Words," *Aeon*, February 22, 2016, https://aeon.co/essays/where-does-swearing-get-its-power-and-how-should-we-use-it.

114 calls *offense escalation*: Roache, "Naughty Words."

114 aren't the sorts of stories: See Melissa Mohr's *Holy Shit: A Brief History of Swearing* (New York: Oxford University Press, 2013).

116 called this *conventional morality*: Ronald Dworkin, *Taking Rights Seriously* (London: Duckworth, 1978), 73.

119 perceived less pain: Richard Stephens, John Atkins, and Andrew Kingston, "Swearing as a Response to Pain," *Neuroreport* 20, no. 12 (2009): 1056–60, summarized in Emma Byrne, *Swearing Is Good for You: The Amazing Science of Bad Language* (New York: W. W. Norton, 2017), 46–48.

119 stronger swear words: Richard Stephens summarizes these unpublished studies in Byrne, *Swearing Is Good for You*, 58.

119 pain caused by social exclusion: Michael C. Philipp and Laura Lombardo, "Hurt Feelings and Four Letter Words: Swearing Alleviates the Pain of Social Distress," *European Journal of Social Psychology* 47, no. 4 (2017): 517–23, summarized by Byrne in *Swearing Is Good for You*, 61.

119 Chimps that learn: Byrne, *Swearing Is Good for You*, 120.

119 emotionally laden language: Byrne, *Swearing Is Good for You*, 21–45.

119 "good for group bonding": Byrne, *Swearing Is Good for You*, 94.

120 *fuck* acts funny: Throughout this section, I am following the lead of McCulloch, "A Linguist Explains the Syntax of 'Fuck.'" Many of the papers she is relying on are collected in *Studies Out in Left Field: Defamatory Essays Presented to James D. McCawley on the Occasion of His 33rd or 34th Birthday*, ed. Arnold M. Zwicky, Peter H. Salus, Robert I. Binnick, and Anthony L. Vanek (Philadelphia: John Benjamins Publishing Company, 1992).

120 linguist named James D. McCawley: Re the footnote, for an overview of McCawley's argument and a bit of the history behind the paper, see Gretchen McCulloch,

"A Linguist Explains the Syntax of 'Fuck,'" *The Toast*, December 9, 2014, https://the-toast.net/2014/12/09/linguist-explains-syntax-f-word.

121 **John J. McCarthy's epic paper:** John J. McCarthy, "Prosodic Structure and Expletive Infixation," *Language* 58, no. 3 (1982): 574–90.

121 **predict how they'll react:** Byrne, *Swearing Is Good for You*, 37–38.

122 **by five or six:** Re the footnote, see Kristin L. Jay and Timothy B. Jay, "A Child's Garden of Curses: A Gender, Historical, and Age-Related Evaluation of the Taboo Lexicon," *American Journal of Psychology* 126, no. 4 (2013): 459–75.

125 **the sacred, the profane:** The contrast between the sacred and the profane was introduced by Émile Durkheim, but I'm using the phrase differently than he did. See his *Elementary Forms of the Religious Life*, trans. Joseph Ward Swain (Mineola, NY: Dover, 2008).

126 **is a scandal:** John McWhorter makes this point in "The F-Word Is Going the Way of *Hell*," *The Atlantic*, September 6, 2019, www.theatlantic.com/ideas/archive/2019/09/who-cares-beto-swore/597499. He suggests that *fuck* is on its way out as a swear word. It's quickly becoming *hell*—a word that only kids bristle at. Extending Roache, we could call this process *offense de-escalation*. The more we say a word, the more we become accustomed to it, and the less offensive it seems.

126 **what a kike is:** For discussion, see Geoffrey K. Pullum, "Slurs and Obscenities: Lexicography, Semantics, and Philosophy," in *Bad Words: Philosophical Perspectives on Slurs*, ed. David Sosa (New York: Oxford University Press, 2018), 168–92.

126 **key to understanding slurs:** Eric Swanson, "Slurs and Ideologies," in *Analyzing Ideology: Rethinking the Concept*, ed. Robin Celikates, Sally Haslanger, and Jason Stanley (Oxford: Oxford University Press, forthcoming).

126 **interlocking set of ideas:** Swanson, "Slurs and Ideologies."

127 **slurs *cue* ideologies:** Swanson, "Slurs and Ideologies."

127 **operate within the ideology:** Swanson, "Slurs and Ideologies."

128 **James Baldwin's letter:** James Baldwin, "The Fire Next Time," in *Collected Essays*, ed. Toni Morrison (New York: Library of America, 1998), 291.

128 **Martin Luther King Jr.'s:** Martin Luther King Jr., *Letter from the Birmingham Jail* (San Francisco: Harper San Francisco, 1994).

128 **Ta-Nehisi Coates's letter:** Ta-Nehisi Coates, *Between the World and Me* (New York: Spiegel & Grau, 2015).

129 **moral seriousness of a slur:** Re the footnote, see Swanson, "Slurs and Ideologies."

130 *sparing* **is the key word:** For further discussion sympathetic to the use/mention distinction, see John McWhorter, "The Idea That Whites Can't Refer to the N-Word," *The Atlantic*, August 27, 2019, www.theatlantic.com/ideas/archive/2019/08/whites-refer-to-the-n-word/596872.

130 **"help his mom":** Swanson, "Slurs and Ideologies."

CHAPTER 6: SEX, GENDER, AND SPORTS

138 **question their femininity:** Re the footnote, see Emilia Bona, "Why Are Female Athletes Criticised for Developing a 'Masculine' Physique?" *Vice*, July 29, 2016, www.vice.com/en_us/article/pgnav7/why-are-female-athletes-criticised-for -developing-a-masculine-physique.

139 **"no grown-up ever says it":** Grown-ups do sometimes say this. In a study by the Women's Sports Foundation, nearly one-third of parents "endorsed the belief that boys are better at sports than girls." N. Zarrett, P. T. Veliz, and D. Sabo, *Keeping Girls in the Game: Factors That Influence Sport Participation* (New York: Women's Sports Foundation, 2020), 5.

141 **season ranked 801st:** "Senior Outdoor 2019 100 Metres Men Top List," World Athletics, accessed January 27, 2021, www.worldathletics.org/records/toplists /sprints/100-metres/outdoor/men/senior/2019.

141 **a dozen boys under eighteen:** "U18 Outdoor 2019 100 Metres Men Top List," World Athletics, accessed January 17, 2021, www.worldathletics.org/records /toplists/sprints/100-metres/outdoor/men/u18/2019.

141 **That time is disputed:** Re the footnote, see Nicholas P. Linthorne, *The 100-m World Record by Florence Griffith-Joyner at the 1988 U.S. Olympic Trials*, report for the International Amateur Athletic Federation, June 1995, www.brunel.ac .uk/~spstnpl/Publications/IAAFReport(Linthorne).pdf; and "Senior Outdoor 100 Metres Women All Time Top List," World Athletics, accessed August 22, 2021, www.worldathletics.org/records/all-time-toplists/sprints/100-metres/outdoor /women/senior.

142 **third in the world:** At least, that's the family lore. We can't track down records of the rankings. But we know from a news account that Benny fought an elimina- tion fight for a shot at the flyweight title. Had he won, he would have faced Midget Wolgast—who, despite the nickname, was an inch and a half taller. Benny lost, so he didn't get the chance. A list of his pro fights is available on BoxRec, accessed January 17, 2020, https://boxrec.com/en/proboxer/431900.

142 **"two separate sports":** Serena added, "I love to play women's tennis. I only want to play girls, because I don't want to be embarrassed." Chris Chase, "Serena Tells Letterman She'd Lose to Andy Murray in 'Five or Six' Minutes," *For the Win*, August 23, 2013, https://ftw.usatoday.com/2013/08/serena-williams-playing -men-andy-murray.

143 **running set plays:** Sarah Ko, "Off the Rim: The WNBA Is Better Than the NBA," *Annenberg Media*, September 20, 2019, www.uscannenbergmedia.com/2019/09/20 /off-the-rim-the-wnba-is-better-than-the-nba.

143 **appear to be biomechanical differences:** Re the footnote, see Reed Ferber, Irene McClay Davis, and Dorsey S. Williams 3rd, "Gender Differences in Lower Ex- tremity Mechanics During Running," *Clinical Biomechanics* 18, no. 4 (2003): 350–57.

144 **died tragically young:** Michael D. Resnik, E. Maynard Adams, and Richard E.

Grandy, "Jane English Memorial Resolution, 1947–1978," *Proceedings and Addresses of the American Philosophical Association* 52, no. 3 (1979): 376.

144 **she published an article:** Jane English, "Sex Equality in Sports," *Philosophy & Public Affairs* 7, no. 3 (1978): 269–77.

144 **"just plain fun":** English, "Sex Equality in Sports," 270.

144 **"no reason to deny Matilda":** English, "Sex Equality in Sports," 270.

144 **"people of all ages":** English, "Sex Equality in Sports," 274.

144 **set a 10K record:** Resnik, Adams, and Grandy, "Jane English Memorial Resolution," 377.

144 **let alone first place:** English, "Sex Equality in Sports," 271.

145 **prominent role in sports:** English, "Sex Equality in Sports," 273.

145 **won a silver medal:** "Angela Schneider to Serve as New Director of ICOS," International Centre for Olympic Studies, accessed January 17, 2020, www.uwo .ca/olympic/news/2019/angela_schneider_to_serve_as_new_director_of_icos .html.

145 **"positions of power":** Angela J. Schneider, "On the Definition of 'Woman' in the Sport Context," in *Values in Sport: Elitism, Nationalism, Gender Equality and the Scientific Manufacturing of Winners*, ed. Torbjörn Tännsjö and Claudio Tamburrini (London: E & FN Spon, 2000), 137.

145 **"systematically denied positions":** Schneider, "On the Definition of 'Woman,'" 137.

145 **fight racial inequality:** Cindy Boren, "Michael Jordan Pledged $100 Million to Improve Social Justice Because 'This Is a Tipping Point,'" *Washington Post*, June 7, 2020, www.washingtonpost.com/sports/2020/06/07/michael-jordan-pledged -100-million-improve-social-justice-because-this-is-tipping-point.

146 **"shape and define our images":** Schneider, "On the Definition of 'Woman,'" 137.

146 **they'd excel, equally:** Schneider, "On the Definition of 'Woman,'" 134.

146 **Men don't bother:** Melissa Cruz, "Why Male Gymnasts Don't Do the Balance Beam," *Bustle*, August 11, 2016, www.bustle.com/articles/178101-why-dont-male -gymnasts-do-the-balance-beam-this-olympic-event-could-use-a-modern -update.

147 **crushed the competition:** Jason Sumner, "Fiona Kolbinger, 24-Year-Old Medical Student, Becomes First Woman to Win the Transcontinental Race," *Bicycling*, August 6, 2019, www.bicycling.com/racing/a28627301/fiona-kolbinger-transcon tinental-race.

147 **twelve hours faster:** Angie Brown, "Nursing Mother Smashes 268-mile Montane Spine Race Record," BBC News, January 17, 2019, www.bbc.com/news /uk-scotland-edinburgh-east-fife-46906365.

148 **what traits researchers count:** Re the footnote, see Claire Ainsworth, "Sex Redefined," *Nature*, February 18, 2015, www.nature.com/articles/518288a.

149 **two started wildfires:** Sarah Moon and Hollie Silverman, "California Fire

Sparked by a Gender Reveal Party Has Grown to More Than 10,000 Acres," CNN, September 8, 2020, www.cnn.com/2020/09/08/us/el-dorado-fire-gender -reveal-update-trnd/index.html.

149 **killed by a cannon:** Nour Rahal, "Michigan Man Dead after Explosion at Baby Shower," *Detroit Free Press*, February 8, 2021, www.freep.com/story/news/local /michigan/2021/02/07/harland-cannon-explosion-baby-shower/4429175001.

149 **homemade pipe bomb:** Sandra E. Garcia, "Explosion at Gender Reveal Party Kills Woman, Officials Say," *New York Times*, October 28, 2019, www.nytimes .com/2019/10/28/us/gender-reveal-party-death.html.

151 **"The generally accepted rule":** Quoted in Jeanne Maglaty, "When Did Girls Start Wearing Pink?" *Smithsonian Magazine*, April 7, 2011, www.smithsonia nmag.com/arts-culture/when-did-girls-start-wearing-pink-1370097.

152 **Some kids don't identify:** For a helpful overview of current research on trans kids, see Kristina R. Olson, "When Sex and Gender Collide," *Scientific American*, September 1, 2017, www.scientificamerican.com/article/when-sex-and-gender -collide.

152 **trans men playing men's sports:** See, for instance, Talya Minsberg, "Trans Athlete Chris Mosier on Qualifying for the Olympic Trials," *New York Times*, January 28, 2020, www.nytimes.com/2020/01/28/sports/chris-mosier-trans-athlete-olympic -trials.html.

152 **performance of trans athletes:** Katherine Kornei, "This Scientist Is Racing to Discover How Gender Transitions Alter Athletic Performance—Including Her Own," *Science*, July 25, 2018, www.sciencemag.org/news/2018/07/scientist -racing-discover-how-gender-transitions-alter-athletic-performance-including.

152 **issue is testosterone:** Joanna Harper, "Athletic Gender," *Law and Contemporary Problems* 80 (2018): 144.

152 **reduced her speed:** Briar Stewart, "Canadian Researcher to Lead Largest Known Study on Transgender Athletes," CBC News, July 24, 2019, www.cbc.ca/news /health/trans-athletes-performance-transition-research-1.5183432.

152 **In a recent Gallup poll:** On the poll in the footnote, see Jeffrey M. Jones, "LGBT Identification Rises to 5.6% in Latest U.S. Estimate," Gallup, February 24, 2021, https://news.gallup.com/poll/329708/lgbt-identification-rises-latest -estimate.aspx.

153 **competition was slower:** Joanna Harper, "Do Transgender Athletes Have an Edge? I Sure Don't," *Washington Post*, April 1, 2015, www.washingtonpost .com/opinions/do-transgender-athletes-have-an-edge-i-sure-dont/2015/04/01 /ccacb1da-c68e-11e4-b2a1-bed1aaea2816_story.html.

153 **Harper has gathered data:** Joanna Harper, "Race Times for Transgender Athletes," *Journal of Sporting Cultures and Identities* 6, no. 1 (2015): 1–9.

153 **study is controversial:** For concerns about Harper's study, see Rebecca M. Jordan-Young and Katrina Karkazis, *Testosterone: An Unauthorized Biography* (Cambridge, MA: Harvard University Press, 2019), 188–89.

153   **no consistent relationship**: The chapter on athleticism in Jordan-Young and Karkazis, *Testosterone*, 159–201, provides a comprehensive review of the research on testosterone and performance in sports.

153   **"to provide women athletes"**: Harper, "Athletic Gender," 148.

154   **"not unduly alter"**: Harper, "Athletic Gender," 148.

154   **key eligibility for women's sports**: "Eligibility Regulations for the Female Classification (Athletes with Differences of Sex Development)," International Association of Athletics Federations, May 1, 2019, www.sportsintegrityinitiative .com/wp-content/uploads/2019/05/IAAF-Eligibility-Regulations-for-the -Female-Classi-2-compressed.pdf.

154   **"depression, fatigue, osteoporosis"**: Jordan-Young and Karkazis, *Testosterone*, 199.

154   **This is a point that Veronica Ivy has made**: Ivy was previously known as Rachel McKinnon. For her argument about Phelps, see Fred Dreier, "Q&A: Dr. Rachel McKinnon, Masters Track Champion and Transgender Athlete," *VeloNews*, October 15, 2018, www.velonews.com/news/qa-dr-rachel-mckinnon-masters-track -champion-and-transgender-athlete. Ivy writes, "If you look at elite athletics, every single elite athlete has some kind of genetic mutation that makes them amazing at their sport. Michael Phelps, his joint structure and body proportion, make him like a fish, which is awesome. But we shouldn't say that he has an unfair competitive advantage."

154   **eight inches taller**: See Rachel McKinnon, "I Won a World Championship. Some People Aren't Happy," *New York Times*, December 5, 2019, www.nytimes .com/2019/12/05/opinion/i-won-a-world-championship-some-people-arent -happy.html.

155   **received legal recognition**: McKinnon, "I Won a World Championship."

155   **If a person sees herself**: For a similar argument, see Rebecca Jordan-Young and Katrina Karkazis, "You Say You're a Woman? That Should Be Enough," *New York Times*, June 17, 2012, www.nytimes.com/2012/06/18/sports/olympics /olympic-sex-verification-you-say-youre-a-woman-that-should-be-enough.html.

155   **Men can't capture**: Thanks to Daniel Halberstam and Ellen Katz for help on this point.

155   **athletes involved were intersex**: Harper, "Athletic Gender," 141.

156   **marking out that category**: Robin Dembroff, "Real Talk on the Metaphysics of Gender," *Philosophical Topics* 46, no. 2 (2018): 21–50.

156   **known as *conceptual ethics***: See Alexis Burgess and David Plunkett, "Conceptual Ethics I," *Philosophy Compass* 8, no. 12 (2013): 1091–1101.

157   **defer to self-identification**: For further reflections on the meaning of the word *woman* and another argument in favor of using the word in a way that tracks self-identification, see Talia Mae Bettcher, "Trans Women and the Meaning of 'Woman,'" in *The Philosophy of Sex: Contemporary Readings*, 6th ed., ed. Nicholas Power, Raja Halwani, and Alan Soble (Lanham, MD: Rowman & Littlefield, 2013), 233–50.

158   **embrace the identity**: Robin Dembroff, "Why Be Nonbinary?" *Aeon*, October 30,

2018, https://aeon.co/essays/nonbinary-identity-is-a-radical-stance-against-gender-segregation.

158 **In a 2015 survey:** Re the footnote, see S. E. James, J. L. Herman, S. Rankin, M. Keisling, L. Mottet, and M. Anafi, *The Report of the 2015 U.S. Transgender Survey* (Washington, DC: National Center for Transgender Equality, 2016), 44, https://transequality.org/sites/default/files/docs/usts/USTS-Full-Report-Dec17 .pdf.

159 **organizing our social relations:** See Dembroff, "Why Be Nonbinary?" See also Dembroff, "Real Talk on the Metaphysics of Gender," 38: "If gender becomes based on self-identification, they worry, the social systems that smoothly determine social expectations, family structures, sexual availability, and gender-based labor divisions will become muddied and inefficient. Here, to my mind, one man's modus tollens is one queer's modus ponens."

159 **choose which competition:** At least one nonbinary athlete plays both men's *and* women's hockey. See Donna Spencer, "Non-binary Athletes Navigating Canadian Sport with Little Policy Help," CBC Sports, May 26, 2020, www.cbc.ca /sports/canada-non-binary-athletes-1.5585435.

CHAPTER 7: RACE AND RESPONSIBILITY

162 *I Am Rosa*: Brad Meltzer, *I Am Rosa Parks* (New York: Dial Books, 2014).

162 *I Am Martin*: Brad Meltzer, *I Am Martin Luther King, Jr.* (New York: Dial Books, 2016).

162 *I Am Jackie*: Brad Meltzer, *I Am Jackie Robinson* (New York: Dial Books, 2015).

162 *When Jackie and Hank*: Cathy Goldberg Fishman, *When Jackie and Hank Met* (Tarrytown, NY: Marshall Cavendish, 2012).

164 **these superficial differences:** K. Anthony Appiah traces the history of these sorts of views in his "Race, Culture, Identity: Misunderstood Connections," in K. Anthony Appiah and Amy Gutmann, *Color Conscious: The Political Morality of Race* (Princeton, NJ: Princeton University Press, 1996), 30–105.

164 **biology doesn't work:** Appiah, "Race, Culture, Identity," 68–71.

164 **it's all bunk:** For helpful overviews, see Gavin Evans, "The Unwelcome Revival of 'Race Science,'" *The Guardian*, March 2, 2018, www.theguardian.com/news /2018/mar/02/the-unwelcome-revival-of-race-science; and William Saletan, "Stop Talking About Race and IQ," *Slate*, April 27, 2018, https://slate.com/news-and -politics/2018/04/stop-talking-about-race-and-iq-take-it-from-someone-who -did.html.

164 **"no basis in scientific fact":** Evans, "Unwelcome Revival of 'Race Science.'"

164 **variation within racial groups:** Paul Hoffman, "The Science of Race," *Discover*, November 1994, 4, cited in Appiah, "Race, Culture, Identity," 69.

164 **a common ancestor:** See Douglas L. T. Rohde, Steve Olson, and Joseph T. Chang, "Modelling the Recent Common Ancestry of All Living Humans," *Nature* 431 (2004): 562–66.

164 **how ancestry works:** See Scott Hershberger, "Humans Are More Closely Related Than We Commonly Think," *Scientific American*, October 5, 2020, www.scientificamerican.com/article/humans-are-all-more-closely-related-than-we-commonly-think.

164 **Adam Rutherford explains:** Quoted in Hershberger, "Humans Are More Closely Related."

165 **descended from a single population:** L. Luca Cavalli-Sforza and Marcus W. Feldman, "The Application of Molecular Genetic Approaches to the Study of Human Evolution," *Nature Genetics Supplement* 33 (2003): 270.

165 **the *genetic isopoint*:** Douglas Rohde, quoted in Hershberger, "Humans Are More Closely Related."

165 **anything like a rigid division:** For a contrary view, see Quayshawn Spencer, "How to Be a Biological Racial Realist," in *What Is Race?: Four Philosophical Views*, ed. Joshua Glasgow, Sally Haslanger, Chike Jeffers, and Quayshawn Spencer (New York: Oxford University Press, 2019), 73–110. Spencer argues that population genetics reveals that human beings cluster into five racial groups: Africans, East Asians, Eurasians, Native Americans, and Oceanians. But he also makes clear that this clustering does not imply that these groups "differ in any socially important traits (e.g., intelligence, beauty, moral character, etc.)" (p. 104).

165 **don't match up:** See Ron Mallon, " 'Race': Normative, Not Metaphysical or Semantic," *Ethics* 116 (2006): 525–51; Naomi Zack, *Philosophy of Science and Race* (New York: Routledge, 2002); and Appiah, "Race, Culture, Identity."

166 **structures a hierarchy:** For an articulation of this sort of view, see Sally Haslanger, "Tracing the Sociopolitical Reality of Race," in Glasgow et al., *What Is Race?*, 4–37.

166 **"must ride 'Jim Crow' ":** W. E. B. Du Bois, *Dusk of Dawn: An Essay Toward an Autobiography of a Race Concept* (New Brunswick, NJ: Transaction Publishers, 2011), 153.

166 **other people became White:** "The racial designations 'white' and 'Black' were born twins." Kwame Anthony Appiah, "I'm Jewish and Don't Identify as White. Why Must I Check That Box?" *New York Times Magazine*, October 13, 2020, www.nytimes.com/2020/10/13/magazine/im-jewish-and-dont-identify-as-white-why-must-i-check-that-box.html.

166 **"No one was white":** James Baldwin, "On Being White . . . and Other Lies," *Essence*, April 1984, 90–92.

166 **were sometimes lynched:** Brent Staples, "How Italians Became 'White,' " *New York Times*, October 12, 2019, www.nytimes.com/interactive/2019/10/12/opinion/columbus-day-italian-american-racism.html.

166 **establishment of Columbus Day:** Staples, "How Italians Became 'White.' "

167 **race is *socially constructed*:** See Sally Haslanger, "A Social Constructionist Analysis of Race," in *Resisting Reality: Social Construction and Social Critique* (New York: Oxford University Press, 2012), 298–310; and Haslanger, "Tracing the Sociopolitical Reality of Race," 4–37.

167 **other Pluto-sized objects:** Adam Mann, "Why Isn't Pluto a Planet Anymore?" *Space*, March 28, 2019, www.space.com/why-pluto-is-not-a-planet.html.

167 **"clear the neighborhood":** Science Reference Section, Library of Congress, "Why Is Pluto No Longer a Planet?" Library of Congress, November 19, 2019, www .loc.gov/everyday-mysteries/astronomy/item/why-is-pluto-no-longer-a-planet.

167 **"Race does not travel":** The quote in the footnote is from Michael Root, "How We Divide the World," *Philosophy of Science* 67, no. 3 (2000), S631–S632.

168 **When these conversations:** The book mentioned in the footnote is Beverly Daniel Tatum, *Why Are All the Black Kids Sitting Together in the Cafeteria? And Other Conversations About Race*, rev. ed. (New York: Basic Books, 2003), 31–51.

169 **less than 15 percent:** Neil Bhutta, Andrew C. Chang, Lisa J. Dettling, and Joanne W. Hsu, "Disparities in Wealth by Race and Ethnicity in the 2019 Survey of Consumer Finances," *FEDS Notes*, Federal Reserve, September 28, 2020, www.federalreserve.gov/econres/notes/feds-notes/disparities-in-wealth-by -race-and-ethnicity-in-the-2019-survey-of-consumer-finances-20200928.htm.

169 **unemployed at twice the rate:** Jhacova Williams and Valerie Wilson, "Black Workers Endure Persistent Racial Disparities in Employment Outcomes," *Economic Policy Institute*, August 27, 2019, www.epi.org/publication/labor-day-2019 -racial-disparities-in-employment.

169 **spend more to teach:** Clare Lombardo, "Why White School Districts Have So Much More Money," NPR, February 26, 2019, www.npr.org/2019/02/26/696794 821/why-white-school-districts-have-so-much-more-money.

169 **White people live longer:** Max Roberts, Eric N. Reither, and Sojung Lim, "Contributors to the Black-White Life Expectancy Gap in Washington D.C.," *Scientific Reports* 10 (2020): 1–12.

169 **better health care:** David R. Williams and Toni D. Rucker, "Understanding and Addressing Racial Disparities in Health Care," *Health Care Financing Review* 21, no. 4 (2000): 75–90.

169 **Black men were incarcerated:** Becky Pettit and Bryan Sykes, "Incarceration," *Pathways* (Special Issue 2017), inequality.stanford.edu/sites/default/files/Path ways_SOTU_2017.pdf.

169 **Tulsa Race Riot:** History.com editors, "Tulsa Race Massacre," *History*, March 8, 2018, www.history.com/topics/roaring-twenties/tulsa-race-massacre.

170 **arrested for drug offenses:** Equal Justice Initiative, "Study Finds Racial Disparities in Incarceration Persist," June 15, 2016, https://eji.org/news/sentencing -project-report-racial-disparities-in-incarceration.

170 **origins in oppression:** Chike Jeffers, "Cultural Constructionism," in Glasgow et al., *What Is Race?*, 75

170 **"stigmatization, discrimination, marginalization":** Chike Jeffers, "The Cultural Theory of Race: Yet Another Look at Du Bois's 'The Conservation of Races,'" *Ethics* 123, no. 3 (2013): 422.

170 **"joy in blackness":** Jeffers, "Cultural Theory of Race," 422.

171 **present in Black culture:** Jeffers, "Cultural Constructionism," 74–88.

171 **"race is not just":** Belle previously published as Kathryn T. Gines. This quote is from her "Fanon and Sartre 50 Years Later: To Retain or Reject the Concept of Race," *Sartre Studies International* 9, no. 2 (2003): 56.

171 **"positive category that encompasses":** Gines, "Fanon and Sartre," 56.

172 **Whiteness was forged:** In his "On Being White . . . and Other Lies" (p. 91), James Baldwin writes: "America became white—the people who, as they claim, 'settled' the country became white—because of the necessity of denying the Black presence, and justifying Black subjugation. No community can be based on such a principle—or, in other words, no community can be established on so genocidal a lie. White men—from Norway, for example, where they were *Norwegians*— became white: by slaughtering the cattle, poisoning the wells, massacring Native Americans, raping Black women."

173 **actions reveal defects:** Judith Jarvis Thomson, "Morality and Bad Luck," *Metaphilosophy* 20, nos. 3–4 (July/October 1989): 203–21.

173 **The company cut corners:** See David Schaper, "Boeing to Pay $2.5 Billion Settlement Over Deadly 737 Max Crashes," NPR, January 8, 2021, www.npr .org/2021/01/08/954782512/boeing-to-pay-2-5-billion-settlement-over-deadly -737-max-crashes; and Dominic Gates, "Boeing's 737 MAX 'Design Failures' and FAA's 'Grossly Insufficient' Review Slammed," *Seattle Times*, March 6, 2020, www.seattletimes.com/business/boeing-aerospace/u-s-house-preliminary -report-faults-boeing-faa-over-737-max-crashes.

174 **Thomas says corporations changed:** W. Robert Thomas, "How and Why Corporations Became (and Remain) Persons under Criminal Law," *Florida State University Law Review* 45, no. 2 (2018): 480–538.

176 **so says David Enoch:** David Enoch, "Being Responsible, Taking Responsibility, and Penumbral Agency," in *Luck, Value, & Commitment: Themes from the Ethics of Bernard Williams*, ed. Ulrike Heuer and Gerald Lang (Oxford: Oxford University Press, 2012), 95–132.

177 **person who is put off:** Enoch, "Being Responsible," 120–23.

178 **"stress cracks and bowed walls":** Isabel Wilkerson, *Caste: The Origins of Our Discontents* (New York: Random House, 2020), 15–20.

178 **"Many people may rightly say":** Wilkerson, *Caste*, 16.

178 **"we are the heirs":** Wilkerson, *Caste*, 16.

180 **"The signers of the Declaration":** Frederick Douglass, "The Meaning of July Fourth for the Negro," *Frederick Douglass: Selected Speeches and Writings*, ed. Philip S. Foner (Chicago: Lawrence Hill, 1999), 192.

180 **"bequeathed by your fathers":** Douglass, "Meaning of July Fourth," 194.

180 **"the great sin and shame":** Douglass, "Meaning of July Fourth," 195.

180 **"What, to the American slave":** Douglass, "Meaning of July Fourth," 196.

180 **"I do not despair":** Douglass, "Meaning of July Fourth," 204.

181 **never taken responsibility:** The House of Representatives issued an apology for

slavery in 2008. Which is good. But it cannot, by itself, act on behalf of the United States. Danny Lewis, "Five Times the United States Officially Apologized," *Smithsonian Magazine*, May 27, 2016, www.smithsonianmag.com/smart -news/five-times-united-states-officially-apologized.

181 **Ta-Nehisi Coates published:** Ta-Nehisi Coates, "The Case for Reparations," *The Atlantic*, June 2014, www.theatlantic.com/magazine/archive/2014/06/the-case -for-reparations/361631.

182 **repair our relationships:** Daniel Fryer, "What's the Point of Reparation?" (unpublished manuscript, May 11, 2021).

183 **first at bat:** Stephen H. Norwood and Harold Brackman, "Going to Bat for Jackie Robinson: The Jewish Role in Breaking Baseball's Color Line," *Journal of Sport History* 26, no. 1 (1999): 131.

183 **collided with Robinson:** Jackie Robinson and Wendell Smith, *Jackie Robinson: My Own Story* (New York: Greenberg, 1948), 96.

183 **"Listen, don't pay attention":** Robinson and Smith, *Jackie Robinson*, 96–97.

183 **invited Robinson to dinner:** Robinson declined the invitation. He didn't want to make trouble for Greenberg. See Hank Greenberg's autobiography, *The Story of My Life*, ed. Ira Berkow (Chicago: Ivan R. Dee, 1989), 183.

183 **the first encouragement:** See Robinson and Smith, *Jackie Robinson*, 96; and "Hank Greenberg a Hero to Dodgers' Negro Star," *New York Times*, May 18, 1947, https://timesmachine.nytimes.com/timesmachine/1947/05/18/99271179.html.

184 **"We killed him":** Lenny Bruce, *How to Talk Dirty and Influence People* (Boston: Da Capo Press, 2016), 155.

184 **"Everybody blames the Jews":** Quoted in Dana Goodyear, "Quiet Depravity," *New Yorker*, October 17, 2005, www.newyorker.com/magazine/2005/10/24/quiet -depravity.

185 **"Jews will not replace us":** Emma Green, "Why the Charlottesville Marchers Were Obsessed with Jews," *The Atlantic*, August 15, 2017, www.theatlantic.com /politics/archive/2017/08/nazis-racism-charlottesville/536928.

185 **in both directions:** And Jews who are Black are often caught in the middle. Deena Yellin, "Subjected to Anti-Semitism and Racism, Jews of Color Feel 'Stuck in the Middle,'" NorthJersey.com, August 27, 2020, www.northjersey.com /story/news/local/2020/08/27/jewish-people-of-color-grapple-with-bigotry-two -fronts/5444526002.

185 **integrated the Texas League:** Norwood and Brackman, "Going to Bat," 133–34.

185 **castigated other Black leaders:** Ami Eden, "Remembering Jackie Robinson's Fight with Black Nationalists over Anti-Semitism," *Jewish Telegraphic Agency*, April 15, 2013, www.jta.org/2013/04/15/culture/remembering-jackie-robinsons -fight-with-black-nationalists-over-anti-semitism.

185 **"How could we stand":** Jackie Robinson, *I Never Had It Made* (New York: G. P. Putnam's Sons, 1972), 159.

185 **James Baldwin's 1967 essay:** Re the footnote, see James Baldwin, "Negroes Are

Anti-Semitic because They're Anti-White," *New York Times*, April 9, 1967, https://movies2.nytimes.com/books/98/03/29/specials/baldwin-antisem.html.

186 **Jackie had it far worse:** Hank Greenberg wrote in his autobiography, "Jackie had it tough, tougher than any player who ever lived. I happened to be a Jew, one of the few in baseball, but I was white, and I didn't have horns like some thought I did. . . . But I identified with Jackie Robinson. I had feelings for him because they had treated me the same way. Not as bad, but they made remarks about my being a sheenie and a Jew all the time." Greenberg, *Story of My Life*, 183.

CHAPTER 8: KNOWLEDGE

190 **"Once Zhuang Zhou dreamed":** Zhuangzi, *The Complete Works of Zhuangzi*, trans. Burton Watson (New York: Columbia University Press, 2013), 18.

191 **Descartes set out to doubt:** René Descartes, *Meditations on First Philosophy: With Selections from the Objections and Replies*, 2nd ed., ed. and trans. John Cottingham (Cambridge: Cambridge University Press, 2017), 15.

191 **deluded by a dream:** Descartes, *Meditations on First Philosophy*, 16.

192 **sleeping doesn't change:** Descartes, *Meditations on First Philosophy*, 17.

192 **imagined that an evil genius:** Descartes, *Meditations on First Philosophy*, 19.

193 **Descartes saw it too:** Descartes, *Meditations on First Philosophy*, 21.

193 **cool bit of reasoning:** Not everyone thinks so. Friedrich Nietzsche argued that the most Descartes was entitled to conclude was that there was thought, not that there was an "I" who was doing the thinking. I'm inclined to think that Descartes's reasoning was, on this score, sound. For Nietzsche's doubts, see his *Beyond Good and Evil: Prelude to a Philosophy of the Future*, trans. Helen Zimmern (New York: Macmillan, 1907), 22–25. For a defense of Descartes's position, see Christopher Peacocke, "Descartes Defended," *Proceedings of the Aristotelean Society, Supplementary Volumes* 86 (2012): 109–25.

195 **have a *justified true belief*:** For an overview of the traditional analysis of knowledge, and the problems with it, see Jonathan Jenkins Ichikawa and Matthew Steup, "The Analysis of Knowledge," *Stanford Encyclopedia of Philosophy* (Summer 2018 edition), ed. Edward N. Zalta, https://plato.stanford.edu/archives/sum2018/entries/knowledge-analysis.

195 **hadn't written anything:** David Edmonds, "A Truth Should Suffice," *Times Higher Education*, January 24, 2013, www.timeshighereducation.com/a-truth-should-suffice/2001095.article.

196 **Gettier said no:** Edmund L. Gettier, "Is Justified True Belief Knowledge?" *Analysis* 23, no. 6 (1963): 121–23.

196 **none of them work:** For an overview of possible responses and problems with them, see Ichikawa and Steup, "Analysis of Knowledge."

197 **wrote a recipe:** Linda Zagzebski, "The Inescapability of Gettier Problems," *Philosophical Quarterly* 44, no. 174 (1994): 69.

197 **One of Zagzebski's stories:** Zagzebski, "Inescapability of Gettier Problems," 67–68.

197 **a mistake to try:** Timothy Williamson argues for this view in *Knowledge and Its Limits* (New York: Oxford University Press, 2000).

198 **"nothing more to say":** **Gettier, quoted in** Edmonds, "A Truth Should Suffice."

198 **Dharmottara says no:** This story is relayed in Georges B. J. Dreyfus, *Recognizing Reality: Dharmakirti's Philosophy and Its Tibetan Interpretations* (Albany, NY: SUNY Press, 1997), 292. I was introduced to this story (and the one in the following note) by Ichikawa in "Analysis of Knowledge."

198 **Peter of Mantua:** Peter's story went like this: "Let it be assumed that Plato is next to you and you know him to be running, but you mistakenly believe that he is Socrates, so that you firmly believe that Socrates is running. However, let it be so that Socrates is in fact running in Rome; however, you do not know this." The story is relayed in Ivan Boh, "Belief Justification and Knowledge: Some Late Medieval Epistemic Concerns," *Journal of the Rocky Mountain Medieval and Renaissance Association* 6 (1985): 95.

198 **Teresa of Ávila:** Christia Mercer, "Descartes' Debt to Teresa of Ávila, or Why We Should Work on Women in the History of Philosophy," *Philosophical Studies* 174, no. 10 (2017): 2539–55.

199 **celebrate the work of women:** See, for instance, *The Philosopher Queens: The Lives and Legacies of Philosophy's Unsung Women*, ed. Rebecca Buxton and Lisa Whiting (London: Unbound, 2020).

199 **died too young:** "Notes and News," *Journal of Philosophy* 75, no. 2 (1978): 114.

199 **Stine had an idea:** G. C. Stine, "Skepticism, Relevant Alternatives, and Deductive Closure," *Philosophical Studies* 29 (1976): 249–61.

200 *know* **is context-sensitive:** Stine was an early and influential proponent of the idea that standards for knowledge shift, but she wasn't the first, and she was far from the last. For a thorough introduction to the view, see Patrick Rysiew, "Epistemic Contextualism," *Stanford Encyclopedia of Philosophy* (Spring 2021 edition), ed. Edward N. Zalta, https://plato.stanford.edu/archives/spr2021/entries/contextualism-epistemology.

201 **looking at a zebra:** Stine, "Skepticism, Relevant Alternatives, and Deductive Closure," 252.

201 **In Tijuana, Mexico:** Amy Isackson, "Working to Save the Painted 'Zonkeys' of Tijuana," NPR, August 8, 2013, www.npr.org/2013/08/08/209969843/working-to-save-the-painted-zonkeys-of-tijuana.

201 **shift the conversational context:** Stine, "Skepticism, Relevant Alternatives, and Deductive Closure," 256–57.

201 **A zonkey is a hybrid:** Re the footnote, see Emily Lodish, "Here's Everything You Wanted to Know about Zonkeys, the Great Zebra-Donkey Hybrids," *The World*, April 30, 2014, www.pri.org/stories/2014-04-30/heres-everything-you-wanted-know-about-zonkeys-great-zebra-donkey-hybrids.

202 **There's lots we know**: Stine, "Skepticism, Relevant Alternatives, and Deductive Closure," 254.

202 **context of climate change**: N. Ángel Pinillos, "Knowledge, Ignorance and Climate Change," *New York Times*, November 26, 2018, www.nytimes.com/2018/11 /26/opinion/skepticism-philosophy-climate-change.html.

202 **our carbon emissions are responsible**: For an overview of the evidence, see Renee Cho, "How We Know Today's Climate Change Is Not Natural," *State of the Planet*, Columbia Climate School, April 4, 2017, https://blogs.ei.columbia.edu/2017/04/04 /how-we-know-climate-change-is-not-natural.

202 **"I don't know for sure"**: "On Energy, Election Commission, & Education, Sununu Casts Himself as More Pragmatist Than Politician," New Hampshire Public Radio, July 10, 2017, www.nhpr.org/post/energy-election-commission-education -sununu-casts-himself-more-pragmatist-politician.

203 **"emphasize the uncertainty"**: David Roberts, "Exxon Researched Climate Science. Understood It. And Misled the Public," *Vox*, August 23, 2017, www.vox .com/energy-and-environment/2017/8/23/16188422/exxon-climate-change.

203 **"Doubt is our product"**: Phoebe Keane, "How the Oil Industry Made Us Doubt Climate Change," BBC News, September 20, 2020, www.bbc.com/news/stories -53640382.

203 **can't doubt everything**: Re the footnote, Ludwig Wittgenstein put it this way: "That is to say that the *questions* that we raise and our *doubts* depend on the fact that some propositions are exempt from doubt, are as it were like hinges on which those turn." Wittgenstein, *On Certainty*, ed. G. E. M. Anscombe and G. H. von Wright, trans. Denis Paul and G. E. M. Anscombe (New York: Harper & Row, 1975), 44.

204 **Pinillos suggests another strategy**: Pinillos, "Knowledge, Ignorance and Climate Change."

205 **including Elon Musk**: Rich McCormick, "Odds Are We're Living in a Simulation, Says Elon Musk," *The Verge*, June 2, 2016, www.theverge.com/2016/6/2/118 37874/elon-musk-says-odds-living-in-simulation.

205 **a rough version**: The full argument is set out in Nick Bostrom, "Are You Living in a Computer Simulation?" *Philosophical Quarterly* 53, no. 211 (2003): 243–55. That article and many others examining the hypothesis are collected at https:// www.simulation-argument.com.

206 **one of these propositions**: I've simplified Bostrom's alternatives a bit. For the original, see Bostrom, "Are You Living in a Computer Simulation?"

207 **in some sense, enslaved**: These concerns are raised in James Pryor, "What's So Bad about Living in the Matrix?" in *Philosophers Explore the Matrix*, ed. Christopher Grau (New York: Oxford University Press, 2005), 40–61.

208 **made of something surprising**: David J. Chalmers, "The Matrix as Metaphysics," in *The Character of Consciousness* (New York: Oxford University Press, 2010), 455–78.

208 **a subtle confusion**: Chalmers explains the confusion in "Matrix as Metaphysics," 471–72.

CHAPTER 9: TRUTH

216 **claim to believe**: See Seana Valentine Shiffrin, *Speech Matters: On Lying, Morality, and the Law* (Princeton, NJ: Princeton University Press, 2014), 12–14.

216 **a witness at trial**: Shiffrin, *Speech Matters*, 13–14. She credits the example to Thomas L. Carson, "Lying, Deception, and Related Concepts," in *The Philosophy of Deception*, ed. Clancy Martin (New York: Oxford University Press, 2009), 159–61.

216 **a person lies**: I've simplified Shiffrin's account of lying. Here is the complete way she describes a lie (*Speech Matters*, 12): An intentional assertion by A to B of a proposition P such that

A does not believe P, and

A is aware that A does not believe P, and

A intentionally presents P in a manner or context that objectively manifests A's intention that B is to take and treat P as an accurate representation of A's belief.

217 **improv comedy show**: See Shiffrin, *Speech Matters*, 16.

217 **Shiffrin calls situations**: Shiffrin, *Speech Matters*, 16–19.

217 **If you lie to me**: Shiffrin would say that the context is *epistemically* suspended, but that doesn't release you from your obligation to tell the truth. See Shiffrin, *Speech Matters*, 16.

217 **she calls those *justified suspended contexts:*** Shiffrin, *Speech Matters*, 16.

217 **falsifications won't count**: Shiffrin, *Speech Matters*, 18.

217 **"demanded by the social context"**: Shiffrin, *Speech Matters*, 33.

217 **a "competent listener"**: Shiffrin, *Speech Matters*, 33.

219 **manifest their will**: Shiffrin, *Speech Matters*, 22.

219 **Athanasius of Alexandria**: See, e.g., Alasdair MacIntyre, "Truthfulness, Lies, and Moral Philosophers: What Can We Learn from Mill and Kant?" (Tanner Lectures on Human Values, Princeton University, April 6 and 7, 1994), 336, https://tannerlectures.utah.edu/_documents/a-to-z/m/macintyre_1994.pdf.

219 **a paper with that advice**: Jennifer Saul, "Just Go Ahead and Lie," *Analysis* 72, no. 1 (2012), 3–9.

219 **Dave and Charla**: Jennifer Mather Saul, *Lying, Misleading, and What Is Said: An Exploration in Philosophy of Language and in Ethics* (Oxford: Oxford University Press, 2012), 72.

220 **"It seems completely absurd"**: Saul, *Lying, Misleading, and What Is Said*, 72.

220 **might as well lie**: Saul does carve out some exceptions, like lying in court. Saul, *Lying, Misleading, and What Is Said*, 99.

221 **lose "reliable access"**: Shiffrin, *Speech Matters*, 23.

222 **his short essay:** Immanuel Kant, "On a Supposed Right to Tell Lies from Be-
     nevolent Motives," in *Kant's Critique of Practical Reason and Other Works on the
     Theory of Ethics*, trans. Thomas Kingsmill Abbott (London: Longmans, Green,
     1879), 431–36.

222 **"duty to speak truthfully":** Allen W. Wood, *Kantian Ethics* (New York: Cam-
     bridge University Press, 2008), 245.

222 **police officer demanding information:** Wood, *Kantian Ethics*, 244–48.

222 **the French Revolution:** Wood, *Kantian Ethics*, 249.

223 **"conviction of your friend":** Wood, *Kantian Ethics*, 249.

223 **"legal process is illegitimate":** Wood, *Kantian Ethics*, 249.

223 **"turning the process into a sham":** Wood, *Kantian Ethics*, 249.

223 **"duty of politicians":** Wood, *Kantian Ethics*, 249.

223 **list of lies:** See, e.g., David Leonhardt and Stuart A. Thompson, "Trump's Lies,"
     New York Times, December 14, 2017, www.nytimes.com/interactive/2017/06/23
     /opinion/trumps-lies.html; and Daniel Dale, "The 15 Most Notable Lies of Donald
     Trump's Presidency," CNN, January 16, 2021, www.cnn.com/2021/01/16/politics
     /fact-check-dale-top-15-donald-trump-lies/index.html.

223 **he lied about the rain:** Dale, "The 15 Most Notable Lies"; and Nicholas Fandos,
     "White House Pushes 'Alternative Facts.' Here Are the Real Ones," *New York
     Times*, January 22, 2017, www.nytimes.com/2017/01/22/us/politics/president-trump
     -inauguration-crowd-white-house.html.

223 **election had been stolen:** Jim Rutenberg, Jo Becker, Eric Lipton, Maggie Haber-
     man, Jonathan Martin, Matthew Rosenberg, and Michael S. Schmidt, "77 Days:
     Trump's Campaign to Subvert the Election," *New York Times*, January 31, 2021,
     www.nytimes.com/2021/01/31/us/trump-election-lie.html.

226 **the ump tracks the truth:** See H. L. A. Hart, *The Concept of Law* (Oxford: Claren-
     don Press, 1961), 141–47.

227 **philosophers think thoroughgoing relativism:** See Paul Boghossian, *Fear of
     Knowledge: Against Relativism and Constructivism* (Oxford: Clarendon Press,
     2006), 52–54. Boghossian thinks global relativism might overcome the argu-
     ment set out in the text but nevertheless thinks it incoherent, because it re-
     quires nonrelative facts about what sort of views people accept (pp. 54–56).

228 **what Ronald Dworkin thought:** See Ronald Dworkin, "Objectivity and Truth:
     You'd Better Believe It," *Philosophy and Public Affairs* 25, no. 2 (1996): 87–139.

229 **"the universe houses":** Dworkin, "Objectivity and Truth," 104.

229 **woven into the fabric of the universe:** Dworkin, "Objectivity and Truth," 105.

230 **"We can do no better":** Dworkin, "Objectivity and Truth," 118.

231 ***"an informational network":*** C. Thi Nguyen, "Escape the Echo Chamber," *Aeon*,
     April 9, 2018, https://aeon.co/essays/why-its-as-hard-to-escape-an-echo-chamber
     -as-it-is-to-flee-a-cult.

231 **They are "easily shattered":** Nguyen, "Escape the Echo Chamber."

231 ***"a social structure":*** Nguyen, "Escape the Echo Chamber."

231 **Limbaugh taught his listeners:** For a deeper analysis of the echo chamber Lim-

baugh created, see Kathleen Hall Jamieson and Joseph N. Cappella, *Echo Chamber: Rush Limbaugh and the Conservative Media Establishment* (New York: Oxford University Press, 2008).

232 **Robin DiAngelo offers up a list:** Robin DiAngelo, *Nice Racism: How Progressive White People Perpetuate Racial Harm* (Boston: Beacon Press, 2021), 45–47.

232 **organization's "diversity work":** DiAngelo, *Nice Racism*, 46.

232 **"not understanding why":** DiAngelo, *Nice Racism*, 47.

232 **"attempting to insulate her views":** In an interview with Isaac Chotiner, DiAngelo walked back the implication of her list, at least a bit, allowing the possibility of good-faith disagreement among people who accept the central tenets of her view. Isaac Chotiner, "Robin DiAngelo Wants White Progressives to Look Inward," *New Yorker*, July 14, 2021, www.newyorker.com/news/q-and-a/robin -diangelo-wants-white-progressives-to-look-inward.

232 **as Nguyen points out:** Nguyen, "Escape the Echo Chamber."

232 **"Does a community's belief system":** Nguyen, "Escape the Echo Chamber."

233 **Nguyen suggests a reboot:** Nguyen, "Escape the Echo Chamber."

235 **not in a justified suspended context:** Shiffrin, *Speech Matters*, 16, explains that in a justified suspended context, the "normative presumption of truthfulness is suspended because these contexts serve other valuable purposes whose achievement depends upon the presumption's suspension and the fact and justification of the suspension are publicly accessible." Later on, though, Shiffrin allows that ambiguity about whether we are in a suspended context can contribute to "art, play, privacy, and interpersonal self-exploration" (p. 43), so she may be more flexible about the requirement of public accessibility than the first quote suggests.

236 **lift the suspension:** Shiffrin, *Speech Matters*, 42.

236 **after assuring someone:** Shiffrin, *Speech Matters*, 42–43.

236 **It's a war crime:** Shiffrin, *Speech Matters*, 24–25.

236 **"at each other's throats":** Shiffrin, *Speech Matters*, 24–25.

CHAPTER 10: MIND

240 **a dog's nose:** Peter Tyson, "Dogs' Dazzling Sense of Smell," PBS, October 4, 2012, www.pbs.org/wgbh/nova/article/dogs-sense-of-smell.

240 **Dogs see mostly:** Stanley Coren, "Can Dogs See Colors?" *Psychology Today*, October 20, 2008, www.psychologytoday.com/us/blog/canine-corner/200810/can-dogs -see-colors.

241 **"Children aren't just defective adults":** Alison Gopnik, *The Philosophical Baby: What Children's Minds Tell Us about Truth, Love, and the Meaning of Life* (New York: Farrar, Straus and Giroux, 2009), 9–10.

243 **"trade all his degrees":** Gopnik, *The Philosophical Baby*, 106.

243 **shrouded in secrecy:** For an informed guess about what it's like to be a baby, see Gopnik, *The Philosophical Baby*, 125–32.

243 **That sonar sense**: Thomas Nagel, "What Is It Like to Be a Bat?" *Philosophical Review* 83, no. 4 (1974): 438.

243 **"It will not help"**: Nagel, "What Is It Like to Be a Bat?," 439.

244 **"for a *bat* to be a bat"**: Nagel, "What Is It Like to Be a Bat?," 439.

244 **real-life Batman**: Tania Lombrozo, "Be Like a Bat? Sound Can Show You the Way," NPR, January 28, 2013, www.npr.org/sections/13.7/2013/01/28/170355712 /be-like-a-bat-sound-can-show-you-the-way.

244 **scans of Kish's brain**: Kish is featured in Alix Spiegel and Lulu Miller, "How to Become Batman," *Invisibilia* (podcast), produced by NPR, January 23, 2015, www.npr.org/programs/invisibilia/378577902/how-to-become-batman.

244 **Nagel would say**: Nagel, "What Is It Like to Be a Bat?," 442, n. 8.

245 **if you stay yourself**: A. J. Ayer put it this way: "It is suggested that in order really to know what another person is thinking or feeling, I have literally to share his experiences; and then it turns out that to share his experiences, in the sense required, is to have his experiences and that in order to have his experiences I have to be that person, so that what is demanded of me is that I become another person while remaining myself, which is a contradiction." A. J. Ayer, "One's Knowledge of Other Minds," *Theoria* 19, no. 1–2 (1953): 5.

245 **can't have experiences**: Ayer, "One's Knowledge of Other Minds," 6.

247 **he's not conscious**: Here, I'm following David J. Chalmers, *The Conscious Mind: In Search of a Fundamental Theory* (New York: Oxford University Press, 1996), 94.

249 **"How it is"**: Thomas H. Huxley and William Jay Youmans, *The Elements of Physiology and Hygiene* (New York: D. Appleton, 1868), 178.

249 **the Hard Problem of consciousness**: David J. Chalmers, *The Character of Consciousness* (New York: Oxford University Press, 2010), 1–28.

250 **body without a mind**: René Descartes, *Meditations on First Philosophy with Selections from the Objections and Replies*, rev. ed., trans. John Cottingham (Cambridge: Cambridge University Press, 1996), 50–62.

250 **The body is a thing**: Descartes writes, "The fact that I can clearly and distinctly understand one thing apart from another is enough to make me certain that the two things are distinct, since they are capable of being separated, at least by God." *Meditations on First Philosophy*, 54.

250 **mind is not *in* the body**: Descartes, *Meditations on First Philosophy*, 56.

250 **happened in the pineal gland**: See Gert-Jan Lokhorst, "Descartes and the Pineal Gland," *Stanford Encyclopedia of Philosophy* (Fall 2020 edition), ed. Edward N. Zalta, https://plato.stanford.edu/archives/fall2020/entries/pineal-gland.

250 **Elisabeth of Bohemia**: For an overview of Elisabeth's contributions to philosophy and her correspondence with Descartes, see Lisa Shapiro, "Elisabeth, Princess of Bohemia," *Stanford Encyclopedia of Philosophy* (Winter 2014 edition), ed. Edward N. Zalta, https://plato.stanford.edu/archives/win2014/entries/elisabeth -bohemia.

251 **Every physical event**: Quantum mechanics might complicate this story, but not

in a way that makes space for a nonphysical mind to cause a physical body to act. See Chalmers, *Conscious Mind*, 156–58.

251 **How did the ghost:** The metaphor of the ghost in the machine comes from Gilbert Ryle, *The Concept of Mind* (New York: Barnes & Noble, 1950), 15–16.

251 **mental states are the functions of brain states:** For an overview of functionalist approaches to the mind, mentioned in the footnote, see Janet Levin, "Functionalism," *Stanford Encyclopedia of Philosophy* (Fall 2018 edition), ed. Edward N. Zalta, https://plato.stanford.edu/archives/fall2018/entries/functionalism.

251 **most influential stories:** Frank Jackson first presented Mary's Room in "Epiphenomenal Qualia," *Philosophical Quarterly* 32, no. 127 (1982): 130.

254 **How much work:** Saul A. Kripke frames the issue this way in *Naming and Necessity* (Cambridge, MA: Harvard University Press, 1980), 153–54.

254 **tug some philosophers:** Chalmers elaborates on these arguments and adds more in *Conscious Mind*, 94–106.

254 **the basic building block:** Chalmers, *Conscious Mind*, 276–308.

254 **view known as *panpsychism*:** Chalmers, *Conscious Mind*, 293–99.

255 **she'd recognize the ruse:** Daniel C. Dennett, *Consciousness Explained* (Boston: Little, Brown, 1991), 398–401.

255 **denies that qualia exist:** See Daniel C. Dennett, "Quining Qualia," *in Consciousness in Contemporary Science*, ed. A. J. Marcel and E. Bisiach (Oxford: Oxford University Press, 1988), 42–77.

255 **judgments and dispositions:** Dennett, *Consciousness Explained*, 398.

255 **"most virulent memes":** Dennett, *Consciousness Explained*, 389.

256 **"Are zombies possible?":** Dennett, *Consciousness Explained*, 406.

256 **"desperate intellectual dishonesty":** Dennett, *Consciousness Explained*, 406, n. 6.

256 **But to be honest:** For more on the question whether qualia are epiphenomenal, see Chalmers, *Conscious Mind*, 150–60.

256 **Chalmers wonders whether:** Chalmers, *Conscious Mind*, 189–91.

256 **"the sum total":** The quote in the footnote is from Dennett, *Consciousness Explained*, 398.

257 **he changed his mind:** Re the footnote, see Frank Jackson, "Mind and Illusion," *Royal Institute of Philosophy Supplement* 53 (2003): 251–71.

259 **"the silliest claim":** Galen Strawson, *Things That Bother Me: Death, Freedom, the Self, Etc.* (New York: New York Review of Books, 2018), 130–53.

259 **physical stuff experiences the world:** Strawson, *Things That Bother Me*, 154–76.

259 **all matter experiences the world:** Strawson, *Things That Bother Me*, 173.

259 **a constant "bzzzz":** Strawson explains his view in an interview with Robert Wright, "What Is It Like to Be an Electron? An Interview with Galen Strawson," *Nonzero*, June 28, 2020, https://nonzero.org/post/electron-strawson.

260 **We're at the stage:** Chalmers, *Conscious Mind*, 277.

260 **who say we won't:** See, for instance, Colin McGinn, "Can We Solve the Mind-Body Problem?" *Mind* 98, no. 391 (1989): 346–66.

CHAPTER II: INFINITY

264 **philosopher named Archytas**: Thanks to Gordon Belot for putting me on to the fact that Archytas made Rex's argument first.

264 **ship to rescue him**: Carl Huffman, "Archyatas," *Stanford Encyclopedia of Philosophy* (Winter 2020 edition), ed. Edward N. Zalta, https://plato.stanford.edu/archives /win2020/entries/archytas.

264 **"If I arrived"**: This is an excerpt from Eudemus's report of Archytas's argument. Carl A. Huffman, *Archytas of Tarentum: Pythagorean, Philosopher and Mathematician King* (Cambridge: Cambridge University Press, 2005), 541.

265 **something stops the javelin**: Lucretius, *De Rerum Natura*, I.968–979. For discussion, see David J. Furley, "The Greek Theory of the Infinite Universe," *Journal of the History of Ideas* 42, no. 4 (1981): 578.

265 **"Space extends infinitely"**: Isaac Newton, *Unpublished Scientific Papers of Isaac Newton: A Selection from the Portsmouth Collection in the University Library, Cambridge*, ed. and trans. A. Rupert Hall and Marie Boas Hall (Cambridge: Cambridge University Press, 1962), 133.

270 **there is only one thing**: For an overview of Parmenides's thought, see John Palmer, "Parmenides," *Stanford Encyclopedia of Philosophy* (Winter 2020 edition), ed. Edward N. Zalta, https://plato.stanford.edu/archives/win2020/entries /parmenides.

271 **Diogenes is said simply**: Simplicius, *On Aristotle's Physics 6*, trans. David Konstan (London: Bloomsbury, 1989), 114, s. 1012.20.

271 **Aristotle had also suggested**: "Hence Zeno's argument makes a false assumption in asserting that it is impossible for a thing to pass over or severally to come in contact with infinite things in a finite time. For there are two senses in which length and time and generally anything continuous are called 'infinite': they are called so either in respect of divisibility or in respect of their extremities. So while a thing in a finite time cannot come in contact with things quantitatively infinite, it can come in contact with things infinite in respect of divisibility: for in this sense the time itself is also infinite: and so we find that the time occupied by the passage over the infinite is not a finite but an infinite time, and the contact with the infinites is made by means of moments not finite but infinite in number." Aristotle, *Physics*, trans. R. P. Hardie and R. K. Gaye (Cambridge, MA: MIT, n.d.), Book 6.2; available at https://www.google.com/books/edition/Physica_by_R_P _Hardie_and_R_K_Gaye_De_ca/A1RHAQAAMAAJ?hl=en&gbpv=1& bsq=1930.

272 **doesn't completely solve the mystery**: See Aristotle, *Physics*, Book 8.8.

272 **even a single second**: Here and throughout the discussion of Zeno's paradox, I've been helped by Nick Huggett, "Zeno's Paradoxes," *Stanford Encyclopedia of Philosophy* (Winter 2019 edition), ed. Edward N. Zalta, https://plato.stanford.edu /archives/win2019/entries/paradox-zeno.

272 **disagreement on the details**: For discussion of the standard solution and alterna-

tives, see Bradley Dowden, "Zeno's Paradoxes," *Internet Encyclopedia of Philosophy*, accessed November 8, 2020, https://iep.utm.edu/zeno-par.

272 **distances don't pile up:** Carlo Rovelli explains this point clearly in *Reality Is Not What It Seems: The Journey to Quantum Gravity*, trans. Simon Carnell and Erica Segre (New York: Riverhead Books, 2017), 26–28.

272 **super small bits of space:** For discussion, see Rovelli, *Reality Is Not What It Seems*, 169–71.

273 **we experiment with ethical ideas:** For an introduction to Dewey's moral philosophy, mentioned in the footnote, see Elizabeth Anderson, "Dewey's Moral Philosophy," *Stanford Encyclopedia of Philosophy* (Winter 2019 edition), ed. Edward N. Zalta, https://plato.stanford.edu/archives/win2019/entries/dewey-moral.

274 **leads some scientists to doubt:** Neil deGrasse Tyson is perhaps the most prominent scientist to dis philosophy, but he's far from alone. See George Dvorsky, "Neil deGrasse Tyson Slammed for Dismissing Philosophy as 'Useless,'" *Gizmodo*, May 12, 2014, https://io9.gizmodo.com/neil-degrasse-tyson-slammed-for-dismissing-philosophy-a-1575178224.

274 **93 billion light-years:** Chris Baraniuk, "It Took Centuries, but We Now Know the Size of the Universe," BBC Earth, June 13, 2016, www.bbc.com/earth/story/20160610-it-took-centuries-but-we-now-know-the-size-of-the-universe.

275 **turns out to be infinite:** Nick Bostrom, "Infinite Ethics," *Analysis and Metaphysics* 10 (2011): 9–59.

277 **infinity plus any finite number:** For an accessible introduction to Hilbert's Hotel, see World Science Festival, "Steven Strogatz and Hilbert's Infinite Hotel," YouTube video, 9:20, January 7, 2015, www.youtube.com/watch?v=wE9fl6tUWhc.

278 ***Hundred Billion Trillion Stars*:** Seth Fishman, *A Hundred Billion Trillion Stars* (New York: HarperCollins, 2017).

278 **thousand billion trillion stars:** "How Many Stars Are There in the Universe?" European Space Agency, accessed November 8, 2020, www.esa.int/Science_Exploration/Space_Science/Herschel/How_many_stars_are_there_in_the_Universe.

280 **air of absurdity:** Thomas Nagel, "The Absurd," *Journal of Philosophy* 68, no. 20 (1971): 719; and Thomas Nagel, "Birth, Death, and the Meaning of Life," in *The View from Nowhere* (New York: Oxford University Press, 1986), 208–32.

280 **absurd when there's a mismatch:** Nagel, "The Absurd," 718.

280 **it won't matter:** Nagel, "Birth, Death, and the Meaning of Life," 215.

280 **attempt is often absurd:** Nagel, "The Absurd," 725–26.

281 **little importance to themselves:** Sarah Buss, "Some Musings about the Limits of an Ethics That Can Be Applied—A Response to a Question about Courage and Convictions That Confronted the Author When She Woke Up on November 9, 2016," *Journal of Applied Philosophy* 37, no. 1 (2020): 26.

281 **hard trick to pull off:** Buss, "Some Musings," 21–23.

281 **love and sympathy:** Buss, "Some Musings," 17.

282 **presently feel your fear**: Buss, "Some Musings," 21.

282 **should expect others**: Buss, "Some Musings," 18.

282 **That's why I talk to them**: As Nagel points out, the size of the universe is not, on its own, a good reason for thinking us insignificant. But reflecting on it helps us step outside ourselves so that we can see our insignificance. "The Absurd," 717, 725.

283 **doesn't matter much**: Nagel also arrives at the view that our absurdity doesn't matter much in "The Absurd," 727.

CHAPTER 12: GOD

288 **He told a story**: The original is in John Wisdom, "Gods," *Proceedings of the Aristotelean Society* 45 (1944–1945): 185–206. Flew's adaptation is in Antony Flew, "Theology and Falsification," in *New Essays in Philosophical Theology*, ed. Antony Flew and Alasdair MacIntyre (New York: Macmillan, 1955), 96–98.

288 **"invisible, intangible, insensible"**: Flew, "Theology and Falsification," 96–98.

288 **"no gardener at all"**: Flew, "Theology and Falsification," 96–98.

296 **"Suppose someone were a believer"**: Ludwig Wittgenstein, *Lectures and Conversations on Aesthetics, Psychology, and Religious Belief*, ed. Cyril Barrett (Berkeley: University of California Press, 1966), 53.

297 **Buchak has pointed out**: Lara Buchak, "Can It Be Rational to Have Faith?" in *Probability in the Philosophy of Religion*, ed. Jake Chandler and Victoria S. Harrison (Oxford: Oxford University Press, 2012), 225–27.

298 **"If you gain"**: Blaise Pascal, *Thoughts, Letters, and Minor Works* (New York: P. F. Collier & Son, 1910), 85–87.

299 **whether Pascal's Wager works**: For an overview, see Alan Hájek, "Pascal's Wager," *Stanford Encyclopedia of Philosophy* (Summer 2018 edition), ed. Edward N. Zalta, https://plato.stanford.edu/archives/sum2018/entries/pascal-wager.

299 **getting full credit**: William James raised the same worry about the wager in *The Will to Believe and Other Essays in Popular Philosophy* (New York: Longmans, Green, 1986), 5.

301 **proved that God existed**: See Anselm, *Proslogion*, trans. David Burr, in "Anselm on God's Existence," Internet History Sourcebooks Project, January 20, 2021, https://sourcebooks.fordham.edu/source/anselm.asp.

301 **mocked by a monk**: For Gaunilo's reply, see "How Someone Writing on Behalf of the Fool Might Reply to All This," trans. David Burr, in "Anselm on God's Existence." For analysis, see Kenneth Einar Himma, "Anselm: Ontological Arguments for God's Existence," *Internet Encyclopedia of Philosophy*, accessed August 20, 2019, https://iep.utm.edu/ont-arg.

301 **improve the argument**: For an overview, see Graham Oppy, "Ontological Arguments," *Stanford Encyclopedia of Philosophy* (Spring 2020 edition), ed. Edward N. Zalta, https://plato.stanford.edu/archives/spr2020/entries/ontological-arguments.

302 **"whether God had any choice"**: Here, Einstein is quoted by his assistant, Ernst Straus. See Straus's "Memoir" in *Einstein: A Centenary Volume*, ed. A. P. French (Cambridge, MA: Harvard University Press, 1979), 31–32.

302 **whether the laws of physics:** On Einstein's question, see Dennis Overbye, "Did God Have a Choice?" *New York Times Magazine*, April 18, 1999, 434, https://timesmachine.nytimes.com/timesmachine/1999/04/18/issue.html.

302 **biggest question of all:** For a fun romp through possible answers, see Jim Holt, *Why Does the World Exist: An Existential Detective Story* (New York: W. W. Norton, 2012).

303 **"the problem is this":** J. L. Mackie, "Evil and Omnipotence," *Mind* 64, no. 254 (1955): 200.

303 **dropping the idea:** Mackie, "Evil and Omnipotence," 201–2.

303 **calling into question:** Mackie, "Evil and Omnipotence," 203.

303 **"These additional principles":** Re the footnote, see Mackie, "Evil and Omnipotence," 201.

304 **compassion, charity, and heroic acts:** See Mackie, "Evil and Omnipotence," 206.

304 **spite, malice, and callousness:** See Mackie, "Evil and Omnipotence," 207.

304 **"If God has made men":** Mackie, "Evil and Omnipotence," 209.

304 **Leibniz insisted that:** For an overview of Leibniz's thought on the Problem of Evil, see Michael J. Murray and Sean Greenberg, "Leibniz on the Problem of Evil," *Stanford Encyclopedia of Philosophy* (Winter 2016 edition), ed. Edward N. Zalta, https://plato.stanford.edu/archives/win2016/entries/leibniz-evil.

305 **So did Voltaire:** Voltaire satirizes the view that we live in the best of all possible worlds in *Candide and Other Stories*, trans. Roger Pearson (New York: Alfred A. Knopf, 1992).

305 **God had to answer:** Marilyn McCord Adams, "Horrendous Evils and the Goodness of God," *Proceedings of the Aristotelian Society, Supplementary Volumes* 63 (1989): 302–4.

305 **listed the sort of evils:** Adams, "Horrendous Evils," 300.

305 **"means to His end":** Adams, "Horrendous Evils," 303.

305 **"Could the truck driver":** Adams, "Horrendous Evils," 302.

305 **"good or loving":** Adams, "Horrendous Evils," 302.

305 **draw on religious ideas:** Adams, "Horrendous Evils," 309–10.

306 *engulf* **a person's life:** Adams, "Horrendous Evils," 307.

306 *defeat* **the evil:** Adams, "Horrendous Evils," 307–9.

306 **patch of a painting:** Adams ("Horrendous Evils," 299) attributed the idea to Roderick Chisholm.

306 **"human experience of horrors":** Adams, "Horrendous Evils," 307.

306 **God might express gratitude:** Adams ("Horrendous Evils," 305) credits this idea to Julian of Norwich, the first woman known to have written a book in English (sometime in the late 1300s). For more on Julian, see "Julian of Norwich," *British Library*, accessed May 1, 2021, www.bl.uk/people/julian-of-norwich.

306 **"too immature to fathom":** Adams, "Horrendous Evils," 305.

306 **convinced of his "mother's love":** Adams, "Horrendous Evils," 305–6.

306 **argued with God:** What follows is a slightly edited version of the conversation that takes places between Abraham and God in Genesis 18.

CONCLUSION: HOW TO RAISE A PHILOSOPHER

310 **According to Plutarch**: Plutarch, *Plutarch's Lives*, vol. 1, trans. Bernadotte Perrin (London: William Heinemann, 1914), 49.

311 **Hobbes tacked a new puzzle**: Thomas Hobbes, *The English Works of Thomas Hobbes*, vol. 1, ed. William Molesworth (London: John Bohn, 1839), 136–37.

311 **Millions of dollars**: For a fun exploration of questions about identity and art, listen to Michael Lewis's "The Hand of Leonardo," *Against the Rules* (podcast), https://atrpodcast.com/episodes/the-hand-of-leonardo-s1!7616f.

313 **Reason with your child**: For more advice on talking to kids about philosophy—and a longer list of questions you might ask—see Jana Mohr Lone, *The Philosophical Child* (London: Rowman & Littlefield, 2012), 21–39.

315 **"arguments so powerful"**: Robert Nozick, *Philosophical Explanations* (Cambridge, MA: Belknap Press, 1981), 4.

315 **The way Bertrand Russell did**: Bertrand Russell, *The Problems of Philosophy* (New York: Oxford University Press, 1998), 6.

INDEX